MASTERING

OFFICE P

CW00506727

MACMILLAN MASTER SERIES

Basic Management
Biology
Chemistry
Commerce
Computer Programming
Computers
Data Processing
Economics
Electronics
English Language
French
German
Italian
Marketing
Mathematics
Modern World History
Office Practice
Physics
Principles of Accounts
Sociology
Spanish
Statistics
Study Skills

OTHER TITLES BY PAUL BAILEY PUBLISHED BY MACMILLAN

Comprehensive Typing (2nd edition)
Typing Task Books (comprising *Typing Problems; Letters, Postcards and
    Memoranda; Displays and Tabulations*)
Typing for Colleges (revised edition)
Typing for Colleges 2
Typing for West Africa
Typing for East Africa

MASTERING
OFFICE PRACTICE

P. BAILEY

First published 1982 by
THE MACMILLAN PRESS LTD
Companies and representatives
·throughout the world

ISBN 0 333 27000 2 (hard cover)
      0 333 27199 8 (paper cover – home edition)
      0 333 29522 6 (paper cover – export edition)

Reprinted 1982

Typeset in Great Britain by
REPRODUCTION DRAWINGS LTD
Sutton, Surrey

Printed in Hong Kong

For MAB

Who has advised, edited and
encouraged throughout
and to the memory of

EAB

CONTENTS

CONTENTS

CONTENTS

PREFACE

Mastering Office Practice is a comprehensive text covering all the elementary and intermediate examinations in Office Practice, Clerical Duties, Secretarial Duties and Secretarial Practice. It is suitable for students taking all public examinations connected with the office and its environment, and it is appropriate for those involved in commercial teacher training.

It has been written in an easy-to-read and understand style and in such a manner as to enable teachers and students to come to terms with the rapid changes which are taking place in the office and its connected worlds. The chapters have built-in Activity sections which are designed to test knowledge and understanding to date and to suggest areas for further discussion and individual research. Questions are offered at the end of each chapter together with some projects. It is expected that teachers and students will be selective about the activities/projects undertaken, but each one is designed to be of value to the student compiling a portfolio which will be of practical value when at work.

The author has provided a comprehensive framework which will enable teachers and students to expand and develop individual ideas and interests while simultaneously preparing students for public examinations and the practical problems associated with office and secretarial work. It has been written by a practising teacher for teachers and students and throughout the text is the thread of modern technology and associated developments – particularly in the microcomputer world.

Paul Bailey

ACKNOWLEDGEMENTS

It is impossible for any one individual to produce a book of this nature without much support, and the author is indebted to those who have supplied him with details of latest developments and so enabled the text not only to be up to date but, hopefully, predict future developments.

The author and publishers wish to thank the following who have kindly given permission for the use of copyright material:

Banda, Berol Ltd, Commodore, Expandex Ltd, Peter Flewitt, Gestetner Ltd, IBM United Kingdom Ltd, ITR International Time Ltd, Lanier Business Products, Her Majesty's Stationery Office, Midland Bank Ltd, Nashua Copycat Ltd, National Girobank, Olympia International, Pitney Bowes Ltd, The Post Office, Rexel Ltd, Spicers Ltd, Swift Business Equipment Ltd, Twinlock UK Ltd, 3M United Kingdom Ltd.

CHAPTER 1

THE OFFICE IN ITS ENVIRONMENT

1.1 DEFINING AN OFFICE

All those about to begin study for examinations in Office Practice, Secretarial Duties, Clerical Duties or other related subjects should be familiar with the terms used to describe an office and its functions. The function of 'offices', whatever they may be, should be seen as part of the whole *commercial process*. 'That group of activities concerned with getting goods from those who first produce them to those who finally consume (use) them.' A *chain of production* often suggests points at which the office function may take place (see Figure 1.1).

Fig 1.1 *chain of production showing the movement of bricks from a manufacturer to a wholesaler/retailer and finally to a consumer*

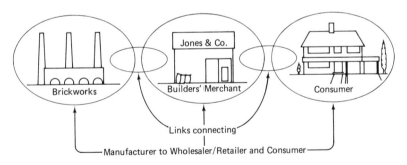

For example, a brickworks digs clay from the ground (nature) and mixes it with various other material before firing it to make bricks. The works does not produce bricks on the off-chance that they will sell – if it did it would soon be out of business. While its productive work force actually digs the clay, moulds and makes the bricks other workers are engaged in activities which enable the brick-makers to get on with the job for which they are employed and best suited – making bricks. Managers have to decide how best to manufacture the bricks, the sales force has to ensure that orders come in to enable production to continue without costly breaks, other employees have to take the actual orders and ensure that they are met, arrange for the bricks to be transported to where they are required, conduct research to enable the company to keep ahead of its competitors – and so on. Add the fact that money has to change hands when payments are paid to and from the company, that insurance has to be taken out against a whole range of risks and it can be seen that what appears to be a simple process is, in fact, a very complex one involving literally hundreds of people who are not directly involved in the process of making bricks. Once the bricks have left the brickworks and been sold to a builders' merchant more processes are involved since the merchant cannot just sell bricks – he must advertise, employ sales staff, staff to take orders and arrange deliveries, staff to collect payments, calculate the salaries of those employed – and so on. Even the consumer, the householder who actually uses the bricks to construct an extension to his house, has to arrange to buy the bricks, accept delivery and pay for them (possibly with borrowed money).

A little thought will show that a large range of activities is involved in all production. While a great many activities do not actually produce goods they do aid, or assist, production. You should now be able to give a definition of the word *'office'*. As an aid to your thoughts consider 'A place for conducting business' or 'A place where clerks work'. If you accept the first definition what about business conducted over a meal in a hotel? If you accept the second do you consider that all office workers are clerks? At the end of your discussions you will probably come to the conclusion that no one definition covers the term 'office' and that the term can be applied to anything which plays a part in assisting the commercial process – be it the back room of a house where a small shopkeeper keeps his records to a vast complex controlling some huge multinational commercial enterprise.

1.2 DEFINITION OF COMMON TERMS

Office practice may well be thought of as 'the whole process of what is considered to be the normal work undertaken in an office'. Firms and organisations need to have a routine to handle the various tasks performed by those workers who directly assist the production or commercial process and can include such functions as receiving and directing visitors, *reception*, answering and directing telephone calls, *telephone reception*; dealing with orders, *purchasing*; dealing with sales, *sales*; typing dictated replies to inquiries and other correspondence, *shorthand-typing* or *audio-typing*; calculating and paying wages, *wages*; hiring and firing staff, *personnel*; taking care of the legal side of affairs, *legal department* – and so on. No matter how many functions there are, they all have to work with some understanding of all the other functions which take place, not only within an individual firm but also in other firms with which the firm is dealing.

Clerical duties may well be thought of as 'The functions carried out by individuals working in the many sections which make up an office'. A wages clerk will calculate wages and deductions from wages, a purchasing clerk will handle the purchasing documents (order the goods to instructions), etc. A glance through the situations vacant columns of any local newspaper will show a whole range of clerical jobs.

Secretarial duties are probably best thought of as 'The duties performed by a secretary', a person who works for, or with, an individual and undertakes a wider range of tasks than would be undertaken by a clerk. These duties will almost certainly consist of some typing, shorthand or audio work, answering the telephone and dealing with callers, making arrangements (appointments and the like) for the employer, taking copies of documents or arranging for many copies of any particular piece of work to be made – and so on.

It follows from what has been discussed so far that office work is not just shorthand and typing but that it is much more and that training for public examinations is no guarantee of training which will directly qualify a person to work in an office. Those engaged in the commercial world are increasingly aware of the need for speed and efficiency in all transactions. This need demands a knowledge of new ideas and technology. The better the quality of service given to those actually engaged in production the greater is the chance of increased prosperity for all. As in all areas of human activity, workers engaged in 'office work' need to be flexible in their approach to all situations and be ready to take advantage of new technology which will save both time and costs. Increasingly office work involves handling machinery and replacing old ideas and techniques with new ones. Those who take and pass examinations in any of the office, clerical or secretarial examinations must be prepared for change and must keep abreast of new ideas by taking an active interest in new products and ideas.

ACTIVITY 1

Before reading the rest of this book, obtain and read the syllabus of the examining body whose examination you hope to take at the end of your course of study. Note those sections which you are required to study. If you study a range of syllabuses you will see that they are not all the same – examining bodies do not necessarily agree what constitutes Office Practice, Clerical Duties or Secretarial Duties/Studies.

ACTIVITY 2

Write a sentence on each of the following:

Chain of production	An office
A secretary	Office practice
Secretarial duties	Clerical duties
An organisation chart	Office work

1.3 BUSINESS OWNERSHIP

While most examining bodies do not expect candidates to have a knowledge of the ownership of businesses, some bodies require not only a knowledge of ownership but also a closer study of some form of it. It can be argued that all who work in commercial undertakings would be better employees if they understood the ownership, not only of their own particular firm, but of others and the way in which they relate to each other. For further details see R. R. Pitfield: *Mastering Commerce* (Macmillan Master Series, 1982).

(a) The sole trader

The smallest and most numerous business unit is that owned and run by one person, the sole trader. *A sole trader is a person who carries on business on his own account and as a general rule the law treats the person and his business as one* - in other words the person and his business are the same. The number of people employed by the sole trader will depend on the size of the business; he may work on his own, he may be helped by his family or he may employ several people. The office part of the business may be just part of it - undertaken in a room at home after hours or be undertaken by a paid secretary cum general office aid (see Figure 1.2).

The sole trader may call on professional people to help him in certain areas; his bank may advise on financial matters or give help when he needs to borrow money; he may employ an accountant to assist with tax returns and a solicitor to advise on legal matters.

Fig 1.2 *organisational chart for a small firm*

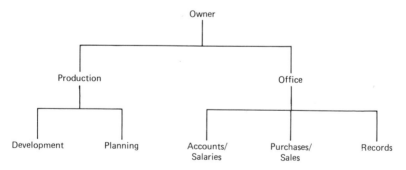

(b) Partnership

In the United Kingdom the 1890 Partnership Act defines a partnership as 'The relationship which subsists between persons carrying on business in common with a view to profit'. As a general rule a partnership consists of not more than twenty persons and, like the sole trader, has unlimited liability - which means that the partners cannot separate their business and private possessions. A partnership may be formed simply by people agreeing to work together at some business but, as a rule, partnerships are formed by means of a written agreement which states all the rules under which the partners intend working. The agreement will cover such matters as the kind or nature of the business, how much money will be involved and what that money will be used for, how much money each partner will provide – and how profits and losses are to be shared. If nothing specific is drawn up then the standard provisions of the 1890 Act apply.

Certain people involved in businesses may wish to keep their business and private affairs separate, and limit their business debts to the amount they invest in the business.

Under the **Limited Partnership Act 1907** partnerships can be formed whereby all the partners enjoy limited liability except one partner who must be responsible for all the debts of the partnership. If a person is a member of a limited partnership and is not the one with unlimited liability, he is able to separate his business and private affairs so that if the business gets into debt he does not have to sell his private possessions to meet his business debts.

(c) Limited liability companies

The most common method of limiting liability for business debts is by taking part in a limited liability company. Limited liability companies may be formed in three ways.

1. Royal Charter
2. Act of Parliament
3. Registration.

The most common method of forming a company is by registration. Companies formed by registration must comply with the Companies Acts of 1948–1976 in the United Kingdom. There are two kinds of limited liability company – private and public. A person wishing to form a limited liability company must find one more person in the case of a private company or six more in the case of a public company and submit the following to the Registrar of Companies:

a Memorandum of Association;
a list of directors and their written consents and promises to buy shares;
a declaration that the Company Acts have been complied with;
a statement of the nominal capital;
the Articles of Association.

The Memorandum of Association regulates the external affairs of the company.
(i) It tells people trading with the company, or intending to buy shares in the company, about the company.
(ii) It gives the *names and addresses* of the first director (private company) or directors (public company) and the first company secretary.
(iii) It shows the *amount of share capital* to be issued and the types of shares. The *nominal*, or *authorised*, *capital* is the maximum amount of money a company is allowed to raise by issuing shares.

The capital of limited companies is raised by the issuing of shares; there are several kinds of share – the most common being *ordinary shares*. If the company has only one class of shares then they, the ordinary shares, will have voting rights.

A preference share is one which has first call on profits – should any be made – and they are usually entitled to interest at a fixed rate.

A cumulative preference share is one which entitles the owner to profits for years when the company failed to pay a dividend.

A voting share is one which entitles the holder to vote at the annual general meeting of the company in proportion to the number of voting shares held.

The capital of a company with £1 000 000 authorised capital could be raised as follows.

1. All in ordinary shares of £1 each (1 000 000 × £1 = £1 000 000).
2. By a combination of shares, e.g.:

	£
500 000 ordinary shares of £1 each	500 000
250 voting shares of £1000 each	250 000
200 000 £1, 6% preference shares	200 000
50 000 £1, 5% cumulative preference shares	50 000
Total	£1 000 000

In the first example all shares carry one vote. In the second example only the 250 voting shares carry the vote.

The Articles of Association. The internal rules by which a company is governed. They state the classes of shares to be issued and how they are to be issued; the rights of the shareholders; the qualifications required to become a director; the rules concerning the holding of company meetings; the procedure for voting; the procedure to be used for keeping accounts and for their auditing; the rules for winding up the company – and the powers of the company to borrow money. Under the Companies Acts a model set of tables is printed and these articles are binding on all companies issuing shares unless the company's own articles specifically change them on some particular point.

A debenture is, basically, *a loan to a company*, offered for a fixed period in return for a fixed rate of interest. There are two kinds of debenture: a *mortgage debenture* which is issued with the ownership of the assets of the company offered as security, and a *naked or unsecured debenture* which is issued without security. Debentures should not be confused with shares, which are actually parts of companies.

A private limited company is one which is limited to fifty members maximum and is not allowed to issue a prospectus. Membership is limited to the fifty maximum and shares can be bought and sold on the agreement of the members – providing the number of members does not exceed fifty. A private limited company need only have two members and one director. There is some privacy as to the affairs of the company and although accounts must be published in limited form details of turnover do not have to be given unless it exceeds an amount fixed by Parliament.

A *public limited company* must have at least seven members – the maximum number will be decided by the Articles of Association. The shares of public companies can be bought and sold to and by the general public. A *quoted company* is one whose shares are bought and sold on the stock exchange after approval has been given by the committee of the stock exchange. Not all public companies are quoted companies. There is full public knowledge of the affairs of public limited companies. (See Figure 1.3.)

Fig 1.3 *organisational chart for a large company*

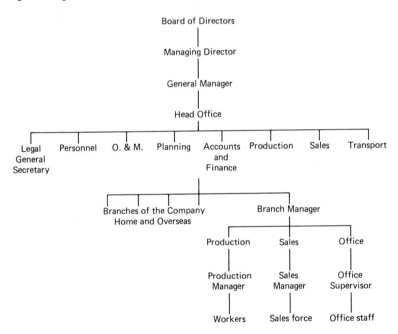

Management. Limited companies are owned by the shareholders but they are actually run by the elected representatives of the shareholders who are entitled to vote at the annual general meeting. Each company is compelled, by law, to appoint a *Company Secretary* and the Company Secretary is the official correspondent of the Board of Directors. It is the responsibility of the Company Secretary to ensure that the company's activities are in accordance with the Memorandum and Articles of Association, that the legal requirements of the business are met and, in some cases, to assume general responsibility for the general supervision of internal administration. Companies are primarily run by a *board of directors* whose activities are presided over by the *Chairman of the Board*. The Chairman may not be a full-time member of the board and may not be in attendance at the head office of the company all the time – but he is usually the person with the widest experience of business matters. The actual running of a company is usually in the hands of the *Managing Director*, who has the responsibility of carrying out the decisions of the board of directors. The board of directors may consist wholly of full-time members or a mixture of full- and part-time members – the part-time members acting in an advisory capacity in such matters as finance, law and technical knowledge while the full-time members may be *heads of important departments* such as accounts, marketing, personnel and production. *Full-time directors* are sometimes called *executive directors*. The board of directors is responsible for formulating and carrying out policy; setting up an efficient organisation structure; appointing qualified people to work within the structure created and to generally provide leadership. While it is the function of the board of directors to formulate and carry out policy, the actual implementation of decisions is left to individual departments which are run by *departmental heads*, who are often directors, and the *section leaders*, who are appointed to assist and advise as required. It is usual for each department to have a chain of command under the chairmanship of the head of department. Appointment to senior positions may be based on length of service, experience, qualifications or some other ability. As individuals leave a company their posts may be filled from within the company, a policy which encourages loyalty to the company but can lead to an atmosphere of 'waiting for dead men's shoes', or from outside the company – a policy which ensures the introduction of fresh blood from time to time. (See Figure 1.4.)

(d) Companies limited by guarantee

Some non-profit-making concerns are companies limited by guarantee – that is *the liability of the members is limited to the amount which they have undertaken to contribute in the event of the company being wound up*.

All registered companies are required by law to produce annual audited accounts and these accounts are usually published, together with a statement from the chairman giving the main points about the company's successes and failures during the year and about its future prospects. Should any profits have been made the accounts will say how much and what each shareholder can expect in the form of a dividend on the nominal value of each share held. Sometimes a company will issue a dividend at the end of six months in anticipation of more to come at the end of the trading year. A dividend paid during the year is called an *interim dividend* and a *final dividend* is the total amount paid for that year.

Fig 1.4 *possible management structure of a company*

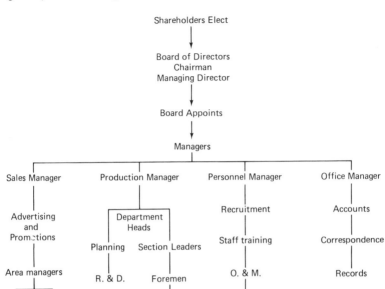

(e) The office in limited companies

The office organisation of limited companies will depend on the size and nature of the company, but might include an *office manager* for each office, an *office supervisor* for each office section and *office workers* within each section. The terms *junior* and *senior* may be used to distinguish between various *grades of office workers* or grades - such as Grade I, Grade II and so on. *A secretary* is not usually considered to be an office worker as such but a person who is responsible to one or two people only - she may have one or more deputies who act on her instructions. Figure 1.4 shows one possible organisation.

(f) Multinational companies

Multinational companies are companies whose operations are based on the good of the companies themselves and because they control operations in many countries, often in a wide range of activities, they are less susceptible to national pressures. They are subject to the laws of the individual countries in which they operate but because they are international they are able to escape full accountability - their affairs in one country may not be made public in another. They act internationally and are able to switch resources between the countries in which they operate to secure the cheapest and best labour, the most desirable locations and most favourable tax situations.

(g) Co-operatives

Co-operatives are basically self-help organisations. Individuals and businesses may join together to control and share the profits or production or obtain economies in buying goods and services. They are found in the fields of production (*worker co-operatives*), farming, banking, insurance and building societies. *Retail co-operative societies* in the United Kingdom purchase their stock from the *Co-operative Wholesale Society* - the CWS.

(h) State ownership

Sometimes called 'public ownership' - some industries are owned by the Government for the people of the country. The Government buys the private companies in a particular industry from their shareholders and runs the many individual companies as one vast national complex - for example the railways, the Coal Board and the Gas and Electricity Boards. Each industry is responsible to a member of the Government and is headed by a chairman nominated by the head of the government department and his colleagues.

Local authorities often run various utilities such as water undertakings or transport services which they own in much the same way as the government owns state undertakings. Local councils consist of elected representatives who are not paid as such but who make decisions about local affairs. The elected representatives are responsible for appointing the paid officials who actually carry out the running of the undertakings or services - and are responsible for setting up the administration to do so.

ACTIVITY

Suggest an office structure for:
a sole trader;
a partnership;
a private limited company;
a public corporation.

QUESTIONS

1. What are the differences and similarities between public and private limited liability companies?
2. What is the difference between a share and a debenture? How many classes of shares are there and what is the purpose of each?
3. What are the duties of:

A company secretary?	The board of directors?
The managing director?	Full-time or executive directors?
Departmental heads?	Section leaders?

4. What is:

Authorised capital?

The Memorandum and Articles of Association?

A multinational company?

A company limited by guarantee?

5. What are the advantages and disadvantages of a sole trader over a partnership and a private limited company over a partnership?

1.4 DEPARTMENTS IN BUSINESS ORGANISATIONS

Throughout this book the various departments of business organisations – sales, purchasing, production, etc. – are dealt with in different chapters covering the relevant office functions. The student should also be aware of the following departments, some of which are only of importance in large organisations (see Figures 1.2 and 1.3).

(a) The personnel department

Basically *the duties of a Personnel Department* are to concern itself with staff welfare, the hiring and firing of staff and training and retraining. The size and scope of a department will depend on the size and nature of the business. When a vacancy arises the section head or department manager concerned will inform the *Personnel Officer*. It may be that the vacancy has arisen because of a resignation, or promotion or expansion within the department. The Personnel Officer and the person in the department concerned will discuss the vacancy and try to arrive at a *job description* – a general statement as to the scope of the job, the responsibilities it carries and the duties a person appointed to that post might be expected to undertake. From the job description *a job specification* may be drawn up – a statement of the mental and physical conditions required to undertake the job, what any person appointed to the job would be expected to know and understand and what judgements the person appointed might have to make. Combining the job description and job specification a *personnel specification* will be arrived at – the kind of person required to undertake the actual job. Once it is agreed what job needs doing, and an outline of the kind of person required to undertake it is arrived at, the job will be advertised.

The job may be advertised on a notice board outside the firm, in the national or local press, by notifying the Careers Office or Jobcentre, informing a Private Employment Agency – or, in the case of a school or college, by telephoning to ask if a suitable student is interested in applying.

The Personnel Department is also responsible for ensuring that a firm complies with the law relating to employing people and the health and safety of employees – see Section 21.1

(b) Welfare

The Personnel Department may also be responsible for staff welfare – the provision of medical rooms/facilities and rest rooms for the sick – and such general matters as working and leisure conditions – and the arranging of holidays. If firms allow employees to take their holidays throughout the year, instead of closing for a period in which all take their holidays at the same time, the Personnel Department may have to draw up a *holiday rota*, which is a list saying who will be away and when. It is important to ensure that the firm can function efficiently while staff are away, so the number allowed away at any one time must be limited. Staff are usually asked to state in advance when they would like to take their holidays and some method must be used to allocate dates which are requested by several staff. The amount of holiday allowed varies from firm to firm, usually with age and experience. When you start to work for a firm it is usual for existing holiday arrangements to be honoured.

(c) Training

The Personnel Department is also responsible for the training of staff, there may be a separate *Training Department* at the firm which is run in consultation with the Personnel Department. Firms may conduct their own training courses, either as part of the normal working week, have centres to which employees are sent from all over the country for varying periods, or link training at work with courses run by local colleges on a day-release or a block-release basis. When a job is no longer required at a firm, for example, because a machine replaces a particular skill, the training department may be responsible for the retraining of staff.

(d) Organisation and Method (O. & M.)

Large firms often have a department which is concerned with general efficiency – the *O. & M. Department*, which is constantly looking for ways of improving production and lowering costs while improving the standard of product. Small firms may not be able to afford such a department and will employ outside firms to advise them when the need arises. The O. & M. Department may, for example, decide that a central typing pool is more economical and efficient than separate typists attached to departments; that an audio bank is to be preferred to shorthand typists; that by redesigning certain forms costs can be saved and processes made simpler, or by doing a job this way instead of that time can be saved. The department is constantly looking at new ideas and machinery to improve standards of efficiency. Very often regular meetings are held with staff or department heads to look at general standards and employees are sometimes rewarded for suggesting methods of improving performance.

(e) Planning

The *Planning Department* may be responsible for the general planning of how to make products and suggesting the ideal layout of the factory/firm to produce new products efficiently.

(f) Research and Development (R. & D.)

The design and development of new ideas is usually the responsibility of the *R. & D. Department* which employs research staff and designers who work on new products, often suggested by the *Market Research Department*, that part of an organisation responsible for finding out what products a firm should be producing. There is little point in designing and developing new ideas and products if they will not sell!

(g) Legal and accounts
The *Legal Department* will be responsible for all the legal aspects of production, employment and the financial structure of a firm. The *Accounts Department* will be responsible for looking after the capital of the firm, its *fixed capital*, that tied up in the fabric and its machinery, its *working capital*, the money used to buy raw materials and make products, to pay bills and wages and so on. It will also be responsible for forecasting future cash requirements, the paying of bills and wages/salaries, receiving payments from customers and generally looking after the interests of the owners of the firm.

All these departments meet on a regular basis, both formally and informally, and from them comes the general efficient running of the firm/organisation. The exact relationships between the departments will vary considerably from firm to firm as a large firm would be expected to have many different departments while a small firm would combine the functions in one department.

QUESTIONS

1. What is a job description?
2. What is a job specification?
3. What the chief functions of the following departments?

Personnel	Welfare
Training	O. & M.
R. & D.	Planning

LAYOUT OF BUSINESS LETTERS

Office workers who have never taken typewriting, and many workers who have taken and passed public examinations in typewriting, may find that the style of layout used varies considerably from firm to firm. This does not mean that the styles taught in English lessons or those accepted by the public examining bodies in typewriting are incorrect – any more than it means that any particular firm does not know what it is doing. It simply means that there are several ways of setting out letters – and each is correct.

There are basically two differing ways of punctuating letters – or not punctuating them – the *fully punctuated* style and what is called *open punctuation*.

Punctuated letters are those in which the normal English style of punctuation, sometimes called *standard punctuation*, is used throughout – for names and addresses, the date and the rest of the letter (see Figure 2.1).

Open punctuation is often used in the interests of economy and speed. While the body of the letter is punctuated as normal, the names and addresses, the date, reference, close – and so on – are left unpunctuated. Even within the body of the letter standard abbreviations and the date may be left without punctuation. As a general rule all punctuation is left out unless to do so would cause some confusion on the part of the reader (see Figure 2.2).

2.1 LETTER STYLES

There are several styles commonly used when laying out letters but the usual styles are the *fully-blocked* and the *semi-blocked*.

Fully-blocked letters are those in which all lines begin at the same point, that is, at the left-hand margin, although the date may be placed as indicated in Figure 2.3.

Semi-blocked letters are set out as in Figure 2.4 – basically the reference and date are typed on the same line and paragraphs are indented. The complimentary close and signatory are typed from the middle of the typing

Fig 2.1 *punctuated letter*

```
WALTER MASON & SON LTD.,
51 St. Martin's Street,
PRESTON.
PR1 6NY                          Telephone 89231
```

```
Ref. MC/BB                       29th November, 19xx

Gardiner & Lancer Co. Ltd.,
76 Bristol Road,
LONDON.
EC99 4RP

Dear Sirs,

        Your Brazilian suppliers, Messrs. Perira
& Tassini, have informed us of a shipment of
750 sacks of coffee by the ship Atlantis, due
to arrive at Liverpool on 9th December.

        We should be glad to hear whether you
wish to have the goods warehoused or forwarded
direct to your London factory.

                        Yours faithfully,



                        Mike Cusford
                        Shipping Manager
```

line. Enclosures may be indicated in a number of ways; with a mark
(usually three hyphens) typed in the left-hand margin at the point where
the enclosure is mentioned, at the foot of the letter at the left-hand margin
(both for the fully-blocked and the semi-blocked letters) or by fixing
pieces of coloured paper to the letter and to the material enclosed.

Fully blocked letters and semi-blocked letters may be typed using open
punctuation or standard punctuation.

Fig 2.2 *letter with open punctuation*

```
Novafield Ltd
The Green
HALIFAX
HX1 1XG
Telephone 778

Ref RT/HG

23 September 19xx

McKechnie & Sterling Ltd
421 Rufford Street
WAKEFIELD
WF9 4RR

Dear Sirs

Further to my telephone conversation with
Mr Simpson this morning I enclose the copy of
Invoice No 4635 sent to me for checking and
the Credit Note received from Crossley Ltd.

I confirm that the original delivery was
returned to Crossley Ltd and that replacements
for the damaged goods were listed on Invoice
No 47869.

Yours faithfully



Robert Tibbitts
Buying Officer

ENCS
```

2.2 PARTS OF A BUSINESS LETTER

The letterhead is usually printed at the head of the first sheet only, since in the interests of economy most firms use plain sheets of paper (the same quality and colour as the first sheet) for continuation sheets should they be required. The letterhead includes the name, address, telephone and/or telex numbers, and such statutory information as may be required – as for example for VAT and company registration purposes. Some firms include a brief description of the business in the address – e.g. Jones & Sons Ltd (Painters and Decorators). If the address has to be typed at the head of the first sheet (because no printed letterhead is available) it may be typed at the left-hand margin, centred or typed to the right of the sheet – either blocked on the longest line or typed so that all lines end flush on the right-hand margin.

The reference is usually typed first, after the letterhead, and helps to identify the sender of the letter and the typist – or other correspondence related to the letter if it is one of a series. Sometimes 'Our Ref' and 'Your

Fig 2.3 *layout of a fully-blocked letter*

```
Reference

Date                              ┌─────────────────────────────┐
                                  │ As an alternative the date   │
Name                              │ may be typed anywhere in     │
and                               │ this area - from the middle  │
Address                           │ of the typing line           │
                                  └─────────────────────────────┘
Salutation

Body of the letterxxxxxxxxxxxxxxxxxxxxxxxxxxxxxxxxxxxxxxxxxxxxxxxxxxxxx
xxxxxxxxxxxxxxxxxxxxxxxxxxxxxxxxxxxxxxxxxxxxxxxxxxxxxxxxxxxxxxxxxxxxxxxxx
xxxxxxxxxxxxxxxxxxxxxxxxxxxxxxxxxxxxxxxxxxxxxxxxxxxxxxxxxxxxxxxxxxxxxxxxx
xxxxxxxxxxxxxxxxxxxxxxxxxxxxxxxxxxxxxxxxxxxxxxxxxxxxxxxxxxxxxxxxxxxxxxxxx

typed in xxxxxxxxxxxxxxxxxxxxxxxxxxxxxxxxxxxxxxxxxxxxxxxxxxxxxxxxxxxxxxxx
xxxxxxxxxxxxxxxxxxxxxxxxxxxxxxxxxxxxxxxxxxxxxxxxxxxxxxxxxxxxxxxxxxxxxxxxx
xxxxxxxxxxxxxxxxxxxxxxxxxxxxxxxxxxxxxxxxxxxxxxxxxxxxxxxxxxxxxxxxxxxxxxxxx
xxxxxxxxxxxxxxxxxxxxxxxxxxxxxxxxxxxxxxxxxxxxxxxxxxxxxxxxxxxxxxxxxxxxxxxxx

blocked paragraphs.  xxxxxxxxxxxxxxxxxxxxxxxxxxxxxxxxxxxxxxxxxxxxxxxxxxxx
xxxxxxxxxxxxxxxxxxxxxxxxxxxxxxxxxxxxxxxxxxxxxxxxxxxxxxxxxxxxxxxxxxxxxxxxx
xxxxxxxxxxxxxxxxxxxxxxxxxxxxxxxxxxxxxxxxxxxxxxxxxxxxxxxxxxxxxxxxxxxxxxxxx
xxxxxxxxxxxxxxxxxxxxxxxxxxxxxxxxxxxxx.

Complimentary close
Name of company - if required

(Signature)

Signatory
Designation

Enclosures
```

Ref' are printed on the paper and the typist has simply to type in the required information.

The date should be typed in the order: day month year, and is usually typed after the reference in the case of a fully-blocked letter or on the same line as the reference in the case of a semi-blocked letter. Sometimes the word 'Date' may be printed on the paper. As a general rule the date is never abbreviated, because this may cause confusion, although some months may be abbreviated – e.g. Aug, Sept.

The name and address of the addressee should be typed in the positions indicated in the charts. The addressee is the name of the person or company to whom the letter is being sent. If a window envelope is being used the postal town must be type in capital letters and the postcode typed in two parts as the last line of the address. It is *never* punctuated – no matter what the style of the letter.

The words *Private* or *Confidential* may be typed at the head of any letter – usually after the date line.

The attention line is usually typed after the last line of the inside address and is used when firms have a rule that all correspondence must be addressed to the firm and not individuals at the firm. The letter should be typed 'For

Fig 2.4 *layout of a semi-blocked letter*

```
Reference                Date

Name
and
Address

Salutation

     Body of the letter xxxxxxxxxxxxxxxxxxxxxxxxxxxxx
xxxxxxxxxxxxxxxxxxxxxxxxxxxxxxxxxxxxxxxxxxxxxxxxxxxxxxxx
xxxxxxxxxxxxxxxxxxxxxxxxxxxxxxxxxxxxxxxxxxxxxxxxxxxxxxxx
xxxxxxxxxxxxxxxxxxxxxxx.

     typed in xxxxxxxxxxxxxxxxxxxxxxxxxxxxxxxxxxxxxxx
xxxxxxxxxxxxxxxxxxxxxxxxxxxxxxxxxxxxxxxxxxxxxxxxxxxxxxxx
xxxxxxxxxxxxxxxxxxxxxxxxxxxxxxxxxxxxxxxxxxxxxxxxxxxxxxxx
xxxxxxxxxxxxxxxxxxxx.

     indented paragraphs.  xxxxxxxxxxxxxxxxxxxxxxxxxx
xxxxxxxxxxxxxxxxxxxxxxxxxxxxxxxxxxxxxxxxxxxxxxxxxxxxxxxx
xxxxxxxxxxxxxxxxxxxxxxxxxxxxxxxxxxxxxxxxxxxxxxxxxxxxxxxx
xxxxxxxxxxxxxxxxxxxxxxxxxxxxx.

                    Complimentary close
                    Name of company - if
                    required

                    (Signature)

                    Signatory
                    Designation

Enclosures
```

the attention of' a particular department or person – 'For the attention of the Sales Department', 'For the attention of Mrs W Yates'. When using window envelopes it is advisable to type the attention line above the inside address.

The salutation or greeting to the letter may be personal, when the addressee is known to the writer (Dear Mrs Matthews; Dear Wendy), or impersonal – when the addressee is not known to the writer (Dear Sir or Dear Sirs, Dear Madam and so on). Use 'Dear Sirs' when the letter has an attention line.

The subject heading indicates what the letter is about and in the fully-blocked style it is typed at the left-hand margin while it is centred about the middle of the typing line in the case of semi-blocked letters. In either style it is usual to underline the subject heading if it is typed with intial capital letters – e.g. Our Order No 3298 – while if it is typed in capital letters it may not be underscored – e.g. OUR NEW CATALOGUE.

The body of the letter is usually made up of more than one paragraph and if so a space is left between each paragraph. Paragraphs may be blocked or indented – depending on the style being used.

The complimentary close – or subscription is typed a single line space below the last line of the last paragraph. If the salutation is impersonal the complimentary close should be 'Yours faithfully' or 'Yours truly', while if the salutation is personal it should be 'Yours sincerely'. The position of the complimentary close will depend on the style of the letter – see Figures 2.3 and 2.4.

Fig 2.5 *the complimentary close*

Yours faithfully

Margaret Hewines
for

Peter Wilkinson

Example A

Yours faithfully

Margaret Hewines

Dictated by Mr Wilkinson and signed in his absence

Example B

Yours faithfully

Margaret Hewines

Margaret Hewines (Miss)
Secretary to
Peter Wilkinson

Example C

Yours faithfully

Margaret Hewines

pp Peter Wilkinson

Example D

The name of the company sending the letter is sometimes typed after the complimentary close – the same as it appears on the letterhead.

The signatory is the name of the person who signs the letter and this is typed in case the signature cannot be read. Space, usually 4 to 8 single lines, is left before the signatory for the letter to be signed. It is not always possible for the person named at the foot of the letter to sign it personally – the person may be away from the office or there may be too many letters to sign personally. In such cases an executive may delegate another to sign letters on his or her behalf. If you are asked to sign a letter by an executive you should sign your own name in the space left but add the word 'for' (Figure 2.5 (example A),). If you are left notes from which you have to type a reply you should sign the letter with your own name and add 'Dictated by . . . and signed in his absence' (example B). If you are asked to write the reply and sign the letter you would indicate the fact in the letter – 'Mr Hughes asked me to write to you . . .' and sign the letter yourself (example C). Where a great many letters are left to another to sign the letters pp or per pro or p. pro or p pro – meaning *per procurationem* – are typed before the name of the person and the letter is signed by the person authorised (example D).

The designation or position held by the signatory may be included, typed beneath the signatory.

Enclosures may be indicated in a number of ways as indicated earlier but if typed they are indicated at the left-hand margin, sometimes with the actual number.

Examples: ENC   Enc   ENCS   Encs   ENCS 2   Encs 2

Continuation sheets must be used if a letter goes on to more than one sheet of paper. *Catchwords*, designed to lead in to the second or subsequent pages, may be typed at the foot of the previous page and such words as 'Continued' (or any abbreviation of it). '/Over', '/over', 'P.T.O.' and 'PTO' may be typed anywhere below the bottom line of the previous page – preceded or followed by dots. The continuation sheet(s) should be plain paper, the same size and quality as the top sheet and should be headed as follows.

Fully-blocked letters should have a continuation sheet(s) which is typed in the same style. It is usual to type the number of the page at the left-hand margin and under it, usually with spaces between the lines; the date (typed as on the first sheet) and the addressee (typed as on the first sheet).

Semi-blocked letters should also have continuation sheets typed in the same style as the first sheet. The addressee is typed (as on the first sheet) at the left-hand margin; the page number is typed in the middle of the typing line and the date is typed (as on the first sheet) towards the right-hand margin.

Short letters – that is, letters of under roughly 130 words using an elite typeface or under 110 words using a pica typeface – should be typed on A5 paper while letters of up to 400 words using elite type or 350 words using pica type may be typed on single sheets of A4 paper. Longer letters will require one or more continuation sheets.

2.3 COMPOSING LETTERS

Letters either convey information or ask for it and should do so in a manner which leaves no doubt on the part of the reader. It is essential that all the required information is given or requested without the letter being made unnecessarily long. The opening paragraph(s) should indicate what the letter is about; the middle paragraphs should contain the information being given or sought. The concluding paragraph should reflect the general tone of the rest of the letter and even if the letter is one of complaint it should not be abusive. Words should never be used unless the writer is absolutely sure of both their meaning and their spelling, while care should be taken never to use words which might confuse the reader or be open to more than one interpretation. No matter what the letter is about, the material in it should be carefully graded and all points covered while exactness of meaning and tone should never be sacrificed in the interests of brevity. If a typist is unsure on any point she should consult the person sending the letter.

It is important to remember that all letters represent the firm sending them – very often they are the only communicatin between the sender and the receiver. All letters must be typed without typing, grammatical or spelling errors and the style of layout should be consistent.

2.4 ADDRESSING

The correct addressing of postcards, letters, packets and parcels is essential if mail is to reach its destination without delay. The *Post Office Guide* gives examples of the way in which addresses should be set out and the regulations published by the Post Office must be followed if items are to be delivered correctly. The rules apply to private and business mail alike.

(a) The correct order of an address
The correct order is:

1. The name of the addressee.
2. The number of the house or firm, or the name of the house or firm if either does not have a number, and the name of the Road, Street or Avenue, etc.
3. The name of the locality – where required by the Post Office.
4. The name of the hamlet or village – in a country district.
5. The name of the postal town, typed in CAPITAL LETTERS.
6. The name of the county – where required.
7. The postcode, shown as the last item in the address, typed on a line by itself, in two parts separated by a single space, UNPUNCTUATED and typed in CAPITAL LETTERS.

Addresses on envelopes should be typed in the *lower part* and towards the *right-hand side* of the front. When *window envelopes* are being used the position may vary slightly – but not the order of the address.

Special instructions such as 'For the attention of', 'Private' or 'Confidential' should be typed two single lines above the address. Special instructions such as 'Express Delivery' or 'Recorded Delivery' should be typed in the left-hand corner of the envelope at the top.

Packets and parcels should have the address and any special instructions typed on sticky paper and stuck on the front – in the appropriate position.

Addresses should be typed in single-line spacing unless the address is a very short one and the envelope, packet or parcel is a large one. If the address must be shortened, because of lack of space or because of addressing machine limitations, the postal town and county may be typed on the same line. If the postcode has to be typed on the same line as either the postal town or county it should be typed two, preferably six, spaces to the right of the item.

The style of punctuation should follow that used for the letter – standard or open punctuation.

Ideally on letters the sender's name and address should appear on the back of the envelope. If this is not possible it should be shown in the left-hand front corner. This will assist the Post Office in returning the item should it prove impossible to deliver it. Packets and parcels should be labelled in the same manner.

(b) Forms of address

Use a courtesy title with a person's name – e.g. Mr Robert Young, Robert Young Esq, Miss Jayne Saunders, Mrs Robert Young (it is usual to use a married woman's husband's Christian name rather than her own), Dr Robert Young or The Misses – when addressing more than one single lady of the same name. Some single and married women prefer to be addressed as Ms – e.g. Ms Jayne Saunders. When addressing a person in a foreign country the equivalent of Mr should be used but if there is any doubt the addressee should be addressed as Mr. When addressing a company do not use a courtesy title – unless you are addressing a person at that company by name – e.g. The Macmillan Press Ltd. The word 'Messrs' (Messieurs) should be used when addressing a partnership – e.g. Messrs Widdowson & Turnock.

The letters in abbreviations in qualifications or decorations should be typed after the name of the person with a space between the groups of letters – e.g. David Anderson BA, Clive Bushell OBE, Miss Sandra Jervis BA FRSA, Michael Flanders Esq BA BSc. The style of punctuation should again follow that used in the letter – standard or open. If there is any doubt about the correct form of address or the correct order for the typing of decorations, honours and qualifications consult a reference book.

2.5 MEMORANDUM FORMS

Memorandum forms (memos for short) are used to send messages to people in a firm either at the same address as the sender or in other parts of the country or the world. The messages are not as formal as letters and so the forms do not have the letterhead or inside name and address. Very often they are not signed and so do not have a complimentary close or designation. It is not usual to use memos for communicating with other firms.

2.6 FORM LETTERS

When standard information can be set out in the form of a letter – many firms find that the same letters can be used to cover particular circumstances such as acknowledgement of an order, advice that an order will be delayed, and so on, they use a form letter. A form letter is the framework of a prepared letter – one with the essential material but lacking a date, inside name and address and salutation (which may be produced simply as Dear – and space left after the word). These routine letters save a great deal of time and since all the typist has to do is insert the missing material before sending the letter off it is highly desirable to use a typeface which exactly matches that used for the preparation of the frame or form letter. If this is not possible then a contrasting face should be used and not one which is vaguely similar.

2.7 REPORTS

There are several kinds of report which a secretary or an executive may be called upon to produce - report of a meeting, an interview, a review of equipment or some discussion. Reports should be headed in such a way as to make it clear what the report is about; Report on Meeting with Area Training Officer; Report on current stocks of Typewriting Materials; Report on Meeting with Mr Eric Owen of Planning Department - and so on.

It is essential that reports are accurate, brief and clear and are set out in a logical sequence in such a way as to make the reader exactly aware of what is going on. *Individual reports* should be written in the first person - e.g. 'I have examined the complaint made by . . .' *Reports of meetings* should be written in the third person - e.g. 'At a meeting of the Area Managers held on Monday 12 October at Head Office it was . . .'.

Reports should contain a reference, to make it easier to refer to in the future, and should state at the top if they are Private or Confidential.

A suggested plan of typing reports is:
the heading or title stating whether the report is Private or Confidential;
the subject of the report;
the date of the subject-matter of the report - or the date of the report if the matter to be reported upon does not require the date of the meeting or interview;
the place - if the report is about a meeting;
a reference number - if the report is to be filed;
the name of the person to whom the report is to be sent or a list of the people to whom copies are to be sent if the report is to be seen by more than one person;
the name of the person making the report.

Each report should begin with a statement as to why it is being made - e.g. 'In response to your request for a report on the state of . . .'. Separate headings should be used for each new point being made, if the headings will make the understanding of the report easier, while the facts should be set out clearly and logically. A report should conclude with a recommendation if the subject-matter calls for one - for example, a report into the typewriters to be used in the office should recommend which machines to use, or where to obtain the machines suggested.

2.8 CARBON COPY NOTATION

If carbon copies of letters, memoranda or reports have to be sent to individuals it is usual to type a note on the original copy, or top copy. The notation is usually typed at the foot of the sheet at the left-hand margin, or at the top. Sometimes copies have to be sent to others, but for various reasons it is not always appropriate for the person receiving the top copy to know. In this case the notation is typed on the carbon copies only – they are called *blind copies*. The notation is typed after the top copy has been removed from the typewriter – sometimes marked 'NOO', or Not on the original.

The usual notation used when sending a carbon copy to an individual is:

c.c. M J Thorrowgood

or

CC: M J Thorrowgood

If copies have to be sent to a number of people the notation is usually:

Copies to: M J Thorrowgood
            J Jackman
            J Theobald

or

c.c. M J Thorrowgood
      J Jackman
      J Theobald

Some firms have their own notation.

The Civil Service has its own regulations concerning the typing of correspondence and details will be found in *Manual for Civil Service Typists* (HMSO, 1975).

Complimentary slips are often used to save the cost of typing a letter when material is sent for information purposes or in reply to a request of some kind. They are printed on small sheets of paper – usually A7 – and contain the name and address of the sender – sometimes with the words 'With the Compliments of . . .'.

QUESTIONS

1. Write a sentence showing that you understand the following parts of a letter.

The letterhead	The reference
The attention line	The salutation
The subject heading	The complimentary close or subscription
The signatory	The designation

2. What are the functions of the following?

A memorandum	A form letter
An individual report	A complimentary slip

PROJECT

Produce a folder containing examples of the following:
Fully-blocked letters – standard and open punctuation.
Semi-blocked letters – standard and open punctuation.
Fully and semi-blocked letters with continuation sheets.
An internal memorandum.
A report.
Complimentary slips.
Carbon copies showing carbon copy notation.
DL envelopes addressed in standard and open punctuation with an attention line; Private; Confidential; special instructions to the Post Office such as Air Mail, etc.

HANDLING THE MAIL

In all organisations the mail presents two basic problems; dealing with the incoming mail and dealing with the outgoing mail. In a small organisation one person deals with all the mail. In a large organisation there may be a special mail room employing many people. What happens in any particular mail room will depend on such factors as the amount of incoming and outgoing mail, the number of staff employed and the amount and range of machinery available. The following describes what might happen in a large organisation.

3.1 INCOMING MAIL

Depending on the size of the organisation the mail may be delivered by the Post Office as part of a normal delivery round; it may be delivered by special delivery when the amounts are very large, or arrangements may be made for an office junior to collect it from the local Post Office sorting office on her way to work. *First-class mail*, which is charged at a higher rate than *second-class mail*, is usually delivered first and includes the more important items – while second-class mail, which includes such things as circulars and advertising material, is often delivered later in the day.

It is essential that the mail is handled efficiently so that correspondence is rapidly available for internal distribution. As soon as the mail arrives:

1. Sign for registered or recorded delivery items and enter a record in a special register.
2. Sort out items marked 'Private' or 'Confidential'. Some firms may require that a register is kept of all such items.

Some firms arrange for the mail to be sorted into departments straight away and these processes take place within individual departments.

3. Open the mail – other than the items which have been signed for or are marked 'Private' or 'Confidential'. In a small office this may be done by hand but in the case of a large organisation this will be done by machine.

Before opening mail by machine tap down the contents so that the machine, which slices a very narrow strip of paper off each envelope, does not cut the contents.

4. Carefully remove the contents from each envelope; you may leave important documents inside if you do not take care. Attach all enclosures to *the front* of the letter. If a letter indicates that there is an enclosure but you cannot find it, mark the letter 'Not enclosed' and put the letter and envelope on one side for your later attention. Initial the letter to show that you have dealt with it.
5. Date stamp *all* the mail – some firms not only date stamp it but also record the time the item was stamped.
6. Keep envelopes, which should also be date-stamped, because they may contain vital information such as when the letter was posted – or indicate a return address when the contents fail to provide one.

Registered, recorded delivery items and items marked 'Private' or 'Confidential' are usually taken to the person or department to whom they are addressed for opening there. In such cases you cannot date/time stamp the contents but you can stamp the envelope.

7. The mail is now ready for sending to the various departments. Some firms require a record of all incoming mail to be kept – usually in a special file or book. Correspondence which contains *remittances*, sums of money for payments in the form of notes (registered mail only), postal orders, stamps or cheques, etc., should be specially checked to ensure just what has been sent – and both the remittance and the letter should be initialled. In some firms all remittances are sent direct to the clerk in charge of mailing or to the chief cashier – who has to sign for all amounts in a special *remittances book*.

In a very large firm the sorting may be made into pigeon-holes, letter trays or wire baskets.

If it is not clear where a particular letter has to go (it may not be addressed to a particular person or department) check for a subject heading which may indicate where it has to go. Any letters which present problems in assigning (deciding where they have to go), put on one side for later attention so that you do not hold up the rest of the mail.

Letters which require the attention of more than one department require special attention.

1. Make a list of all the departments concerned.
   As the letter passes from one department to another the department head initials the letter and passes it on. *A route slip* may be used.
2. The main department may keep the letter and pass on the minor problems to departments concerned.
3. It is sometimes easier to take as many copies of the letter as there are departments concerned and so ensure that all departments receive at

Fig 3.1 *the incoming mail*

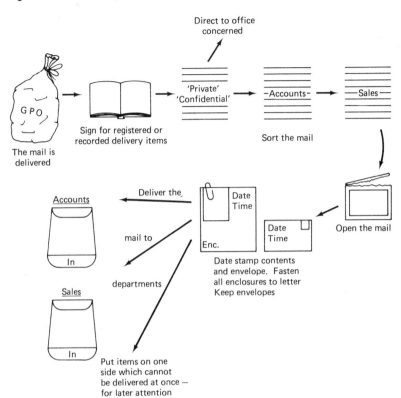

least a copy of it. This may be more expensive than the other two methods – but is the safest and often the quickest.

Once the bulk of the mail has been routed, go back and deal with the mail which presented problems. *Remember*: all mail is important. The letter which fails to reach its destination quickly and accurately may result in the loss of important business.

In a very small office one person will deal with all incoming mail, opening it by hand and dealing with it at that time – of filing it for later attention.

3.2 OUTGOING MAIL

Much will depend on the size of the organisation on the method used for dealing with the outgoing mail. *In a small firm* replies will be typed to letters, which will then be filed together with a copy of the reply, envelopes addressed and stamps attached. An entry may be made in a *postage book*.

The letter may then be posted by the clerk on her way home – registered or recorded delivery items will have to be taken to the Post Office.

In a large firm

1. All correspondence will have to be processed; executives will have to read the letters and compose replies which must be signed. At the same time as the letters are typed the relevant envelopes are addressed and are usually attached to the letters so that the wrong reply does not find its way into the wrong envelope.

   To avoid a last-minute rush on the mail room, many firms encourage executives to sign letters as soon as possible and arrange regular collections throughout the day from offices to the mail room. Firms may insist that mail which is not ready by a particular time will not be dispatched that day.

2. All letters are checked to see that any enclosures are in fact enclosed.
3. Letters and enclosures are checked against envelopes before they are inserted.
4. Envelopes are sealed.
5. Letters and packages are weighed and stamped, or franked by machine. An executive may indicate on the envelope if a letter or parcel is to be sent first- or second-class mail.
6. Details of the mail are recorded in various postal accounts.
7. Special items such as registered or recorded-delivery items are kept apart so that the necessary forms can be filled in and receipts obtained from the Post Office.
8. All the letters are tied in bundles, with the addresses facing the same way for collection by the Post Office (in the case of large firms), or for delivery to the Post Office.

3.3 CIRCULARS

The sending out of a batch of circulars may involve dealing with thousands of circular letters, which may run into several pages, and the envelopes in which to put the circulars. In a large office most of this work is handled by machines.

Addressing machines may be used to address the envelopes. There are several types available. Some use a plate made like a *spirit master* (see Section 18.10). others use a *stencil* in much the same way as stencil duplicating machines (see Section 18.11), others use an *embossed plate* from which the machine prints addresses through an inked ribbon to give the impression that the address has been typed – while others use a *foil master* which works like an embossed plate. Depending on the system used all the addresses stored in the banks can be printed – while other systems make the selection of certain addresses only easy. *Examples*. Every other address can be printed. Certain letters of the alphabet can be chosen – as for example in the case of a selective mailing where only firms/people whose names begin with the letters A, P, S and T are to be mailed. On some machines part of the plate can be masked out, when some information is not required, while other machines can date or number material.

Other uses of addressing machines include heading invoices, statements, advice notes, delivery notes, debit and credit notes, credit transfers, circular letters, pay documents, the printing of price tickets (in large stores), printing insurance renewal notes, completing dividend warrants – as well as addressing envelopes. Labels can be printed to be stuck on large items, such as parcels. Some addressing machines will print a replica of a signature on documents.

Addressing machine plates can be stored, or filed, in several ways: *geographically,* according to area or country, *alphabetically* by name, *by subject* or *numerically* – each customer being given a reference number. In most systems the plates, whether they are made of paper, metal or plastic, are stacked before and after use and again, depending on the system used, print the required information as the material to be printed passes under them. Addressing machines may be *hand-operated* or *fully automatic*. In the former case the material usually passes through the machine as the operator feeds the machine by hand while in the latter case the whole process is performed by machine.

The actual circular may be produced in a number of ways – see Sections 8.3, 8.4, 18.9–12 on duplicating.

If the circular consists of several sheets they may be machine collated rather than a member of the staff having to collate individual sheets by hand and fasten them together. There are several kinds of collating machine. In some the individual sheets are stacked so that the office worker can easily take the top copy from each stack before *jogging*, making sure that all the sheets are straight so that they can be stapled neatly. In others the individual sheets are stacked into the machine, which automatically collates (puts together) the sheets, jogs them and staples them. In addition to stapling documents, some automatic collators will stitch documents together as well as recording the number actually collated.

Once documents have been duplicated, collated and fastened together other machines will *fold the material*; machines can be set to handle various sizes and qualities of paper as well as fold in various ways.

Before franking, other machines will fill envelopes and either seal the envelopes or tuck the flaps in – depending on requirements.

In a large modern mailing room the whole process of collating, jogging, fastening, folding, inserting, sealing and franking is done in one continuous process (see Figure 3.2). If a firm does not have a franking machine the Post Office will frank envelopes free of charge – although a particular mailing may have to be at the Post Office before a certain time for posting that day.

3.4 STAMPING MAIL

All mail should have the correct amount of postage put on it; if too much postage is put on items the firm loses money while if the postage is not

Fig 3.2 *the Pitney Bowes Flowline*

enough the firm receiving the mail may have to pay extra – hardly the way to encourage customers!

In a small office all mail may be weighed on a set of scales and the appropriate *stamps* stuck on each item – after consulting the *Post Office Guide* to see what is the correct postage. A record of each item sent and the amount of postage stuck on is kept in a *Postages Book*. This book provides a check on the number and amount of stamps used and a record of all mailings.

In the example given on 1 November there was a balance of £1.25 in stamps from the previous week and on the same day a further £8.75 worth of stamps were purchased to make up a number it was expected might be used during the week,

On 1 November a packet costing £0.75 in postage was sent to Jenkins of Bristol and a letter costing £0.20 went to Oldfield of Stratford.

On 2 November a parcel costing £2.25 was sent to Macmillan at London, a letter costing £0.25 postage went to Whitehouse at Wrexham and one costing £0.35 went to Samuelson at Chester.

Can you say what happened on 3 and 4 November?

At the end of the week – 5 November, a letter costing £0.30 went to Somerfield at Plymouth while a packet costing £1.90 went to Wiggins at Slough. It was then necessary to balance the book for the week. To do this:

1. All the stamps used were added together – the amount comes to £7.48.
2. The amount used was taken from the balance at the start of the week (£1.25) plus the purchases (£8.75) which, in this case, makes a total of £10.00.
3. The balance in hand is carried forward to the next week and the £2.52 will appear as the opening amount on the next entry.

Fig 3.3 *a page of a postages book*

DATE	STAMPS PURCHASED	NAME	ADDRESS	STAMPS USED	COMMENTS
	£			£	
1 Nov	balance b/d 1.25 8.75				
		Jenkins	Bristol	0.75	Packet
		Oldfield	Stratford	0.20	
2		Macmillan	London	2.25	Parcel
		Whitehouse	Wrexham	0.25	
		Samuelson	Chester	0.35	
3		Anderson	Oxford	0.95	Packet
		Mayfield	York	0.28	
4		Patterson	Nottingham	0.25	
5		Somerfield	Plymouth	0.30	
		Wiggins	Slough	1.90	Parcel
				7.48	
		balance b/f		2.52	
	10.00			10.00	
	2.52	6 Nov balance b/d			

The person in charge of the postages book should check to see that stamps used plus stamps in hand equals the value of stamps issued to the postage book.

In a large office a franking machine may be used.

(a) Franking machines
A franking machine prints the postage on mail and saves the problem of sticking stamps. If letters are being sent the machine will print, in red, the amount of the postage together with the sender's code, the date of posting and the cancellation mark. Some firms print *a slogan* or some message with the franking. *If large objects* such as parcels are sent the postage is printed on sticky paper and stuck on.

Franking machines may be leased or purchased from the supplying companies authorised by the Post Office. Firms wishing to use a franking machine must obtain authority from the local Head Post Office first. Advance payment for postage, or value cards, must be made at a specific Post Office. The mail must be *faced* (arranged with all the addresses facing one way), *bundled* (tied in bundles), and either handed in at a specific Post Office or posted within special envelopes in posting boxes agreed by the local Head Postmaster.

To check that each machine is working correctly a completed control card must be sent to the agreed Post Office, even if the machine has not been used, each week. The machines must be checked for accuracy, by the manufacturers of the franking machines or their agents, twice every six months or as specified by the Post Office.

Each machine has a meter which can be set to various amounts; it is usual for the amounts to be in units of $\frac{1}{2}$, so that for a letter costing £0.20 the dial on the machine would be set to 40 units – $40 \times \frac{1}{2}$ = £0.20. The user purchases a number of units from the Post Office in advance and the amount is recorded on a card. As post is franked the number of units purchased is used up. When the number of units has been totally used up the machine stops working until further units have been purchased. A lock is fitted to each machine to prevent unauthorised use and each machine should be locked at the end of the day. The person operating the machine is responsible for keeping the card record up to date, changing the date each day, cleaning the printing head on the machine and ensuring that the supply of red dye is sufficient.

Fig 3.4   *franking machine control card*

FRANKING MACHINE CONTROL CARD

User   SERVALL ELECTRICS CO

Machine (or Meter No.)   G 7436   Setting or Recording Unit $\frac{1}{2}$ p

Meter Office (as shown on Record Card)   BIRMINGHAM

I certify that the following entries for the above machine for the week ended   22 OCTOBER 19XX   are correct and that the correct date has been shown on each day's posting

CHECK DATE DAILY

Put initials in column below to show date has been changed		ALL MACHINES Reading of Ascending Register (Totalisator)	LOCKING MACHINES Reading of Descending Register (Credit Meter)	ALL MACHINES Last entry in col. "Total Deposits" or "Total Settings" on Record Card
DG	Mon.	10980	4020	15000
DG	Tue.	13020	1980	15000
DG	Wed.	14770	230	15000
DG	Thur.	16970	8030	25000
DG	Fri.	18940	6060	25000
	Sat.			

NOTE 1.   Whether or not the machine has been used, this card must be posted on Saturday, or on Friday if no postings are made on Saturday.

Signed   Doreen Gardner

22 October   19XX

NOTE 2.   The daily entry must be made on completion of each day's postings.

Post Office Examining Officer's initials

In the example given the licensee is Servall Electric Co. and their local meter office is Birmingham. The number of their meter is G7436 and the machine is set in $\frac{1}{2}$ units. The card is for the week ended 22 October 19XX.

At the start of the week the firm had purchased 15 000 units; the amount appears in the right-hand column. This is worth 15 000 ÷ $\frac{1}{2}$ = £75.00.

At the end of the previous week the firm had used 9 750 units – it had 5 250 in credit (15 000 less the 9 750 used or 15 000 – 9 750 = 5 250).

On Monday the firm used 1 230 units (615 or £6.15 worth of postage). These 1 230 units reduced the amount of credit held from 5 250 to 4 020 (5 250 − 1 230 = 4 020) – the amount appears in the middle column. At the same time the meter showing the number of units used, the left-hand column, increased from 9 750 to 10 980 (9 750 + 1 230 = 10 980).

On Tuesday the firm used 2 040 units. The amount in credit in the middle column decreased from 4 020 to 1 980; the reading in the first column increases from 10 980 to 13 020. On Tuesday night the firm has 1 980 units of $\frac{1}{2}$ (£9.90) in credit.

On Wednesday the firm used 1 750 units, decreasing its credit from 1 980 to 230; the ascending meter increased from 13 020 to 14 770. This means that unless further units are purchased the machine will stop once the 230 remaining units have been used up.

On Thursday the firm purchased an extra 10 000 units. This increased the total deposits column, the one on the right, from 15 000 to 25 000 (15 000 + 10 000 = 25 000). During the day 2 000 units were used. This means that there were now 8 030 units in credit – the middle column (25 000 − 16 970 = 8 030). The ascending column showed an increase from 14 770 to 16 970 – the difference being the 2 200 units used.

On Friday 1 970 units were used – the amount in credit fell from 8 030 to 6 060; the ascending column shows an increase from 16 970 to 18 940.

The card was signed by Doreen Gardner.

(b) The advantages of a franking machine
1. No problem of sticking stamps on mail.
2. Increased security; no problems of stamps being lost.
3. No need to keep a postages book.
4. 'Free' advertising if a slogan is printed.
5. Mail is speeded up – no waiting at the Post Office to get mail franked there.
6. Good credit control – you can see at a glance how much credit you have.

(c) Disadvantages of a franking machine
1. It is expensive to hire or purchase – a small firm will not find it economical.
2. If the machine is incorrectly set postage can be wasted – if the operator moves from franking small parcels to second-class mail he or she may not reset the meter at once. (A refund can be obtained from the Post Office for mail franked in error but this takes time and costs 5 per cent of the amount claimed.)
3. Although security is improved there is the problem of what happens when the machine has been locked up for the night. Either the mail has to wait for the machine to be unlocked next day or stamps have to be used.
4. No record is kept of where mail is actually sent to.
5. Franked mail cannot be posted as easily as mail which has been stamped.

If departments have to keep a record of all money spent on postage the franking meter has to be read before and after that department's mail has been franked – and a record kept for the department.

(d) Postage stamp machines

Some firms still use postage stamp machines. A roll of stamps is locked into the machine which records the postage, on a counter, as stamps are used. Some machines will take several rolls of stamps of differing values. Theft is prevented by the fact that the rolls are locked into the machine and the stamps are marked, often by perforating the initials of the firm on the stamps, before being locked into the machine. The machines themselves are locked when not in use. Postage stamp machines can be used with a postage book.

3.5 REFERENCE BOOKS IN THE MAIL ROOM

The Post Office Guide – published each year with regular supplements showing changes – will show current information on many aspects of the post.

The Postal Addresses and Index to Postcode Directories – again published each year – will assist in correctly addressing mail.

Various *street guides* or *classified trade directories* will provide added information. The *Post Offices in the United Kingdom* and *London Post Offices and Streets* published by the Post Office provide details of Post Offices in the United Kingdom and specific information on the London area.

3.6 OTHER MAIL ROOM EQUIPMENT

Post rate scales compute the exact postage for airmail and letter post. Some will compute up to 20 kg for parcels. The particular machine used in an office will depend on what is normally mailed.

Shredding machines may be used to destroy confidential documents and so provide useful packing material for packets and parcels.

Packet tying machines will tie string or plastic bands round parcels or packets.

Rolling and wrapping machines are used for preparing printed material, newspapers, magazines and so on, for posting.

Dispensers of various kinds can be used for glue, sealing wax, sticking tape and so on.

A moist sponge or roller moistener will be useful for moistening envelopes and stamps.

Rubber stamps may be used for a number of purposes – identifying documents, stamping signatures on circulars and so on.

QUESTIONS

1. What are the advantages and disadvantages of franking machines?
2. The office junior has been delegated to collect, sort and distribute the incoming mail. Draw up a list of the points she should follow.
3. Suggest ten items of equipment you would expect to find in the mailing room of a large concern. State the purpose of each chosen item.
4. Prepare the entries for a Postages Book covering a period of a week and containing twenty items of postage.
5. Draw up a list for dealing with the outgoing mail in a large concern.

PROJECT

Produce a folder containing detailed particulars of the equipment you would expect to find in the mailing room of a large concern. Suggest alternative uses for the relevant items where possible and suggest points at which it might be more economical to replace machines with human labour or to replace simple machines with more complex ones.

MAIL – CHOOSING THE BEST METHOD

The dispatch side of the mailing and/or sales departments of any organisation can save large sums of money each year if the personnel working in those departments keep an up-to-date check on the methods available for the dispatch of parcels and mail. While the information given here is accurate at the time of writing, readers must check to see the position at the time of reading – because the services change. If an organisation does not deliver its own parcels and mail it must choose from the alternatives and of these, those offered by the Post Office and British Rail are the most important.

4.1 POST OFFICE SERVICES

Full details of current Post Office services and regulations are published each year in the *Post Office Guide* and it is essential that those concerned with the dispatch of mail and parcels are aware of the current situation. Monthly changes are notified to purchases of the *Post Office Guide* who return the supplements card to their local Head Postmaster. These supplements must be inserted into the *Guide* as indicated.

Post Office mailing service
The Post Office mailing services can be split into four categories:

inland letters; overseas letters;
inland parcels; overseas parcels.

The *Post Office Guide* also lists other Post Office services including *National Girobank and Postal Order Services* and *Savings and Other Services*.

4.2 INLAND LETTER SERVICES

Letters and cards may be sent by two classes of service known as *first class* and *second class*. The class of service is determined by the amount of postage paid. Second-class mail is normally delivered up to two working days later than first class except that long or difficult journeys, or large postings, may take a little longer. Both first- and second-class mail may be sealed and it is not normally necessary to indicate on the letter, other than by using a stamp, if the letter is first or second class.

(a) Post Office Preferred (POP) envelopes and cards
In order to assist its sorting and franking services the Post Office has laid down a number of recommendations as to sizes of envelopes and post-cards and may, in the future, introduce a surcharge for non-POP envelopes and packets.

(b) Second-class letters posted in bulk
Second-class letters, posted in bulk, qualify for a reduction in postage – subject to special conditions of posting and delivery. The reduction is a progressive one – which means that the more posted, the greater the reduction. Your *Post Office Guide* will give the current reductions.

(c) Business reply service
This service enables people to communicate with firms without paying postage. Firms send out business reply cards or envelopes with correspondence or include the design of one in newspaper or other advertisements. This service can be used for first- or second-class mail. Before a firm can use the Business Reply Service it has to obtain a licence from the local Head Postmaster and an advance sum of money is paid to cover the expected deliveries for a period of approximately a month. Once the sum of money has been used up a further sum must be paid. The printed designs must comply with Post Office regulations – see a current edition of the *Post Office Guide* – and designs which fall outside this range are liable to an additional charge in future, as non-POP items. Designs of cards to be used have to be sent to the local Head Postmaster for his approval. Once he approves them he allocates a licence number and the firm is charged first- or second-class postage for all items delivered – plus a small extra fee.

ACTIVITY

Collect an example of a first- and a second-class business reply advertisement from a newspaper or magazine.

(d) Freepost
A firm wishing to obtain replies from others without putting them to the expense of paying postage may include, in its correspondence or advertisements, a special address. The reply, using the special address, can be posted in the normal way but without a stamp. The firm, or person, receiving the mail pays postage on all the replies received plus a small additional fee. The service, which can be used by anyone who obtains a licence, is only sent as second-class mail.

Anyone wishing to use the service must obtain a licence from the local

Head Postmaster and pay an annual fee. An advance fee, to cover a period of approximately a month, is payable and as this is used up more money has to be paid. The Head Postmaster will insist that the word FREEPOST appear in the address – which again must meet with his approval.

ACTIVITY

Use the *Post Office Guide* to find details of the *Household Delivery Service* and *Admail*. Make notes on these services and keep them in your folder.

(e) Newspapers
Publications, registered at the Post Office as newspapers, are given first-class service at the newspaper postage rate if specially posted by publishers or their agents and are prominently marked NEWSPAPER POST. All other newspapers are transmitted as first- or second-class post. The *Post Office Guide* will give all details, such as limits of weight and size and the postage rates, which are lower than those for first-class letters when posted according to the regulations.

(f) Articles for the blind
Packets containing literature which conforms to Post Office regulations will be transmitted free by first-class letter post. Consult the *Post Office Guide* for current regulations as to admissible articles and their maximum/minimum sizes and weights. The letter, or packet, containing the material must be clearly marked ARTICLES FOR THE BLIND and should also contain the address of the sender.

(g) Registration
Any first-class letter, other than an airway, railex or railway letter, may be sent by registered post. Consult the current *Post Office Guide* for the current minimum fee which is charged to cover the cost of Post Office clerical services in connection with the registration and to provide, subject to certain conditions, compensation for loss or damage. A higher fee provides for higher amounts of compensation and all fees are in addition to the normal postage. The Post Office does not undertake to deliver a registered letter to the addressee in person.

Instructions for registering can be found in the *Post Office Guide*; they state that letters and packets must be fastened in such a way as to make their opening without detection impossible – and that means sealing wax or tape or other appropriate means. Money may only be sent using special envelopes sold by the Post Office (this ruling applies to a range of other matter such as cheques made payable to bearer and coupons, vouchers and tokens, etc., exchangeable for money, goods or services).

Registering. Anything intended for registration must be handed to an official at a Post Office and a certificate of posting, carrying an acknowledgement that the registration fee has been paid, must be obtained. The registration fee must be paid by postage stamps. If a higher fee is paid for greater compensation the amount must be recorded on the certificate of posting by the official receiving the letter/item. Any items which are posted and are discovered, by the Post Office, as falling within the range of items which must be registered are compulsorily registered and the person receiving them has to pay the registration fee.

The sender of a registered item may pay an extra fee for an advice of delivery to be sent to him. The purpose of registration is, in effect, to insure items of value which have to be sent by post. The amounts of compensation currently payable in the event of loss or damage in the post are given in the latest edition of the *Post Office Guide*, together with the fees payable. The amount of compensation paid is, to some extent, related to the fee paid.

(h) Recorded delivery

The recorded delivery service provides a record of posting and delivery and limited compensation in the event of loss or damage in the post. All kinds of postal packets except parcels, railway letters, railway parcels, railex packets, airway letters and cash on delivery packets can be sent by recorded delivery. A fee, additional to normal postage, is payable. The rules for packing are similar to those for registered items.

Method of posting. The Post Office provides special recorded delivery labels and receipts which have to be filled in with the name and address to whom the item is being sent – as it appears on the item. The receipt end of the label is stuck on the front of the item, above and to the left of the address, and the whole packet is handed in at a Post Office. A Post Office official will stamp the label and hand it to the person posting as proof of posting. Like registered mail, recorded delivery items must *not* be dropped into a letter box.

Delivery. Recorded delivery items travel with the normal unregistered post and are given no special treatment except at the time of delivery a receipt is obtained, though not necessarily from the person named – somebody else can sign for them. If a sender requires advice of delivery they must pay an extra fee at the time of posting. The purpose of recorded delivery is to provide proof of postage and delivery and to provide limited compensation in the event of loss or damage.

(i) Royal Mail special delivery

This service, which is offered in the United Kingdom, enables first-class letter items to be delivered on the next working day in all areas except some remote areas. The item is dispatched from the posting office by the next ordinary mail and is specially picked out at the delivery office and any intermediate office through which it may have to pass. See the *Post Office Guide* for current regulations.

(j) Express delivery

The Express Delivery service is only available for items addressed to places in the Channel Islands, the Isle of Man and the Irish Republic. See the *Post Office Guide* for current regulations.

(k) Airway letters

British Airways, by agreement with the Post Office, will accept first-class letters from the public at certain airport offices and take them on the next available direct flight to the destination, either to be called for or to be transferred to the normal post by the airline. See the *Post Office Guide* for current regulations.

(l) Cash on delivery

Under this service registered letters and packets may be sent and the amounts, called the *Trade Charge*, specified by the sender, may be collected on delivery by the Post Office and sent to the sender by means of a special order. Parcels must be sent by the Compensation Fee service.

Method of posting. The Cash-on-Delivery service only applies to goods requested by the person receiving them. The sender must fill in the trade charge form and ensure that the item is marked on the cover with the following information:

the name and address of the person to whom the item is being sent;
his/her own name and address;
the amount of the trade charge.

The information is usually written on an adhesive address label provided by the Post Office. There are various other services available in connection with the Cash-on-Delivery service but under normal conditions the amount collected is sent to the sender by means of a crossed order (special arrangements are available for people who do not have bank accounts).

(m) Datapost

Datapost provides an overnight, door-to-door service throughout the country. The regulations regarding size, weight and contents are similar to those for letter post although charges are negotiated with individual customers – taking into account weight, frequency of service and the requirements of the customer. Packages are collected from customers at agreed times and are delivered next day on a contractual basis for daily, weekly and monthly packages and for packages sent on a schedule of dates. There is a fixed charge for an item up to 5 kg irrespective of distance and at the time of writing the maximum weight is 10 kg, although special arrangements can be made for larger items. There is also an *International Datapost* service – see a current edition of the *Post Office Guide* for details.

Datapost 'D', an On-Demand service, operates from over 1 000 Post Offices into and out of London and between provincial centres. The packet must be handed in at selected posting points – usually Head Post Office counters.

(n) Poste restante

Letters and parcels to be called for may, as a rule, be addressed to any Post Office except a town sub-Post Office. The words 'To be Called For' or

'Poste Restante' should appear in the address. Poste Restante is provided solely for the convenience of travellers and may not be used in the same town for more than three months. To ensure delivery to the proper person (of Poste Restante letters) callers must provide proof of identity.

(o) Private boxes and bags

An addressee may rent a *private box* at the normal delivery office so that he may call to collect mail as an alternative to delivery by the postman. Correspondence may be handed to callers, or at some offices it will be placed in a locked box – to which the renter is given a key.

A lockable *private bag* may be used for posting and receipt of correspondence. The bag must be delivered to the Post Office by the user although for a fee it may be delivered to the addressee. The bag and key must be supplied by the user and if it is to be delivered by the postman it must be of an acceptable weight when empty.

(p) Railway letters

Under an agreement with the Post Office certain railway companies may accept first-class letters at certain of their railway stations on weekdays (some have Sunday facilities) for transmission on their own lines only. The letters may be collected from the station of address or be transferred to the post. Subject to Post Office approval the railway companies may agree among themselves to transfer railway letters between their respective companies until they reach the station of address.

(q) Redirection

Any kind of a postal packet, other than a Business Reply or FREEPOST packet, may be redirected to the same person (addressee) at another address either by an official of the Post Office or by a person at the original address – after delivery. Business Reply and FREEPOST packets may only be redirected by an official of the Post Office.

Redirection by the public must be undertaken not later than the day after delivery – not counting Sundays and public holidays. The old address may be crossed out and the new address written it – or a label may be used (providing it does not cover the original addressee). Registered postal packets and recorded delivery packets must be taken to a Post Office for posting. If redirected mail is not posted the day after delivery an extra charge is payable.

Redirection by the Post Office has to be paid for on a sliding scale – depending on the length of time the service is required. Notice of a person or a firm moving to a new address must be sent to the local delivery office serving the old address together with the new address and the fee.

(r) Selectapost

Where the local Head Postmaster can make the necessary arrangements, an addressee's mail may be sorted into sections before delivery – providing that a suitable indication of the divisions required appears as part of the address. The charge for the service is negotiated with each customer and the initial period must be a year. After the first year the arrangement operates on a quarterly basis.

4.3 OVERSEAS LETTER SERVICES

(a) Postage rates
The overseas postage rates and fees are not shown in the *Post Office Guide* but in the *Postal Rates Overseas Compendium* – a separate booklet issued free of charge as a supplement to the *Guide*.

(b) Airmail services
Letters and postcards (including letter packets) for Europe are sent by air as the normal means of transportation – if this will ensure earlier postal delivery. The service, also known as the *All-up Service*, does not require special air mail marking or an extra charge. For countries outside Europe the air postage must be paid and a blue air mail label, obtained from the Post Office, affixed on the left of the address side. If no label is available the words PAR AVION (by air) may be written or typed in the same place. *Air Letter Forms* are available in two sizes and may be sent to all countries. The forms may be obtained from the Post Office with the stamps printed on them – privately manufactured forms approved by the Post Office must have stamps stuck on them or they may be franked. In either case the letters must not contain enclosures.

(c) Surface mail
Surface mail is mail sent by land and sea.

4.4 LETTER POST SERVICES

(a) Letters
Packets which might be mistaken for other mail categories, because of their size, must be clearly marked LETTER. The letter service is the speediest service for sending letters or goods up to 2 kg (check the current limits).

(b) Postcards
Postcards must fall within the maximum (105 x 148 mm) and minimum (90 x 140 mm) sizes to qualify for the postcard rates. Larger cards travel at letter rates while small cards are not allowed at all.

(c) Small packets
This is a cheap service for goods up to a certain limit. The packet must be open for easy examination and be clearly marked *Small Packet*. Letters or any form of personal correspondence may not be included.

(d) Printed papers
There are special cheap rates for commercial items – advertising material,

price lists, etc. There are even cheaper rates for literary items such as newspapers and books. Packets must be open for easy examination and be clearly marked as required – for example *Printed Papers*. Letters or any form of personal correspondence may not be included.

(e) Literature for the blind
A special service is available for certain articles for the blind – letters and books in braille, for example. The air mail rates are greatly reduced, while surface mail is entirely free.

ACTIVITY

Find out:
the all-up rates for letters and postcards;
the surface mail rates for newspapers and small packets, for Europe and then for the rest of the world.

Use the *Post Office Guide* to find out about:
accelerated surface post (ASP);
bulk postings;
bulk air mail (BAM);
International Datapost.

(f) International reply coupons
These coupons, available from the larger Post Offices, are exchangable in virtually all countries of the world for a stamp or stamps representing the minimum international postage payable on a letter sent abroad. The coupons are a convenient means of prepaying the cost of a reply from abroad. International Reply Coupons may be accepted from customers with meter franking machines as part or whole payment of meter credit.

Customers who have unused reply coupons purchased in Great Britain or Northern Ireland may apply for a refund of their total cost.

(g) Registration
Letters, small packets, printed papers and items for the blind may all be registered on the payment of a fee and the completion of the necessary documents at the Post Office. They must not be posted in a letter box. Small packets, printed papers and items for the blind cannot be insured.

4.5 INLAND PARCELS

(a) Posting parcels
The postage on a parcel must be prepaid unless the sender has a postage account or the parcel is sent by the postage forward parcel service. A parcel must not be posted in a letter box; it must be marked *Parcel Post* and be handed in at a Post Office where an official will check the weight and size in order that the correct postage may be ascertained.

Parcels may be sent via the Post Office at two rates:

The national rate applies to parcels posted in the United Kingdom and from the United Kingdom to the Isle of Man, the Channel Islands and the Irish Republic.

The area rate is lower than the national rate and applies to parcels posted and delivered within a group of postal counties – see the *Post Office Guide* for national and area rates. *County parcels* are charged the same as *Local parcels* – current details will be found in the *Post Office Guide* or at any Post Office.

A certificate of posting may be obtained for an ordinary parcel in return for a small fee.

(b) Posting parcels in large numbers

The Post Office provides special contracts for *regular* postings of large numbers of parcels. Details are available from the local Head Postmaster.

(c) Compensation fee parcel service

This service, also known as the *C.F.* service, is available for parcels addressed to places in Great Britain, Northern Ireland, the Channel Islands, the Isle of Man and the Irish Republic. A blank certificate form, obtainable from any Post Office, should be completed by filling in the name and address of the addressee and ticking the box which shows the relevant fee. If parcels are posted in bulk a C.F. posting list may be used instead of separate certificates. The completed certificate of posting form and the parcel should be handed to a counter clerk and the appropriate stamp(s) will be stuck on the parcel before the clerk initials and date-stamps the top portion of the certificate of posting – to be kept by the sender as proof of posting. The compensation fee does not entitle a parcel to special treatment during its journey.

The purpose of the C.F. service is to provide higher compensation (insurance) cover in the event of loss or damage than is offered in the ordinary parcel service. The amount of compensation offered is given in the current edition of the *Post Office Guide* and it will be seen that a higher fee is charged for greater amounts of compensation. See the *Post Office Guide* for current rules and regulations.

(d) Claims

Claim forms are available from the Post Office and must be supported by a certificate of posting. Claims must normally be made within three months.

(e) Postage forward parcel service

The service enables individuals and organisations to receive parcels from others without putting others to the cost of paying the postage. The client is sent an unstamped addressed label, wrapper or container which conforms to Post Office regulations. The parcel is posted in the normal way but without a stamp. The person or firm receiving the parcel pays the postage. Before the service can be used the person or firm issuing the labels must obtain a licence from the local Head Postmaster and pay an advance sum to cover the deliveries expected for a given period – usually a month. Further payments must be made as required.

(f) Postage: prepayment in money
Subject to certain conditions, see the *Post Office Guide*, individuals or firms receiving parcels can arrange for the prepayment of any postal packets in money. This enables clients to post parcels at agreed Post Offices without having to pay the postage at the time of posting.

(g) Deposit accounts
Individuals and firms can be saved the trouble of paying postage in money at the actual time of posting by depositing a sum of money, sufficient to cover a week, month or any agreed period, and agreeing to pay any outstanding money at the end of that time. Applications should be made to the local Head Postmaster.

(h) Railway parcels
Railway parcels can be handed in at any express delivery office to be taken by a Post Office messenger to a railway station for dispatch by train. The sender may arrange for a Post Office messenger to collect the parcel when it arrives at the station of destination and deliver it. In addition to paying for the parcel to be taken to the railway station, the sender must check what the railway charge will be – so that the messenger can pay the railway officials.

4.6 OVERSEAS PARCELS

Consult the *Post Office Guide* for maximum sizes and weights of overseas parcels.

(a) Addressing
In addition to the name and address of the addressee, the name and address of the sender must appear on parcels.

(b) Forms
Parcels are posted over the counter at Post Offices, unless special arrangements have been made with the Post Office. The contents of parcels must be declared to customs on special *customs forms* obtained from Post Offices – the forms vary according to the country of destination. Instructions should be given on the form to indicate what should be done in the event of non-delivery or other irregularity.

Air parcels must bear blue air mail labels positioned close to the address.

(c) Express delivery
Subject to the conditions laid down by the Post Office, packets can be sent by the Express Delivery service to certain countries. An extra fee is

paid at the time of posting and although the item is sent by the normal methods it is given the earliest possible delivery from the office of delivery – by messenger if required.

(d) Cash on delivery

A *Trade Charge*, specified by the sender, can be collected when parcels are delivered to many countries. Such parcels may be insured. The system works similarly to that of the inland service – see the *Post Office Guide* for details.

(e) Registration

Parcels cannot be sent by registration overseas – but they may be sent under an insurance service.

(f) Insurance service

In the overseas service, insurance provides a means of covering losses, part losses or damage beyond that covered by the registration service. The service is not universal – it applies only to certain countries. Items to be insured must be handed over a Post Office counter and the appropriate fee paid before a certificate of posting is obtained. Use the *Post Office Guide* to find current regulations.

4.7 RAILWAY SERVICES

British Rail provides a range of services for the collection and delivery of packets and parcels.

(a) Red Star service

The Red Star service provides a fast station-to-station service for parcels. Local stations offering the service issue booklets each year outlining the service and the train times. Parcels to be sent by this service should be taken to the local station offering the service some 45 minutes before the train is due. A fee, which depends on the destination and the weight of the parcel, is charged. Large items often require prior notice. The parcel should show the name (not the address) of *the consignee* (person receiving the parcel), the destination station and the sender's name and address. Parcels are sent by passenger train – the Inter-City links provide a fast and efficient service – to be collected at the station of destination. If you are sending a parcel by the Red Star service you must tell the person receiving the parcel what train to meet. He or she must give the correct name and be able to prove identity. Uncollected parcels are taken to a warehouse for safe-keeping – and a charge may be made.

(b) Red Star links to airports

Parcels to be sent overseas or to be received from overseas through Heathrow Airport can be sent or received through the Red Star service.

(c) City Link

The City Link, run in conjunction with British Rail, provides a collection and delivery service using both road and rail. Parcels can be collected (telephone the local City Link Office) at short notice and are sent by scheduled parcels trains which run at high speed. Under a TOPS system – *Total Operation Processing System* – British Rail is, by using a computer, able to tell exactly where each parcel or consignment is at any given time. Special rates are offered for regular dispatchings and arrangements can be made for quantities. Parcels are delivered against a signature, although if a person is not available a card may be left indicating that a particular parcel is in a garage, or outbuilding, at the delivery address, with a neighbour (who has signed for it) or is awaiting collection at a local depot. Copies of the delivery note are kept in case of problems concerning delivery.

(d) Jetlink

Using the Red Star service and City Link, British Rail offer a service whereby parcels conforming to certain standards are taken to Heathrow Airport, cleared through the customs and sent to the USA on Concorde for collection or onforwarding.

(e) Other services

The range of services offered by British Rail is constantly expanding and it is now possible for parcels to be collected and delivered to many parts of Europe. Other services include provision for the collection of items to be sent by the Red Star service – to save people having to take parcels to the nearest relevant station.

(f) Compensation

Parcels sent by train may be sent by either Board's risk or owner's risk.

Board's risk is a service which provides compensation in the event of loss or damage to goods. There is a limit to the amount of compensation which is based on so much per tonne.

Owner's risk provides for compensation only in the event of a total loss.

In both bases there is minimum limit – in other words payment will not be made unless the sum involved is more than £10 (at the time of writing).

ACTIVITY

Keep advertisements from national and local newspapers advising of new and/or improved mail/packets/parcels services offered by the Post Office, British Rail and local carriers. Add details of these services to your notes.

Use the *Post Office Guide* to find details of the *Printed Postage Impression* (PPI) facility.

QUESTIONS

1. What are the differences between the Registered Mail and Recorded Delivery services?
2. When might a firm use private boxes and bags?
3. What is the postage forward parcel service and how does it operate?
4. List the railway services available for the collection and delivery of packets and parcels, and write a paragraph on each.
5. What factors must be taken into account by individuals and firms when sending letters and parcels by the various means available?

THE TELEPHONE

The telephone is probably the most commonly used item of office equipment and, if used correctly in the office or home, it can save both time and money. It is often much cheaper to make a telephone call than to write a letter. Despite its convenience and versatility the telephone can, like all equipment, be easily misused and thus become expensive and inefficient. Just as a letter represents a firm, so does the person who answers the telephone, whether that person is the telephonist, a secretary, an office junior or an executive. The field of telecommunications is one of the most rapidly expanding, and the wise student takes care to update knowledge, consistently using the relevant guide (e.g. *British Telecom Guide*). The advent of the microcomputer has led to an explosion of facilities available in the field of telecommunications and it is essential to keep the *Guide* up to date by using the supplements issued from time to time. *Telephone directories* are issued for all parts of the country. They are printed on white paper and are arranged in alphabetical order. They also contain the *Green Pages* – details of telephone services. The classified business (*Yellow Pages*) directories are printed on yellow paper and contain details of a wide range of goods and services. The *commercial classified directories* list, in classified order, businesses which are of interest to the business world. *Local and community alphabetical directories* serve local communities and areas. *Business directories*, listing large businesses in alphabetical order, cover wide areas. Telephone subscribers are issued with the *Telephone Dialling Codes* which contain details of the various services and codes offered; the blue *International Telephoning Guide* provides details of international telecommunications.

ACTIVITY

Use any telephone directory to find the following definitions:

The dialling tone – the tone you will hear when you first pick up the telephone.
The ringing tone – the tone you will hear when you make a telephone call.

The engaged tone - the tone you will hear should the number you require be engaged.

The number unobtainable tone - the tone you will hear should the number you have dialled be unobtainable. The **pay tone** - the tone you will hear should you make a call from a pay telephone and the person answers the telephone.

What should you do when you hear the dialling tone?
What should you do should you hear the engaged tone?
What should you do should you hear the number unobtainable tone?
What should you do should you hear the pay tone when telephoning from
  a pay telephone?

5.1 USING THE TELEPHONE

Local calls are telephone calls made within a specified local area. All calls within a given area can be dialled direct - by dialling the number required. **Trunk calls** are telephone calls outside a locality - on another telephone exchange. Most trunk calls can be dialled direct by means of **STD** - Subscriber Trunk Dialling - to make a call to a number on another exchange. Use the Telephone Dialling Codes to find the number of the exchange and dial that number before dialling the number required. If the exchange you require is not in the Telephone Dialling Codes you must contact the operator (dial 100), give your telephone number and then ask for the number you require. The operator will then connect you. **Calls via the operator** are usually more expensive than those dialled by STD. **Certain overseas countries** can be dialled direct using the codes in the relevant Dialling Codes Booklet or Directory and the **International Direct Dialling (IDD)** service. All other calls overseas must be made via the operator - in which case guidance as to the passage of time is normally given by *pip* signals - the first *pip* coming roughly twelve seconds before the end of each three minute period.

ACTIVITY

Use any telephone directory to find how to make an emergency call. How would you dial 999 in the dark?

Use the Telephone Dialling Codes to find out how to dial:

enquiries and difficulties;
maritime services;
telegrams.

How many services are offered under the heading 'Enquiries and Difficulties'?

Calls made via STD are charged by a system of equipment called 'Group routing and charging equipment' - GRACE for short.

5.2 RECORDED INFORMATION SERVICES

In addition to the range of operator services offered, British Telecom offers a range of recorded information services - details will be found in the *dialling Codes*. The services included are:

bedtime stories;
Financial Times index and business;
food price news;
gardening information;
motoring;
recipes;
ski-ing information;
teletourist;
time;
weather.

5.3 TELEPHONE RATES

It will be seen from the above that the cost of a telephone call depends on the following:

Where the call was made from - a private line or a coinbox;
The distance over which the call was made - local calls are cheaper than long-distance calls;
The time of day or week when the call was made;
Whether the call was made direct or through the operator.

Peak rate calls are the most expensive - from 9 a.m. to 1 p.m. Monday to Friday.
Standard rate calls are those which are made between 8 a.m. and 9 a.m. and 1 p.m. and 6 p.m. Monday to Friday.
Cheap rate calls are made at all other times.

5.4 MAKING TELEPHONE CALLS

Remember that when you make a telephone call the person to whom you are speaking cannot see you and that you will not be able to use your hands or facial expression to emphasise a point. You must use your voice to make all points absolutely clear.

1. Make sure that you have the number you require before you make a call - and see that you have the relevant dialling code should the call require one.
2. Have with you a pad for taking down messages and something with which to write. A pencil can break so have a spare one or some alternative writing instrument handy.
3. Pick up the telephone receiver in the hand you do not use for writing - this will leave your writing hand free.
4. When you hear the dialling tone dial the number you require. Place

your first finger in the correct hole, rotate the dial firmly round to the stop and let it return by itself - do this for each figure that you need to dial. Do not pause for too long between each number dialled.

5. When the telephone is answered, identify yourself before proceeding with your message. Speak into the mouthpiece - not across it as this will distort your voice - and speak more slowly than you normally do, pitching your voice slightly lower.

6. If you make a mistake when dialling, replace the telephone receiver for a few moments and then pick up the receiver and dial the number you require again. If you are connected to a wrong number offer an apology - the fault may be yours or the telephone operator's but it is certainly not the fault of the person called.

7. If the person you require is on a telephone extension, ask for the extension number, or if you do not know the number of the extension give the name of the department and the person to whom you wish to speak.

8. If the number is unobtainable, dial the operator and ask for assistance.

If you are seeking information on the telephone plan your call before you make it - noting the points you wish to raise on a pad so that you can ensure that you cover all the points in that call.

When you answer the telephone

1. Pick up the receiver correctly.
2. Speak in a cheerful voice and identify your firm at once - either by giving its name or its telephone number or both. Time is money and failure to identify your firm's name or number can result in a person in a pay telephone losing his money.
3. If the caller wishes to speak to a person who is not available:
   (a) do not keep them waiting;
   (b) ask if they would like to speak to another person;
   (c) ask if they would like to be called back by the person they require when that person is available;
   (d) ask if they can ring for the person they require later;
   (e) ask if they would like to leave a message.
4. If you have to leave the telephone for a time, let the caller know how long you expect to be away and give him the option of waiting or calling back later - or arrange to call him yourself.
5. If the call has to be transferred to an extension, explain what you have to do and ask the caller for his/her name so that you can announce him/her. If there is a delay, inform the caller.
6. If the caller is cut off, replace the telephone and wait - the caller may wish to call you back.
7. If the caller has the wrong number accept his/her apology, when offered; the caller did not call the number intentionally.

If you have to take a message, make sure that you have a telephone message form to hand - if not, use a pad to record the information in a logical fashion.

5.5 TELEPHONE MESSAGES

To make sure that all points in a telephone call are correctly recorded use a telephone message form - any typist can easily prepare a stencil and run off copies. The points should be recorded as they are given and it is advisable to check with the caller that the points have been correctly noted, by reading them back, before you replace the receiver. The telephone message form should contain the following information:

the name of the person called;
the department called;
the name of the caller;
the telephone number of the caller;
the name of the firm represented by the caller;
the message;
details of the person taking the call;
the time of the call;
the date of the call.

The form might also contain space indicating what action was taken to make sure that the message was forwarded to the person called.

ACTIVITY

Prepare a telephone message form and use it to record the following information:

Mrs Sandra White in the Accounts Department was called by Mr Peter Anderson of Hodge & Rowley Ltd - telephone number 0332 (Derby) 89312. Mr Anderson wants Mrs White to call him back before 4.45 p.m. today about last month's account - number 9032. The call was taken by Rosemary Cresswell at 11.30 a.m. today. The message has been placed on Mrs White's desk for her attention when she returns.

5.6 USING THE FIRM'S TELEPHONE FOR PRIVATE CALLS

Some firms do not like employees using their telephones for private calls, except in cases of emergency, and the rules of the firm must be kept. Other firms do not mind employees using their telephones providing that all private calls are noted and paid for and that they are not made at peak times. If you are allowed to use the firm's telephone for private calls, make sure that all are paid for and that you do not spend longer on the telephone than is absolutely necessary - you may prevent a vital call from reaching your firm.

5.7 SWITCHBOARDS

Most firms have two kinds of telephones - those for making external calls and those used for making internal calls - telephone calls within the firm.

Sometimes the two systems are separate and the outside line(s) cannot be connected to the internal system. Most firms have a system whereby one or more outside lines can be connected to a number of extension lines by means of a switchboard. Generally switchboards are one of two kinds – manual or automatic.

(a) Manual switchboards
Manual switchboards, sometimes called *PMBX* (Private Manual Branch Exchanges), are those by which all connections between the extensions within a firm and the incoming and outgoing calls are made through the operator. The system may have a cordless switchboard, it may have a series of switches which the operator must manipulate, or it may have a cord system which consists of a series of plugs and jacks which must be connected as required.

(b) Cordless PMBX
There are several sizes of cordless switchboards currently available including:

PMBX 2 + 6 which has 2 exchange lines with up to 6 extensions;
PMBX 3 + 12 which has 3 exchange lines with up to 12 extensions;
PMBX 4 + 18 which has 4 exchange lines with up to 18 extensions.

Each exchange line, each extension and the operator's telephone has a signalling lamp with a column of keys underneath it – the keys are used to answer and connect calls. On the 3 + 12 and 4 + 18 models the exchange line calls are held automatically if the operator has to leave the line to make an inquiry. On the 2 + 6 model exchange line calls are held manually by operating the associated hold key. The lamp above the operator's keys glows continuously while any exchange line is being held. Extensions are called by pressing down the associated key in the bottom row. The number of two-way conversations is dependent on the size of the switchboard. Extensions can be internal, external or inter-switchboard. Extension telephones are provided with dials so that calls can be dialled direct when the operator has connected the extension to an exchange line. Each extension telephone has a pressdown button which can be used to signal the operator while a call is in progress – the operator can then assist as required or transfer the call to another extension. The operator can also speak to an extension without being overhead – while holding an exchange call. A glowing lamp reminds the operator that the exchange line is being held.

The PMBX 5 + 25 panel-mounted system provides the above facilities and has up to 5 exchange lines and 25 extensions. Night service is provided by connecting each exchange line to an extension and switching on the night service key.

(c) Cord system of PMBX
The variety of systems available is designed to meet the requirements of firms of various sizes; the PMBX 4 single-position system provides up to 10 exchange lines and 40 extensions and the PMBX 4 multiple-position

equipment provides up to 20 exchange lines and 80 extensions. Each exchange line, extension, private circuit and inter-switchboard circuit has a calling lamp and answer jack. Each call is signalled by lights (if required, by an alarm buzzer as well). As each calling cord is plugged into an extension jack the required telephone automatically rings. The ringing continues until the extension answers. Each cord system has similar facilities to the cordless system – meters can be installed on the various circuits to record how many units each uses.

5.8 AUTOMATIC EXCHANGES

A PABX (Private Automatic Branch Exchange) system offers automatic telephone service and public exchange service in a single system – each automatic extension can dial other extensions and make or receive calls on outside lines without using an operator. There are various sizes of system available to meet the demands of firms of various sizes; the PABX 1 system offers up to 10 exchange lines and 49 automatic extensions and the PABX 7 system offers up to 20 exchange lines and 100 extensions and the PABX 2, PABX 5 and PABX 6 systems offer varying capacities. Some systems are cordless; others use the cord-type switchboard – combining a system of automatic exchanges with manual extensions. Systems which have a number of manual extensions (Private Branch Extensions or PBX for short) have fewer automatic extensions and in some cases fewer exchange lines.

Automatic extensions call each other and manual extensions by dialling two-digit numbers between 21 and 69 – the range depends on the size of unit being used. Automatic extensions dial 9 to obtain an exchange line or to make an outside call. If required, selected extensions can be prevented from dialling outside direct – the calls can be routed through the switchboard. Automatic extensions dial 7 to obtain a line connected to another PBX; they dial 0 to call the PABX operator.

(a) PABX switchboard facilities

The operatore calls extensions from the switchboard by pushing buttons in sequence for the required number – the extension telephone automatically rings until it is answered. Calls to or from extensions are released when the extension handset is replaced. If an extension is engaged the PABX operator can let an exchange line caller hold on to be automatically connected to the extension as soon as it becomes free. The operator can interrupt an engaged extension to ask if another call can be accepted – a ticking sound or warning tone tells the extension that the operator is on the line. An exchange call can be held by the operator, who connects it to a special 'hold' number – the call can then be connected to an extension when required. More than one call may be held in this way – without a conversation being overheard. When the *night service* button on the switchboard is pressed, incoming exchange calls cause suitably sited bells to ring continuously. Any automatic extension dials 8 to answer the call – which can be then transferred to any other extension. Another method enables individual exchange lines to be connected to selected extensions.

(b) Conference facilities

A separate unit can be rented which allows up to eight extensions, internal or external, or private circuits to be connected together for a telephone conference. There are various other facilities available – connecting up to ·5 extensions and one exchange line or an amplifier can be rented to allow up to 7 extensions and an exchange line to have a conference.

(c) Summary of dialling codes normally provided on PABX systems

7	To obtain lines to another PBX
8	To answer a call on night service
9	To obtain an exchange line
0	To call the operator
20	Used by an operator for holding calls
21	to 35 for 15 extensions
21	to 44 for 35 extensions
21	to 69 for 49 extensions

5.9 NO-SWITCHBOARD SYSTEMS

Systems such as the PABX 5 use a system which does not involve a switchboard. Incoming exchange calls ring bells situated near specified extensions. The calls can be answered from any of the extensions in the system by lifting the handset. The incoming call can be transferred to another extension by pressing a button on the telephone, dialling the required extension number and, if the person for whom the call is intended agrees to take the call, replacing the handset. If the person cannot take the call it can go to another extension. If a transfer does not succeeed for any reason, the incoming call rings the bells again and any extension user can take the call by lifting the receiver. Specified extensions are usually allowed to interrupt an engaged extension to offer an incoming exchange call by dialling 1. A ticking sound warns of the intrusion.

Keyphones are available for all PMBX systems.

5.10 PRIVATE BRANCH EXCHANGES

There is a range of PBX (Private Branch Exchange) systems available, ranging from a simple extension to a telephone at home to one involving up to ten telephones. Using Keymaster telephones and a PBX system a wide range of extension facilities can be used, including the facility to make an internal conference call on up to 9 *Keymaster telephones*. A Keymaster telephone has a dial and a set of buttons which must be pressed to operate the system.

(a) Extension plans 107, 107A, 105 and 105A

With extension plans 107 and 107A the equipment consists of a main telephone fitted with a switching unit, an extension, a power unit and, if the extension is external, a ringing unit. The extension from the main telephone can be internal or external but if the main telephone is itself an extension from a PBX exchange the extension must be internal. The person on the main telephone can make and receive exchange calls and can call and speak to the person on the extension. The person on the extension can call the main telephone and, when the line is switched through the main telephone, make and receive exchange calls. The exchange call can be held while the person at the main telephone speaks to the extension and this conversation cannot be heard by the caller. An exchange call can be transferred to the extension if required. Plans 107 and 107A are similar in operation but with 107A an extension to exchange call cannot be overheard at the main telephone.

Plans 105 and 105A are used in connection with a telephone exchange line and consist of a main telephone fitted with a switching unit, two extensions, a power unit and, if one or both of the extensions is, or are, external, a ringing unit. The two extensions from the main telephone can be internal, external or one of each but when the main telephone itself is an extension from a PBX the extension must be internal. Plans 105 and 105A are similar in operation but with 105A an extension to exchange call cannot be overheard at the main telephone – although it can be heard at the other extensions. (See Figure 5.1.)

Fig 5.1 *the control panel of extension plans 107 and 107A, 105 and 105A*

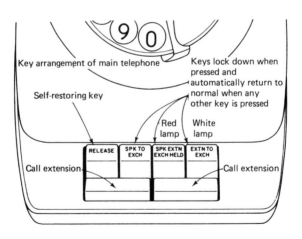

(b) Operation

Pressing down the SPK TO EXCH key connects the main telephone to the line. Pressing down the SPK EXTN EXCH HELD key connects the main telephone to the extension or extensions while a call is held – the red lamp behind the key glows while the line is held. Pressing down the EXT TO EXCH key connects the extension or extensions to the line – the white lamp behind the key glows while the person at the extension (plans 107 and 107A) or extensions (plans 105 and 105A) is using the line. The RELEASE key restores any other key previously pressed. If plan 107 or 107A is used either of the unmarked keys can be used to call the extension but if plan 105 or 105A is being used one key is used for each extension.

(c) Extension arrangement Plan 9

Plan 9 is useful for anyone with an extension from a switchboard who wants to make telephone inquiries while holding the original call. Two extensions are fitted to the same telephone and the extension lines can be internal or external. Calls are normally made and received on the first extension line. A call on the first extension line can be held while an inquiry is made on the second – the original caller cannot hear the inquiry.

5.11 TELEPHONE CALL SERVICES

(a) Advice of duration and charge (ADC)

For an extra fee the cost of a particular call made via the operator will be notified on its completion provided that the operator is asked to advise the cost at the time of booking the call. The duration (time taken by the call) will be advised for the same cost if the operator is asked at the same time that the cost of the call is given.

(b) Alarm calls

For a fee (see the *Telecom Guide*) the local telephone exchange will call a subscriber at a specified time of the day or night – as for example when a subscriber wants a call early in the morning to ensure that he meets an appointment. Any person requiring this service should call the local exchange and give his/her telephone and the time they require the call.

(c) Freefone

This service allows customers or agents to contact firms without paying for their telephone calls. The firm offering the service pays a fee and so much for each call made. (See the *Telecom Guide*). A person making a call to a Freefone number dials the operator and asks for the number required; the call is put through without the caller being required to make payment.

(d) Fixed-time calls

A call may be booked in advance to be connected at an agreed time - for a fee. (See the *Telecom Guide*). Providing that traffic will allow the call to be made, it will be made within ten minutes of the time required. If the call is not made within the time allowance the charge is not made.

(e) Personal calls

A personal call enables a caller to save time and money when calling a particular person. Using the service a caller can:

specify the person he/she wishes to speak to (or a substitute) and give the
telephone numbers or addresses where they may be found;

specify the person to whom he/she wishes to speak by reference to a title
or code or by extension number;

arrange to speak only if two named persons are both available at a particular
number;

arrange for a person, not on the telephone, to be brought to a neighbour's
telephone whose number he/she gives.

The caller may give his/her name, telephone number or extension number
to be passed on to the number called. If the personal call cannot be made
at once the originating exchange operator will leave word at the number
called for the person required to ring the personal call operator as soon as
possible – the call is then connected. The caller or the called number may
specify the time at which a further attempt should be made. If calls are
not made within 24 hours the call is cancelled. An extra fee is charged in
addition to the cost of the call.

(f) Telephone credit cards
A subscriber may ask his General Manager for cards which enable telephone calls and telegrams to be made/sent from any telephone without
payment at the time. The credit card is supplied for a quarterly fee and
each call is charged at the normal operator rate plus an extra fee. To use
the service a subscriber calls the operator, gives the number of the credit
card and is connected by the operator.

(g) Transferred charge calls (reverse charge calls)
A caller may ask the operator to connect him/her to a subscriber in such
a way that the person called pays for the telephone call. The operator will
dial the person requested; if that person agrees to accept the call and the
charge the caller is connected. The normal operator fee is charged plus an
additional fee.

(h) Telegrams by telephone
Inland and international telegrams may be dictated from a private or pay
telephone. Telegrams may be delivered to telephone subscribers by telephone and may be addressed to subscriber's telephone numbers.

(i) Transfer of telephone call
Subscriber-controlled transfer is a facility provided for the customer who
does not want to be disturbed by telephone calls or who has to leave the
telephone for some time. Using equipment supplied, the customer himself
sets up and cancels transfer arrangements from his own telephone without
the assistance of the operator.

Operator assistance is required if the temporary transfer is to a number
on a different exchange.

5.12 OTHER TELEPHONE FACILITIES

There is a range of telephones available for a number of situations.

The standard telephone is available in a range of colours and has the standard telephone dial.

The trimphone is a lightweight table telephone with a tone-caller instead of the conventional telephone bell. The dial is usually illuminated.

The self-contained (SC) keyphone has a keypad instead of the conventional rotary dial.

A wallphone is a wall-mounted telephone for use where space is limited.

Pendant telephones are suitable for fitting in the knee-hole of a desk or on a wall to save space. A separate drawer-type dial unit can be fitted beneath the edge of the desk – the bell is wall-mounted.

A wall-mounted weatherphone contained in a metal case can be provided for use at outdoor locations.

The explosive atmosphere telephone is designed for use where an accumulation of explosive gases may occur in normal circumstances – as for example in some store rooms.

Loudspeaking telephones are useful for those who want both hands free during a call. The loudspeaking facility can be used on all outgoing and incoming calls and can be used to enable a small group of people to take part in a telephone call. The line can be switched from loudspeaker to handset any number of times during a call.

Customer metering facilities enable customers in STD areas to assess the cost of a call or a series of consecutive calls. There are two types of meter available: the *clock meter*, which can be fitted to exclusive exchange line telephones, most switchboard extensions and the smaller cordless switchboards; and *the cyclometer*, which can be associated with all other British Telecom provided switchboards. The clock meter has a clock-type face with three hands; the cyclometer shows the number of units behind a window on the face of the meter.

Tape Callmakers can save time finding and dialling a telephone number. The Tape Callmaker can be used with most types of telephone from which calls can be dialled and the telephone can be used in the normal way for numbers not stored on the Callmaker. A magnetic tape stores 400 telephone numbers – numbers can be added or changed or removed when necessary. A motor drive controlled by the two-way key quickly moves the tape up or down to the required section of the alphabet – indicated by movement of the red line – it takes about twelve seconds to move from A to Z. The final positioning of the tape for making a call or recording a number is made with the manual control wheel. The 'wait' lamp on the Callmaker glows while a number is being transmitted. The unit can be used to call an engaged number until that number is available.

Card Callmakers use a punched card to call the number for you. The Callmaker is housed in a plastic case which also contains a power unit. A card well, which holds up to fifty cards, a card slot, a red pilot lamp and a cancel button are contained in the top of the unit. Telephone numbers are stored on white plastic cards - each card holds one number. Each card has feed-holes down each side and spaces for writing the name of the person to be called and the digits (figures) in the number. The red pilot lamp glows when the Callmaker is switched on. When the handset on the telephone is lifted and the dial tone is heard, the required card is dropped into the slot at the front of the Callmaker. The card works its way through the slot, step by step, dialling the number automatically - then drops into the tray below. A call can be cancelled while the card is working its way through the slot by pressing the cancel button; if the engaged tone is heard the card can be reinserted to make a second or further attempts. Numbers are changed by punching a fresh card. Index dividers are provided to help keep the cards in order and speed location of numbers.

Private circuits are for business users who need frequent or prolonged contact between particular locations. No call charges are payable because the customer rents the circuit for his exclusive use - the rent is based on the distance and type of circuit and not on the number of calls made. Private circuits can be used for a wide range of purposes other than speech - the transmission of signals such as data, telementary, telegraph and the remote control of alarms, lights or radar.

Radiopaging enables people who are on the move to be contacted quickly and easily. Each user is supplied with a pocket-size unit with its own paging number which is activated when the number is called - provided that the user is not in a place where reception is impossible - such as in a basement or underground. When the number is called the unit bleeps until the user takes some action - usually switching it off and finding the nearest telephone to find out why he/she is required. Should a user not wish to be disturbed each unit has a built-in memory which will store a call until the unit is switched to normal use. The radiopaging service is not available for the whole of the country but is limited to certain areas.

Radiophones enable users to make and receive telephone calls from any telephone in this country and many overseas countries. The mobile equipment consists of a handset and control unit, a special aerial and a transmitter and receiver unit which can easily be fitted into a car or other vehicle.

Confravision is not a specific telephone service but combines the telephone with television. It links individuals or groups of people in different cities by sound and vision - users can conduct discussions, meetings and presentations between studios at distant locations as though they were face-to-face in the same room. The service enables people to hold face-to-face discussions without the inconvenience and waste of time involved in long-distance travel. A display camera is also provided to transmit black-and-white pictures of documents, graphs, charts and small objects. Screens can be provided to allow a large group of people to see and hear what is going on - even though the initial system limits the number of people able to take part in meetings to a small group of about five at each end of the circuit. (See Figure 5.2).

A *Conference Call* service is available to most countries. It allows up to six

Fig 5.2 *Confravision: some modes of use*

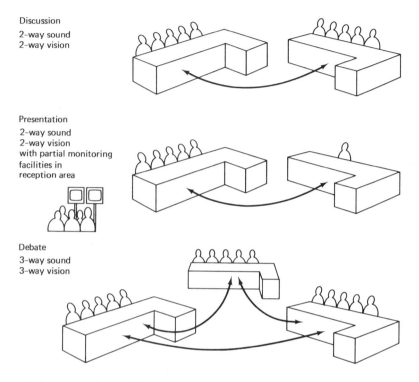

Discussion
2-way sound
2-way vision

Presentation
2-way sound
2-way vision
with partial monitoring
facilities in
reception area

Debate
3-way sound
3-way vision

telephones, each requiring separate connection, to be connected at the same time on an international call. Up to five of the telephones may be abroad.

Telephone answering machines may be used when staff are not available to receive telephone calls. They provide a means of giving a caller information which may be of value. The telephone is connected to a machine on which a message has been recorded – the message can be changed when required. When a caller dials the subscriber's number he will hear the ringing tone which, after a few seconds, will stop and the recorded message will be played. The message may indicate when the subscriber will be available – or where he is available (as for example when a firm moves to a new location).

Telephone answering and recording machines are similar to telephone answering machines except that they consist of a machine with two tapes which is connected to the telephone. The first tape is a loop tape on which a message is recorded; the second tape is to enable a caller to record his/her own message. A caller who dials a subscriber's telephone connected to a telephone answering and recording machine will hear, after the ringing tone, the recorded message which will inform him/her that it is a telephone answering machine and invite him/her to leave a message when the caller hears a bleep at the end of the recording. Once the bleep is heard the caller can leave his/her message - after taking care to identify him/herself. The subscriber can see at a glance, from the amount of recording media used while he has been away, the number of messages left. A telephone answering and recording machine provides a 24-hour service. Some machines can be used for centralised message collection - callers contact a number of machines placed in various localities and the messages can be collected by the centre over the telephone. A business man who has been away from the office, which might have been closed in his absence, can use the centralised message-collection system to hear messages recorded in his absence - various controls on the machine in the office can be set to enable him to do this - providing they are set up before he leaves.

Some telephone answering and telephone answering and recording machines can also be used as dictation machines. Both telephone answering and telephone answering and recording machines are usually hired from private suppliers.

Reports may be recorded on a dictation machine or telephone recording machine after the initial call has been answered by a person at the receiving telephone. This *'handing on'* is often used by newspapers when reporters dictate their copy to a machine rather than a shorthand writer.

The Midnight Line Service enables an unlimited number of inland STD calls to be made between the hours of midnight and 6 a.m. daily. The user pays a rental for each exchange line and a connection charge.

Paging is a system used by some large organisations to contact officials who are moving about the concern. It may consist of sets of coloured lights placed at strategic points, a pocket bleeper or a loudspeaker announcement. The person responds by going to the nearest telephone.

The transmission of documents by telephone is a rapidly expanding service by which copies of documents or photographs can be transmitted by telephone or radio (see also Section 6.3). If a customer wishes to discuss a document with a supplier - or two departments need to discuss a document which one does not have - a copy of the document can be transmitted. The sender has a machine which copies the document and transmits it while the receiver has a machine which reproduces the document sent. The machines may be called *telecopiers, facsimile transceivers, transcopiers* or *remote copiers.*

THE TELEPHONE ALPHABET

The telephone alphabet is used when spelling names or giving information over the telephone. The following could be used when spelling names:

A - Albert	C - Charles	E - Eric
B - Barry	D - David	F - Frank

G - George	N - Nine	U - Uncle
H - Henry	O - Orange	V - Victor
I - Ian	P - Peter	W - Walter
J - John	Q - Quick	X - X-Ray
K - Keith	R - Robert	Y - Yellow
L - Lion	S - Simon	Z - Zebra
M - Mark	T - Trevor	

A person spelling the name 'Ely' would spell
it as follows:
E for Eric; L for Lion; Y for Yellow.

When dictating numbers care must be taken to ensure accuracy. Read numbers in pairs counting from the last figure. The number 53165 would be given as five, three one, six five. A double number at the beginning is always read separately - 55165 would be given as five five, one six, five. Nought is given as zero. Double numbers are given separately - 456199 would be given as four five, six one, nine nine.

5.13 DATA TRANSMISSION FACILITIES

All data transmission facilities offered by British Telecom in the United Kingdom are grouped under the title *Datel* - a contraction of *Da*ta and *Tele*communications.

Computers are an expensive business tool to purchase but because they are so versatile they are rapidly becoming essential to the efficient running of all kinds of businesses. Some firms have their own computer which is linked to their branches - for example, banks link their computers to all their branches so that information of all kinds can be transmitted, stored and analysed with vast savings of time. Firms which cannot afford to purchase a computer may share one with several other firms or rent time and space in one supplied by one of the many firms now offering a computer service. Computers enable calculations to be made quickly and accurately by scientists and business men; they can store information and advise - as for example those used to keep records of purchases and sales by firms and so prevent overstocking or supplies running out; they can make decisions which are based simply on facts and which are not clouded by human emotion, as for example when firms are planning new factories and products; daily, weekly and monthly details of such matters as workers' attendances, salaries, wages, deductions and so on can be made on a continuous basis.

A **Datel service** consists of a telephone line connected to a translation device called a *modem* which allows privately owned data processing equipment to work over the telephone network. There is a Datel service for each of a range of speeds up to 50 000 bits per second and optional extras are available which make more efficient use of telephone line used for data transmission. The range of Datel services includes Datel 200, Datel 600, Datel 2 400, Datel 2 400 Dial Up Service, Datel 2 412 Datel 48K as well as the DCE 1A, DCE 2A, DCE 3A and DCE 3A with Dialling Unit control equipments, the Midnight Line Service and Dataplex Systems (see Figure 5.3).

Fig 5.3 *the Datel 200 system*

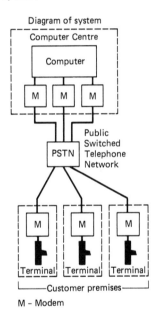

Diagram of system

M – Modem

The **Datel 200** service is useful where access to a computer is required by a large number of low-speed terminals – typically a time-sharing bureau and its customers.

The **Public Switched Telephone Network** (PSTN) is normally used although private circuits sometimes provide an economical alternative. Information to and from the data terminal is translated by a modulator-demodulator (called a *modem* for short) into a signal suitable for transmission over a telephone circuit. When using the PSTN the modem must be provided by British Telecom. A choice of two modems is offered – the standard modem is housed in a case for table-mounting and racks can be provided to house several modems should they be required at a particular computer centre. A miniaturised modem is available which is housed in a plinth under a telephone.

A telephone connected to a modem is used to call the distant end; when the connection has been made the line is switched to the modem. There are three methods of switching the modem to the line:

by press buttons on the telephone instrument;
by a switch on the private terminal equipment;
automatically from the private terminal equipment.

In other systems the modem is permanently connected by a privately leased circuit to a remote location - which could be virtually anywhere in the world. The systems can be used for:

international working;
automatic answering of incoming calls;
automatic origination of calls;
speech and signalling on private circuits;
remote testing of modems;
controlling by computer centres.

Private circuits can be used for point-to-point circuits - linking two points directly - or for multipoint circuits which allow from two to twelve terminals to be connected to a central station and enables data to be transmitted from the central station to any terminal and from the terminals to the central station. It is not possible to transmit information between terminals directly - they must go through the central station.

International data transmission can be arranged over privately leased circuits - whether or not the International Datel Service is available to the country concerned.

International Datel 200, 600 and 2 400 Services provide for the transmission of data over the PSTN to most of Europe, the United States and several other countries - see the *Telecom Guide*. The **International Packet Switching Service** (IPSS) is a public automatic switched data service giving access by U.K. data terminals to computing systems abroad and vice versa. **Euronet** is a data network provided on behalf of the European Economic Community to scientific and technical retrieval services. See the *Telecom Guide* for full details. See also *Prestel* (Section 23.5).

ACTIVITY

Find the telephone numbers required to dial the following:

Fault Repair Service - used when reporting a telephone which is broken or out of use.
Directory Enquiries - when you cannot find a telephone number.
The operator - when you have difficulty in obtaining a call.

Other Enquiries and the *Supervisor* - when you have a problem not covered above.
Calls to Malta, Poland and Australia.

QUESTIONS

1. What do the following abbreviations stand for? IDD, STD, GRACE, PMBX, PBX, PSTN and ADC.
2. What are the main differences between a PMBX and a PABX system?
3. Draw up a list of the points any user of the telephone should follow when making and receiving telephone calls.
4. Write not more than three sentences on each of the following to show that you understand them:

Datel services	Freefone
Telephone credit card	Transferred charge call
Tape Callmaker	Telephone answering machine
Radiopaging	Telephone answering and recording machine

TELEGRAM, TELEX AND CABLE SERVICES

All inland and overseas telecommunications services in the United Kingdom are operated by British Telecom and details of the current services will be found in the British *Telecom Guide* which should be kept up to date using the free supplements issued from time to time. The Post Office handles some telegrams, those handed in at offices offering telegraph business, and details of these will be found in the *Post Office Guide*.

6.1 TELEGRAMS

Telegrams may be sent in a number of ways, as follows, and there are two kinds - inland and international.

6.2 INLAND TELEGRAMS

(a) By hand
Telegrams should be written in BLOCK CAPITALS and handed in at any Post Office which handles telegrams or given to a messenger delivering a telegram or express letter. Special forms are provided for inland and international telegrams and the correct form should be used. Telegrams may be written in plain language, code or cipher or a combination of these.

ACTIVITY

Obtain an inland telegram form from your local Post Office and keep it in your folder.

(b) By telephone
A telegram may be dictated from a private telephone or public call office. To obtain the telegraph office a caller should follow the instructions given in the *Telecom Guide* or the preface to a *telephone directory*. When the operator answers, the caller should give the telephone number and exchange from which the call is being made and dictate the message two or three words at a time.

ACTIVITY

Use a telephone directory or the *Telecom Guide* to find how to send a telegram over the telephone.

(c) By telex
Telex may be used to hand in a telegram for transmission as a telegram. The normal telegraph charge is made but no charge is made for the telex call. The dialling codes card supplied to telex subscribers shows all the telex numbers of telegraph offices.

(d) In advance
Greetings telegrams (except those for delivery with a telegraphic money order – see Section 12.7) may be handed in in advance for delivery on a specified date. Delivery will be made as near as possible to the time specified – within normal hours. Notice must be given in advance if it is intended to send large numbers of telegrams from a particular office.

If a telegram is handed in at a Post Office the sender's name and address should be written in the space provided on the back; if it is made over the telephone, on other than a private line, the name and address of the sender must be given.

(e) Delivery of telegrams
Telegrams may be delivered in a large number of ways, but usually by hand or by machine.

Delivery by hand is to the address indicated. If delivery cannot be made to the person named the telegram will be put through the letter-box – unless there is some doubt about the address. Special instruction regarding delivery may be made to the local Head Postmaster. A telegram may be delivered to a *temporary address* such as a caravan or holiday home – either to the person named or the proprietor for delivery. A telegram may be delivered to a stationmaster at a railway station for delivery to a *railway passenger*. It may be handed to an airline company for delivery to a *passenger* or member of the crew *of an aircraft*. A telegram intended for a passenger or a member of the crew of *a ship in port* is given to the Purser's Office for delivery. A *poste restante* telegram, one to be collected from a Post Office, will normally be kept for two weeks at the counter – after which time it will be filed with other undelivered telegrams.

Machine delivery includes telegrams delivered *by telephone*. A telegram addressed to a telex address will be normally delivered *by teleprinter*.

ACTIVITY

Use the *Telecom Guide* to find the answers to the following:

When is there no hand delivery of telegrams?
When will a telegram not be delivered by telephone?

What is a prepaid reply telegram?
What is a telegraphic address?
What is an overnight telegram?

(f) Counting for charges

The words in the name and address as well as those in the message are all counted for charging purposes with some exceptions. All the required words in an address after the name of the road, street, lane and so on are charged for as a word. *Telephone and telex addresses* are charged for as two words. *Special instructions* are charged for as part of the message. *The text of the message* is charged for according to the number of words contained in the message. Names of towns, compound words, words normally coupled by hyphens and abbreviations in normal use are charged as single words – for example Much Wenlock, La Trobe, Newcastle upon Tyne, cannot. Foreign words, with the exception of Latin words and words in any modern European language (including Esperanto), are charged at the rate of five characters to a word. Latin words and modern European languages (including Esperanto) are charged at the same rate as English words. *Combinations of letters or figures* – but not letters and figures combined – are counted at the rate of five characters to a word. *When figures and letters are mixed* they are counted separately – for example; 75p counts as two words, Bc7D counts as three words and 1660X counts as two words.

ACTIVITY

Use a copy of the *Telecom Guide* to find the current cost of sending telegrams. How would the following be charged?

1. 23a High Street
2. $4\frac{1}{2}$
3. 8%
4. ono
5. *Quickly*
6. c/o

6.3 INTERNATIONAL TELEGRAMS

Telegrams sent overseas must be sent on an international telegram form if they are to be handed in. Like inland telegrams, international telegrams may be handed in at any Post Office at which telegraphic business is conducted, or they may be dictated over a private telephone or from a telephone call office or be sent by telex.

ACTIVITY

Obtain a copy of an international telegram form and keep it in your folder.

On an international telegram the letters URGENT mean Urgent telegram; LT mean letter telegram; GLT mean Commonwealth Social Telegram; TF mean by telephone.

ACTIVITY

Use the *Telecom Guide* to find how much it costs to send an international telegram and how words are counted for costing purposes. What is a Press telegram? What is Sender's Risk?

Delivery of international telegrams is as described for inland telegrams.

Picture services

Pictures, photographs, drawings, plans, etc., typed or written material, documents and shorthand, etc., may be telegraphed in facsimile from London over line circuits and over radio links to many places in the world. The **phototelegrams** may be posted from the office of receipt by express or registered post. **Intelpost** is an electronic letter service which allows customers of the Post Office to send urgent copies of documents around the country and have them delivered within hours. The service is intended for those customers who do not have their own facsimile service and it provides a national service with some international service (Canada, Holland and the east coast of the United States). One idea is to encourage large business customers to transmit bills and accounts to local centres where they can be printed out and posted – thus cutting handling costs.

ACTIVITY

Use the *Telecom Guide* for full details of the Picture Services.

6.4 TELEX

The telex service uses *a teleprinter* to transmit messages and receive messages from all over the country and many parts of the world. The telex service in the United Kingdom is a fully automatic teleprinter switching system which enables subscribers to call each other at any time of the day or night and to communicate in print. Calls can be made to telex subscribers in most other parts of the world. The service combines the speed of the telephone with the authority of the printed word and the service is especially useful when accuracy is important – for example when an order or a complex message has to be sent. Messages can be sent to a subscriber even when his office is closed – providing his telex machine is switched on. The service is extremely useful when messages to overseas customers are involved and there are time zone differences. A subscriber can receive messages even if he is away from his business, providing his machine is switched on, and up to five copies of every message received are available if required – as, for example, for accounting and record purposes. Nearly all calls to telex subscribers abroad can be made direct, but some calls have to be made via the operator (see Figure 6.1).

(a) Charges

Inland telex calls which are dialled are charged according to the distance

Fig 6.1 *a telex keyboard*

between the telex centres and the duration of the call. Those connected through the operator are charged at the same rate as dialled calls but for a minimum period of three minutes and then for one-minute periods thereafter.

International calls which are dialled to North Africa and Europe are measured in metered units. The time per unit depends on the country dialled. The cost per unit multiplied by the number of units used gives the cost of the call. Calls beyond Europe are charged in one-minute periods with a one-minute minimum charge. Overseas calls through the operator are charged for a three-minute minimum period and for one-minute periods thereafter.

Telex bills are usually sent out quarterly and cover one month's rental in advance and calls for the previous quarter.

The United Kingdom Telex Directiory lists subscribers in alphabetical order by name, followed by address, telex number and 'answer-back code'. A fully revised directory is normally issued every April and October.

Stationery and other supplies, such as ribbons, have to be provided by individual subscribers and must conform to prescribed standards.

The telex service is usually provided for a period of a year – temporary service can be provided for shorter periods.

(b) Training
Instruction is usually given by one of the experienced members of a firm or by personnel from British Telecom who regularly visit each installation

to ensure that the service is satisfactory. Any person who can type should have no difficulty in operating a telex machine.

6.5 PRIVATE TELEPRINTER SERVICE

Printed messages can easily and quickly be sent between teleprinters linked by private circuits; no call charges are payable by a customer who rents the teleprinter circuit for his exclusive use. There is a range of attachments and facilities, including one which permits one transmitter to broadcast to several terminals on a network at the same time. Such a facility is the *Private Automatic Telegraph Branch Exchange (PATBX)* which combines a private teleprinter system with access to the whole telex system. To contact a PATBX system, telex subscribers have to dial two extra digits (figures) to the telex number they would normally call. *A card callmaker* attachment can be used with a telex installation (see Section 5.12).

6.6 TELEX CALL OFFICES

The *Telecom Guide* lists the addresses from which inland and overseas telex calls may be made. The form supplied by the telecommunications service is normally used and there is an additional fee payable per call in addition to the normal call charge.

ACTIVITY

Obtain a copy of a telex form and keep it in your folder.
Use the *Telecom Guide* to find the addresses of telex call offices.
What is the fee charged for a call from a telex office?

Make notes on the Telegraphic Maritime Services.
What is a radiotelegram?

6.7 CABLES

The term 'cable' is used to distinguish the service which used undersea cables as the means of transmitting international telegrams or cables. Today, with the use of satellites, radios and other methods, the terms 'cables' and 'telegrams' mean the same.

QUESTIONS

1. What is a radiotelegram?
2. Write brief notes explaining how a telex machine is operated.
3. Your employer has been suddenly taken ill and cannot keep an important engagement with a Mr R A Burgess, 24 Station Drive, Basingstoke, Hants, RG21 2XS. Draft a telegram to Mr Burgess informing him of the situation. Use the *Telecom Guide* to find the *cost of sending your telegram*.

PROJECT

Prepare an illustrated folder showing the current Telex services available. Include details of the telex machines available and how they are operated.

SHORTHAND AND AUDIO SYSTEMS

7.1 SHORTHAND

There are many shorthand systems in use and their main purpose is to enable the spoken word to be recorded visually in less time than writing in longhand. Although shorthand and typewriting are usually spoken of in the same context the skills are not related and the ability to do one does not equate with the ability to do the other. The reason why the skills are associated is that most shorthand is typed back rather than written in full. Shorthand systems either use symbols to record speech or they use some system based on letters of the alphabet.

The most commonly used symbol systems are Pitman shorthand and Gregg shorthand. Many secretaries use the 'old-fashioned' New Era Pitman system while the modern system commonly taught is Pitman 2000. Symbol systems usually take a lot of time to master but have the claimed advantage that high speeds can be obtained – up to 200 words a minute by a very good writer – while speeds of 100 words a minute are to be desired by people who hope to work as shorthand writers.

Systems based on letters of the alphabet include Speedwriting and Pitmanscript. These systems are usually considered easier to learn than symbol systems, but it is claimed that they do not enable speech to be recorded at high speeds – speeds of 80 words a minute being the norm. To counter this claim it is often stated that most dictation is given at about 80 words a minute and the ease of learning gives the systems an 'edge' over the more traditional methods.

(a) Advantages of shorthand systems
1. The writer's notebook provides a valuable record – and can be referred to if queries arise during the course of taking dictation.
2. Queries concerning the dictation can be handled at the time the dictation is given.
3. Spelling and other problems – for example, grammar, sentence-structure and paragraphing – can be handled during dictation.
4. Notes can be used as legal evidence.

5. The actual process of taking dicatation is more personal than using a machine.
6. Confidential matters are kept private between the dictator and the secretary.

Further considerations Shorthand can be used for taking notes at a meeting and can be used to identify individual speakers; it is useful for taking notes from which the secretary can compose replies to letters or other communications such as memos; it can be used to take dictation from authors who may be unfamiliar with dictation machines – although most organisations using dictation machines provide training for both the authors and the secretaries using the equipment.

(b) Taking dictation
Secretaries who take dictation are advised to keep two notebooks – one for notes and reminders – the other for dictation. A spiral bound notebook is preferable for dictation, as the pages can be turned back flat. A notebook with a board cover will provide some support. Number all pages for ease of reference and draw a wide margin down each sheet so that important items can be noted – in colour if possible, for ease of reference – and any additions made easily. Write special instructions on each piece of work – the number of copies required, urgent or confidential, etc. Rule off each piece of dictation and when you type back notes, lightly draw a line through the notes used to indicate that you have finished with them. Date and store old notebooks. If you are nearing the end of a book make sure you have a spare book to hand. If possible write in ink – the notes are more permanent than those written in pencil while ballpoint notes are not as clear as those written with a pen and ink. If you must use a pencil, keep it sharp and have a spare available should it break or the point wear. Always face the dictator. If there are any queries, about words missed or spellings and so on, wait until the dictator has finished before asking for assistance.

7.2 AUDIO–TYPING

Instead of dictating material to shorthand writers some executives dictate their material into a machine which can then be played back by a typist. There is a wide range of machines available.

The authors (people who give dictation) make their recordings using a microphone on to whatever medium (method of recording the information) the machine they are using takes. Many microphones have facilities for stopping and starting, rewinding and playing back so that if the author is interrupted he can stop, rewind to listen what he has previously said and then continue. Corrections are made, in some cases, by rewinding and then re-recording the new material. In other cases a note has to be made at the end of the dictation. Some machines require a mains power supply while the more modern machines can be both battery and mains operated. The length of the dictation is recorded either on a marker sheet or the amount of dictation given is recorded on a counter. Portable dictating machines have a built-in microphone and counting mechanism. Flexible plastic belt and disc machines have a medium which can only be used once; tape and cassette machines have the advantage that the tapes and cassettes can be used over and over again if required.

An audio-typist takes back dictation by playing back the material on her machine, which usually has a head set through which the dictation is heard. Some machines have a speaker, rather like a small radio, through which the dictation is amplifier. There is a volume control and a hand or foot mechanism for stopping and starting the machine, rewinding to listen to what the author says and typing it – stopping the machine, rewinding to play back material which was not heard accurately the first time, and starting the machine again to hear more dictation – until the whole is typed back.

(a) Using a dictation machine – recording

If full efficiency is to be obtained the information given to the audio-typist must be given in such a way as to avoid confusion and delay. If several people are giving dictation, as for example when a central bank of machines is in use, they must all be trained to give it in the same way. The training of authors is just as important as training the audio-typists.

1. Before starting dictation make sure that there is sufficient medium available so that the dictation is not split over more than one tape or disc, etc.
2. Identify yourself so that the typist knows who to contact with finished work or contact if there are problems.
3. State how many copies are required and what paper/material is to be used.
4. Indicate the length of the material being dictated – unless you do this the typist can only guess from the amount of recording medium used. For example, if a letter of 100 words or thereabouts was being dictated – a short letter, begin 'Mr Jenkins dictating. Take two carbon copies of this short letter which is to be sent today to . . .' The typist then knows exactly what to expect and can carry on without fear of having the wrong paper – or having to retype to produce extra copies. *A short letter* would be one of roughly 100 words pica type or 125 words elite type; an *average letter* would contain roughly 100 to 250 words pica type or 125 to 350 words elite type while *longer letters* would require continuation sheets.

It can be seen from this that the author must collect his thoughts before starting dictation and train himself to think well in advance.

5. Speak clearly, directly into the microphone. Some machines have a switch which enables the machine to be used either for individual dictation or for recording several people speaking in a room – as for example at a meeting. If the machine has this facility check the position of the switch before dictating.

6. Indicate punctuation. With training an author can indicate commas by the inflection in his voice. It is usual to indicate full stops (a good author does not need to do this), and new paragraphs.
7. Names and unusual spellings must be spelt out.
8. If the machine has a correcting facility, use it to correct errors – if not, indicate the position of errors on the recording slip and make the corrections at the end of the passage.
9. Send any documents or papers which have to go with the recording.

Be polite – act as though the typist was with you actually taking the dictation.

(b) Using an audio machine – playing back

To play back material the typist places the recording medium on to her machine – the same machines used for recording can be used for playing back – and checks the length of the passage(s) and the slip for any corrections or instructions. If there are corrections it is usual to play through the passage and the corrections before attempting the typing. Once the material has been typed the medium can either be stored for future reference – or returned to be reused. The typed material should be sent to the author for signature.

(c) Points for and against audio systems

The points 'for' might include the following:

1. It is easy and cheap to train audio-typists. Many people learn to type by audio methods and learn to audio-type as quickly as they learn to type. To train an audio-typist from a copy typist only takes five to six hours as a rule.
2. Authors can dictate at any time they are free – at home, while on trips, in the car – and so on, and post the material to the office. Audio machines can be linked to the telephone so dictation can be telephoned in. Some audio machines can be used as telephone answering machines.
3. Portable machines can be used in any situation – stocktaking, making reports and while on tours for example.
4. Time is saved because the shorthand writer is not kept waiting while the author deals with matters which crop up while dictation is being given. Typists can get on with other work while waiting for dictation and the work flow can be evened out.
5. If a centralised system is being used all the recording can be taken in one place and maximum use can be made of the typing pool.
6. Running costs are cheap because the medium can be used over and over again.
7. There is no problem of waiting for a shorthand writer to catch up and there is not the problem of poor outlines which cannot be read.
8. Dictation machines can be used to record conferences as well as individual dictation.

The points 'against audio systems might include the following:

1. Shorthand writers will lose their hard-earned skills through lack of use and the cheapness of training audio-typists may lessen the value in terms of salary of a shorthand writer.
2. The system is impersonal because there is no contact between the author and the typist.
3. The system is expensive to install. (The point about power failure making the machines useless has no value because if the audio machines cannot operate neither will the lights or the electric type-writers.)
4. Authors may not identify themselves or dictation might be poor. (The answer to both problems is to train the authors correctly.)
5. No record is usually kept of dictation other than the typed copy. Material which has been posted can be lost in the post – although carbon file copies can help to resolve the problem of loss of information.
6. On some machines it is impossible to correct at the point of error and time is wasted playing through material and the error. (The answer is to insist on suitable equipment.)
7. If a typing-pool arrangement is used, confidential matters are difficult. (The author should use the head of the typing pool, a senior typist or his secretary.)
8. If meetings are recorded it is often impossible to distinguish voices and define who is speaking on any given point.
9. Tapes are not normally a legal record.
10. It is not as easy to refer back to previous matters relating to the dictation as when a shorthand writer makes reference to past notes in her dictation book.
11. If there are problems it may be difficult, if not impossible, to contact the author at once.

7.3 CENTRALISED SYSTEMS

Some firms have centralised dictation systems in which all the recording machines are located at one point – usually the typing room. All authors are equipped with an internal telephone which is connected to the bank of machines. To make a recording an author simply picks up the telephone which automatically connects him to an available machine. In the Lanier system (see Figure 7.1) the supervisor has a visual record of the current position on a screen. Controls on the telephone permit recording, playing back, stopping and starting so that in the event of interruption dictation can continue – the machine in the bank is engaged as long as the receiver is lifted off the cradle. When dictation is finished the indication light on the machine in the bank records the fact and the supervisor simply gives the recording to the typist who happens to be available.

Fig 7.1 *Lanier monitor*

The monitor is linked to a centralised dictation system and uses a micro-processor with a visual display unit to enable the supervisor to control the whole system. The monitor's control centre automatically displays and stores essential information about each individual unit of dictation. The keyboard accepts human language commands from the supervisor for the control of external entries, such as information from executives travelling about the country and telephoning in, hard copy, revisions and information from all dictation machines. One monitor controls up to 16 PBX- or PABX-controlled recorders and can process the dictation from up to 9 999 telephone originators or up to 96 direct-wire originators. It automatically receives and displays a five-point description of every unit of incoming dictation:

cassette and recorder number;
day and time of input;
author identity;
length of dictation.

The monitor can display information on all work or just that of a particular individual. The supervisor can request status reports on work in progress and recall from the system memory up to 1 200 entries. A printed display for survey and charging purposes gives a summary of the work by individual typists or departments.

For and against centralized systems

The arguments against a centralised dictation system are much the same as those 'against' a typing pool – and the points 'for' are again about the same. Some typists do not like head sets, while others prefer them. A poor office supervisor will tend to overload the better audio-typists but in a well-managed office it is easy to pay good typists for the extra work they do – and give all a range of work to do so that they do not become bored with the same kind of task. Training is made easier and there is not the problem of recruitment of shorthand writers – who may not all be using the same system so that a typist who can read one system finds the notes of an absent typist using another system useless.

7.4 MACHINE SHORTHAND

Machine shorthand or *stenotyping* is the system whereby an operator uses a machine to take down dictation instead of a shorthand notebook and pen. Both hands are used to operate the keyboard which records syllables or words on a continuous roll of paper. The machine is silent in its operation and presents outlines which are as clear as normal typing – so that reading back is very easy.

QUESTIONS

1. Prepare a list of the advantages and disadvantages of shorthand systems over dictation machines.
2. What steps should be taken to ensure that any person taking dictation is able to do so efficiently?
3. What points should authors bear in mind before dictating information into a dictating machine?

TYPEWRITERS

Typewriters may conveniently be thought of as three distinct types: manual, electric and word-processing.

8.1 MANUAL MACHINES

Manual machines have remained basically the same for many years and even an old machine can be readily identified for what it is. The basic or 'standard' office machine has four banks of keys, a tabular mechanism, a choice of ribbon positions and a choice of carriage lengths. The keys are struck manually and operated by a series of levers, springs and type bars; the harder the typist strikes the keys the harder the keys strike the roller or platen. Figure 8.1 illustrates a typical machine and you should learn the names of the parts.

ACTIVITY

Can you name the parts numbered in Figure 8.1?

Most modern manual machines offer a touch adjustment – to make the keys harder or ligher to operate; half-line spacing; a line indicator to tell the typist how many lines of type she has available on any particular sheet; special centring scales; automatic tabulator clearance as opposed to the clearance of individual tabulator keys; a choice of platens – hard for the typing of carbon copies as well as the normal platen – and the facility to replace such keys as fractions with other keys. Most machines have a half-space correction facility so that a typist can replace a word with one letter longer than the error, as for example:

He wil come ...   He will come ...

All manufacturers of manual machines offer a choice of *typeface sizes* and *typeface styles*. Most manual machines are either *pica* or *elite* size. *Pica type* gives 10 letters to every inch (about 25 mm.) across a sheet of paper while *elite type* gives 12 letters to every inch across a page. Pica type is

90

Fig 8.1 *the parts of a typewriter*

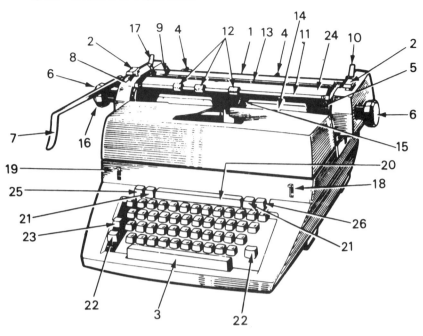

probably easier to read than elite, because it is slightly larger, but elite type is more economical because more words can be typed on any given page. Both pica and elite machines give six lines of type to every inch (about 25 mm.) down a sheet of paper. Some *continental machines* give 14 or 16 letters to every inch across a sheet of paper with eight lines of type to every inch down a sheet of paper.

The usual carriage length of a standard office machine is 13 inches or 14 inches although longer carriages are available for legal or statistical work - when up to 18 inches may be required.

Typing ribbons for manual machines are made of carbon film, silk, nylon or cotton. All ribbons are supplied on spools and the usual lengths are 10 or 20 metres. A typing ribbon is basically fabric soaked in ink and many different colours are available. If only one type of work is being undertaken it makes economic sense to buy a one-colour ribbon - sometimes called a *record ribbon* or a *monochrome ribbon*. *Two-colour ribbons* - sometimes called *bichrome ribbons* - are the most common although three-colour ribbons are available. The usual colours are black, black/red, blue, blue/red, red, green, purple, orange, brown - and each in combination with black. *Silk* and *carbon film ribbons* give a sharp, clear image of very high quality and are ideal for all kinds of high-class work - including the production of offset litho plates. Carbon film ribbons can be used once only. *Nylon* ribbons are good for general work and produce good carbon copies while *cotton* ribbons are very durable (they last a long time), but do not produce work of the same quality as silk, film or nylon – they are much thicker and so the keys cannot produce a sharp image so easily. It will save a great deal of time if the typist orders the correct ribbon to replace a worn-out one; while most ribbons are the same length and width, the spools on which they are wound vary. If a ribbon with the wrong spool is purchased the typist must clear the old ribbon off both spools on her machine before winding the new ribbon on to one spool – before replacing as normal. All typists should learn how to change the ribbon on their machine – if you have to change one on a strange machine have a look in the instruction book for details. Ribbons dry out – so only purchase them as you require them.

(a) Care of the manual machine

1. Keep the typeface clean by brushing daily with a hard brush to remove ink. This is particularly important after typing stencils. If the ink is hard, use some spirit to dissolve it first – manufacturers supply various kinds.
2. When erasing, make sure that the carriage is moved to one side or the other so that all dust falls outside the machine and never into the workings. If using one of the liquid correcting materials make sure that the plastic card holders at the front of the machine are wiped clean – again with some spirit.
3. Wipe the machine regularly with a soft cloth and use a long-haired brush to flick dust out of the workings. Clean under the machine to prevent dirt and dust building up and entering the machine – use a mat when typing. *A typing mat* will make the machine quieter to operate and cause less vibration. Manual machines are best stood on thick felt mats – or cushioned plastic. Shake the mat when you clean the machine.
4. Oil only the metal parts – and then very carefully. If in doubt, leave the oiling to the mechanic and in any case never oil the type bars. Too much oil will encourage dust and dirt to stick to the working parts of machines – and speed up wear.
5. When the machine is not in use, cover it with the cover supplied. When it is in use ensure that the typing cover is on the back of the typing chair or some suitable dust-free place – never on the floor where it will pick up dust which will find its way into the machine.
6. Centre the carriage by bringing the two margins together when the machine is not in use – this will prevent accidental damage should the machine be moved causing the carriage to move from side to side.
7. Never lift a machine unless you must. When moving machines make sure that they are picked up with the base of the machine, not the carriage, and with the keyboard facing away from you.
8. Always use a backing sheet when typing. If possible have two platens (rollers) available – a hard one for typing carbons and a normal one. If a hard platen is used for normal work, undue wear will be caused to the typeface.

9. Never keep a typewriter near a radiator or in the sun – the heat will damage it.
10. If anything should go wrong with the machine and the fault is not apparent at once – send for a mechanic.

(b) Erasing using a manual machine

.1. Read through material before taking it out of the machine – it is easier to correct while still in the machine than when it has been taken out.
2. If using a *typing eraser*, move the carriage to one side or the other so that any dirt or dust caused in the process of correcting the error falls outside the workings. Many machines have an *erasure platform* on to which work can be turned before erasing. Take care when erasing – it is all too easy to wind the paper out of the machine. If this is likely to happen wind the paper back into the machine and erase as it comes round the erasure platform. It is a good idea to move the eraser from side to side, rather than up and down when erasing, it prevents the paper moving so easily. In either case hold the paper between finger and thumb while erasing. Take care never to rub a hole in the paper and if the paper is roughened, smooth it with the 'wrong' end of a pen before winding to the typing point and typing the correction.

If making a correction *while taking a carbon copy*, place a piece of scrap paper, or a thin plastic sheet, between the carbon paper and the carbon copy while removing the error on the top copy. Erase the error on the carbon copy before typing the correction. Take care to remove the protecting piece of paper or sheet of plastic.

Typing erasers are made in various shapes and sizes but are generally rubber mixed with some abrasive material, such as pumice or carborundum, which cuts into the ink. An ordinary soft 'India' rubber has little effect on ink because it lacks the abrasive material. Soft rubbers are used for erasing the carbon on carbon copies. Some manufacturers offer a dual-purpose eraser – one with a hard core for erasing ink and two soft outside layers for erasing errors on carbon copies.

3. *If using a correcting fluid*, wind the paper on to the erasure platform and use the small brush supplied with the fluid to paint out the error – taking care to paint it out completely. If taking a carbon copy remember to correct the error on the copy – preferably using an eraser or a fluid the same colour as the copy sheet. Wind the paper back to the typing point before continuing. *Thin the fluid* with the liquid supplied by the manufacturer from time to time – to prevent it becoming too thick. Always keep the container screwed up tight when not using the fluid, even between corrections, because the solvent will rapidly evaporate.

4. *If using a correcting paper*, backspace to the point of the error and place a sheet of the correcting paper, coating side away from you, between the type face and the copy. *Type the error* (the correcting paper will cover it up) before backspacing again to type the correction.

Take care to ensure that you insert some protective material, scrap paper or plastic film, between the carbon paper and the carbon copy if taking a carbon copy and correct the copy before continuing to type.

The use of *erasing shields* – which are pieces of plastic with holes of various shapes and sizes – helps to protect work when erasing or correcting. The sheet is placed over the work and the error corrected through one of the holes in the shield.

8.2 ELECTRIC MACHINES

There are basically three kinds of electric machines; those with type bars, those with a golf-ball or daisy-wheel head and automatics (see Figure 8.2).

Electric machines with type bars look very similar to normal manual machines and operate in much the same way except that the keys are operated by a light touch – yet strike the platen with a constant pressure, giving the work a much more even appearance. A key is used to automatically return the carriage and turn up the paper. By altering the position of one lever the amount of pressure required to trigger the keys can be adjusted to suit the needs of the typist, while the operation of another lever determines how hard the keys strike the platen so that adjustments can be made, as, for example, when cutting stencils or taking carbon copies. Many type-bar electric machines allow the typist to use a carbon ribbon, used once, for high-grade work, and a normal ribbon for routine material. This facility saves the high cost of carbon film ribbons. In most other respects electric type-bar machines are the same as manual machines – the other major difference being the angle of the keyboard which is 'flatter' on the electric machine than the steeper angle of manual machines.

The correction of errors is much the same as for manual machines.

Single-element electric machines differ from other machines in a number of ways.

1. Instead of using type bars the machine is fitted with a golf-ball or daisy-wheel head which revolves as keys are touched.
2. The head moves across the page as the machine is operated – the carriage does not move. This means that less space is required either side of the machine.
3. The head of the machine can be changed very quickly and simply so that a wide variety of styles of typeface may be used as the situation demands.

Many single-element machines are *dual pitch*. Instead of talking about pica and elite the term *pitch* is used to describe the size of typeface. A *10-pitch* head gives 10 letters, or spaces, to the inch while a *12-pitch* machine gives 12 letters, or spaces, to the inch. A dual-pitch machine is one which may be used with a 10-pitch or a 12-pitch head. Some machines even offer

Fig 8.2 A: *daisy-wheel*; B: *golf-ball*

A

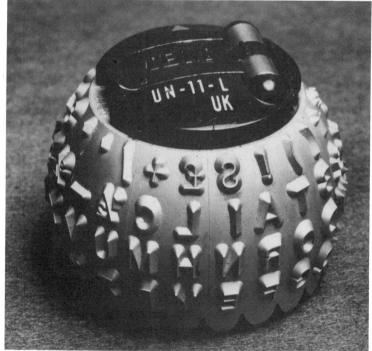

B

further choices – such as 11-pitch. In addition to the variation in pitch, a 10-pitch head may be used with the machine on 12-pitch spacing – or the reverse, there is a wide variation of styles available.

4. Many single-element machines have a dual tabulator so that when new tabulator settings are required for a subsection of a piece of work they can be set while the original settings are stored by the machine for later use.

5. Most single-element machines use *carbon film ribbons* which are supplied in a disposable case. When a new ribbon is required, the old ribbon, which is encased in a plastic cover, is removed and a new ribbon inserted.

Film ribbons are normally of two kinds: *correctable film*, which are used once and thrown away, and multi-strike. Correctable film ribbons are usually used with machines which have an *easy erasing feature*. When an error is made the typist presses the self-erasing key. This causes the machine to backspace and operates *a correcting (or lift-off) ribbon*, which is a ribbon coated with a sticky substance. When the original error is typed the sticky ribbon pulls the ink off the page – allowing the typist to make the correction. Carbon copies still have to be corrected in one of the normal ways. Most film ribbons are about 160 m. long. Each lift-off tape will permit about 2000 corrections – depending on the pitch being used.

Multi-strike ribbons use a micro-porous plastic impregnated with a molecular solvent ink, which means that the ribbon is like a miniature thin sponge. When the typewriter key strikes the ribbon it releases the ink into the paper. By means of capillary action ink flows from unused areas of the film to those areas which have been used, allowing the film to be used several times. In order to make a correction *cover-up tapes* have to be used which coat the original error rather than remove it. Multi-strike ribbons are usually 90 m. long and twice the cost of correctable film ribbons. It is claimed that they last much longer and are cheaper to use in the long term.

6. Electric machines, type-bar and single-element alike, have *repeat keys*. If pressure is maintained on these keys – usually the x, the underscore, hyphen and full point – the machine will continue to type them until the pressure is removed.

Proportional spacing machines do not have a consistent space for each letter. Each letter, or character, is allowed a space which varies from key to key – for example, the letters f, i, j and l are allowed less space than say w or m. The allowance for each key depends on the manufacturer. These machines offer work which looks attractive but problems are presented in the calculation of display material or corrections – as, for example, when the letter i has been typed instead of m and there is the problem of 'fitting in' the correction.

8.3 AUTOMATIC TYPEWRITERS

Automatic typewriters type material, previously typed and recorded, without the typist operating any of the standard controls. The machines are thus able to produce, at high speed, individually typed pieces of work. They have a normal keyboard with the addition of such control keys as STOP, START, EDIT and PARAGRAPH. The keys may be part of the actual typewriter or be operated by an attachment. The machines work as follows:

1. The original document must be typed in the normal way and, as this is being done, the material is recorded in various ways - punched tape, punched card, magnetic tape or disc.
2. The machine is instructed to type the document automatically and as it does so the material is checked, edited and corrected/amended as required.
3. The record is filed for future use.
4. When required the recording is fed into the machine, which is ordered to type. The typist is able to type in such information as the date, inside address or instructions within individual letters, such items as dates and figures. If a whole batch of the same recording is required the date may be fed into the recording to save further time.

The work and range of automatic machines is constantly being improved - some will now transmit material via the telephone, including the signature, to another machine, which receives it and reproduces an exact copy - thus saving time and postage.

As automatic typewriters become more and more sophisticated manufacturers use a range of terms to describe their products. *Memory typewriters* and *electronic typewriters* are very similar inasmuch as both have a *memory display* or a *visual display* - all typing is initially shown electronically on a small screen which shows fifteen or twenty characters as they are typed. Any errors in the typing can be seen and corrected on the small screen before the edited typing is stored in a *working memory* (see Figure 8.3). The machine can be instructed to type the whole or part of the working memory at any time so that adjustments to a whole passage can be made before instructing the machine to record the working memory on to a *mini-disc* for future use. The size of the working memory and the amount which can be stored on a mini-disc depends on the manufacture of the machine - some will store only phrases or paragraphs; others will store up to 70 000 characters (50 A4 sheets). Material can be taken from a mini-disc and recorded in a working memory and vice versa.

The contents of most memories can be printed as many times as required - machines enable additions and deletions to be made at any point in text - the layout of the material is automatically adjusted. The right-hand margin can be repositioned or centered as required as well as justified while the machines will undertake such tasks as underscoring as the material above the line is typed, indenting paragraphs, bold printing.

Fig 8.3 *diagram showing how a memory typewriter works*

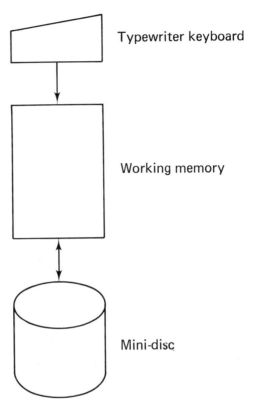

Typewriter keyboard

Working memory

Mini-disc

double printing and spaced lettering. Most are *microprocessor*-controlled and have a multi-lingual keyboard capability; they can be programmed to type several languages without changing the print wheel. They all offer a variable-pitch facility and a range of type styles as well as a range of ribbon colours in various cartridges – most ribbons can be used with correctors.

Advantages of automatics
There are several advantages, the chief ones being:

1. Much correspondence is of a routine nature – typists have to type, monotonously, the same series of letters over and over again. Automatic machines do this for them with great speed (up to 350 words a minute) and with total accuracy.
2. One typist is able to operate several automatic machines and so save the high cost of wages.
3. Instead of an author (also called a dictator) dictating whole passages he is able to dictate only those sections which require change.

4. The machines can transmit and receive messages – saving time and money – as well as store information either for immediate or future use.

5. The machines can *justify the right-hand margin*. Printed work usually has both left and right margins justified, that is both are a straight line. This adds to the appearance of the work. It is possible, by typing a passage first, finding the average and using the half-space mechanism to close up the required number of spaces to justify the right-hand margin on some manual machines. Automatic machines can be instructed to do this on their own and so produce work of total accuracy coupled with a printed appearance. Only machines with proportional spacing produce a right-hand margin which is justified in an acceptable way to the critical eye – most machines justify the margin by opening extra spaces between some words.

6. Machines can be instructed to underscore material as it is typed and to produce bold printing and double printing.

Before deciding which automatic/memory/electronic typewriter to purchase, a firm must consider such factors as cost, the use to which the machine will be put and the facilities offered by the machine. Many machines have built-in features which few firms require and there is a danger of spending money on sophistication which is not required.

8.4 WORD-PROCESSING

Just as automatic machines are marketed under a range of titles so are word processors and such names as *text processors* and *wordplex* are used to describe what is basically the same process. The machines consist of a keyboard which is linked to a *visual display unit* – a screen rather like a television screen on which the typed material appears. Once material has been inserted it can be corrected and edited on the screen very easily – insertions and deletions can be made simply and quickly without resetting the whole passage and machines will automatically adjust the text as required. Some visual display units (vDUs) will show a whole A4 page while others show any required part of a page – they can scroll horizontally and vertically over the whole memory. Material is stored in a working memory until the operator is satisfied with it; it can then be transferred to a memory, which usually takes the form of a floppy disc which can store up to 250 000 characters. The discs can transfer the information stored on them to a working memory and be edited as required (see Figure 8.4).

A text printer has to be used to produce the prepared information in printed form. A memory disc is fed into the machine, which produces the text at very high speed – over 45 characters a second. As the text printer is producing the required material the vDU and word-processor can be used to prepare more information and some units have several processing units to one print unit.

Word-processors are very versatile and can produce a vast range of material including flow charts, block diagrams and other graphics – the

Fig 8.4 *a word-processing unit*

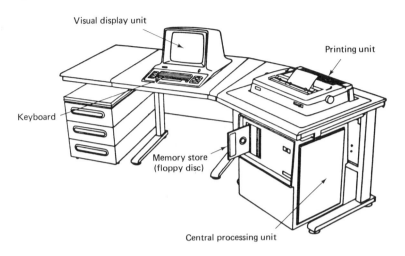

text sections can be prepared before or after the graphics. They have all the facilities of the memory/electronic typewriters and much more, and can be used for the whole range of typed/printed applications. Newspapers use them to enable reporters to type, edit and set their own material while authors use them to edit and alter work to suit any demands made without the need to retype whole texts. They are almost the complete answer to all typing problems – that is, except the one of cost. While many firms could use word-processors to advantage, memory/electronic typewriters are probably a more economical proposition. As *microcomputers* (see Sections 5.13, 8.5, 9.12, 10.1, 11.3(e), 14.11, 16.2, and 19.4) become increasingly used in business organisations it is likely that they will be used as word-processors (this is just one of their functions) and firms will not need to purchase word-processors as such.

8.5 SOME COMMONLY USED TERMS

The development of new forms of electric machines is so rapid that many systems are out of date before the equipment is worn out and as a consequence many firms are using equipment which although 'modern' compared with manual machines is, in fact, 'out of date' compared with the latest machines. The following terms are still in use and it should be noted that, in order to resolve patent problems, firms give various names to what are, in effect, the same or very similar processes.

Magnetic tape typewriters are similar to those automatics described earlier.

Magnetic card typewriters store material on a magnetic card rather than a tape or disc. Both tapes and cards are reusable. Some magnetic tapes and cards can be used with word-processing machines although discs are more commonly used.

Flexowriter is an automatic machine which uses a punched card as a memory store; card or punched tape may be used. This machine can transmit via the Datel services, the telephone or telex (see Sections 5.13 and 6.3).

The Varityper is a machine which can be programmed to a line of a given width; the machine justifies the right-hand margin and can produce work which looks like printers' type. The machine can be used for a number of functions: normal correspondence, specifications, price-lists, etc.

Diskettes are a form of memory store used on certain automatic machines such as the IBM system and the new electronic system. **Mini-discs** are the same as diskettes. The same kind of material may also be called **floppy discs**.

The petal printer or **daisy-wheel** is a system which consists of an electronic machine which uses a wheel (usually of 92 'petals' or 'strokes') instead of a golf-ball head or type basket. The wheel spins in a vertical plane and when a character is to be printed it is spun to the top of wheel and is hit by a hammer against the paper. The typing speed of over 350 words a minute is two or three times as fast as that for the *Selectric* or golf-ball system. There are several styles of typeface available in a range of pitches; proportional spacing is one of the options.

A search facility is a device used on word-processors to enable any point in a text to be located quickly and easily. On some machines the operator simply has to type in the word or words to be located and the machine does the rest.

A visual display unit usually means a screen on which material is displayed – it is rather like a small television screen – particularly when using word-processors. Some firms use the term 'visual display' to refer to a much smaller electronic display panel (15–20 characters) used with some electronic typewriters. The term 'electronic typewriter' is a blanket term used to describe any typewriter which has electronic components – usually a word-processor or memory typewriter. Some firms use the term 'microprocessor' to describe an electronic function.

An ink jet printer can put a range of typefaces on paper at a speed of 92 characters a second without using an impact system (where the keys hit the page). This system is often described as a *dot matrix* system.

It is perhaps true to say that while many typewriters appear to be entirely different when described or named, they are, on close examination, very similar. Students should take every opportunity to examine the latest electric/automatic/electronic machines and see what the actual differences are. It is advisable to concentrate on the system being offered rather than the name given to a particular system by individual manufacturers. The term 'hardware' usually refers to the actual machine; the term 'software' usually refers to the disposable material used when operating the system –

discs and tapes, etc. While the latest machines are, without doubt, able to offer a range of facilities and speeds far in excess of manual and type-bar electric machines, many offer speeds and facilities which are well beyond the needs of many users and there is a danger that machines are purchased which are too sophisticated for the use to which they are put. The more advanced machines are usually sold as part of a package which includes the training of two operators so that if one is away from a firm for any reason the machine can still be used. While good typing technique is important in the operation of any typewriter the more advanced machines, word-processors in particular, require further training on the part of the operator. While many many machines can be cleaned and serviced by the operator the more advanced machines require specialist attention and this is usually offered on a contractual basis.

8.6 CARE OF ELECTRIC MACHINES

Type-bar machines require similar attention to manual machines, but in particular:

1. It is important to see that a plastic or rubber mat is used and not a felt mat because felt may be drawn into the machine by the circulation of air and clog the motor.
2. Always ensure that the machine is switched off when not in use and pull out the plug at night.
3. Never leave an electric motor running with the cover on.
4. Take care when moving type-bar machines; they are usually very heavy.

8.7 SINGLE - ELEMENT MACHINES

1. Some machines suck air in from under the machine – some suck air from the rear. Always check to see where the ventilation ducts are and never place material near them. (If in doubt consult the instruction book.)
2. Before use check to ensure that the pitch setting is the same as the head being used – 10-pitch, 12-pitch, etc.
3. Check the pressure controls to see how much effort is required to operate the keys and how much pressure the head is applying to the ribbon or film. More pressure will be required when typing carbon copies than top copies only.
4. Check the ribbon supply – look at the ribbon cartridge to see how much tape is left.
5. Brush the elements (heads or wheels) *after removing them from the machine when the machine is switched off* with a fairly stiff brush to clean them. Some mechanics suggest using solvent to help the cleaning process. If this is done make sure that the head is perfectly clean before being relocated and *locked in position*.
6. If the machine has an *acoustic shield*, a plastic fitting which encloses

the whole of the top of the machine and so reduces the noise when working, see that it is kept clean.

7. Unplug machines when not in use – to prevent accidental switching on.
8. For maximum efficiency have the machine serviced regularly; single element machines seem to need more attention than type bar machines. If a machine has not been used for some time it is advisable to switch it on several minutes before it is to be used to allow it to warm up. Typists may find that a machine which has not been used for some time requires a higher impact setting than normal for the first few minutes of operation.

8.8 ADVANTAGES OF ELECTRIC MACHINES OVER MANUAL MACHINES

1. They are less tiring to use; the typist only has to touch the keys to operate them.
2. Work of a uniform standard can be produced; there is not the problem of uneven touch.
3. Single-element (golf-ball and petal-print) machines offer a wide range of type styles without changing the machine.
4. They can be used for a wide range of services, including composition, memory storage, setting up of documents to printed standards and to transmit and receive information. The services offered will, naturally, depend on the machine being used.
5. They offer high speeds with total accuracy when used in conjunction with memory banks.

The disadvantages of electric machines used to be cost but many modern electrics now cost less than manual machines. There is the disadvantage of power failure but if the power fails it often means that the lights fail as well so that the typist cannot see to work. Electric typewriters are more expensive to operate than manual machines (the ribbons alone are more expensive), but against that the quality of the work is much higher.

8.9 WHAT MACHINE TO USE

The choice of machine will depend, to a large extent, on the purpose to which it will be put. There is little point in purchasing the latest electronic machine for use in a small office where only one or two letters a week are typed – just as a small manual machine would have little value in a large typing pool where a wide range of work has to be undertaken. Choice must be made after a careful consideration of the work to be undertaken.

Portable machines are machines which are smaller than standard machines and so are easy to carry about. There are manual and electric portables – the latter may even have a single-element head. If the typist is to move about or the amount of work to be produced is small then a portable machine may well be all that is required. The disadvantage of an electric portable over a manual is the fact that a power point is required. Often portable machines lack some of the characters found on a standard machine and lack the width of carriage for more than normal paper sizes.

Lightweight machines are machines which fall between portables and standard machines. Very often they have the same keyboard as standard machines but lack the versatility and size required to take more than standard sizes of paper. As with some portables, they may lack a *stencil-cutting facility* – that is, you might not be able to disengage the ribbon to cut ink stencils. (You might have to take the ribbon out of the machine to cut ink stencils.) Some manufacturers call machines 'lightweight' when they actually mean to imply that their machines are lighter in weight than comparable machines from other manufacturers – and this may not always be an advantage.

Interchangeable carriage machines are machines which can be fitted with carriages of differing lengths according to the task at hand. Single-element machines cannot be used with carriages of differing lengths – neither can most type-bar electrics.

8.10 ATTACHMENTS AND ACCESSORIES

Continuous stationery attachments enable paper or forms (including sheets interwoven with carbon paper) to be fed into the rear of the machine and torn off as required.

The Formalinear is an attachment for feeding pre-collated sheets of documents into a typewriter.

A spirit carbon attachment enables spirit masters to be typed without a sheet of hectographic carbon paper being fed into the machine with the master sheet. The spirit carbon ribbon passes between the back of the master and the platen.

A BTA carbon ribbon attachment can be used with almost any kind of machine and is essentially a container holding carbon ribbon which is fixed to a typewriter. The ribbon from the container can be fed through the appropriate slot on the built-in guide arm so that the typewriter produces a high-quality carbon image. Its main value is improving the appearance of the work produced on any machine which does not have a carbon ribbon facility.

The typit attachment enables the typist to type characters or symbols not on her type-bar machine. The normal type-bar guide on the typewriter is replaced by a special type guide which holds and lines up the typits With the modification fitted the typist selects the required character or symbol and puts it into the type guide. Any key is struck and this forces a small slide to make contact with the surface of the page. There are over 1 000 symbols available.

A front paper feed enables invoices to be inserted from the front of the platen.

A card-holding attachment enables stiff card to be fed into a machine from a roll while the knife, set on the bail bar, cuts paper as required.

A copyholder may be a device for holding copy for the typist, or something more complex which will slide up and down the sheet so that the material being typed is easily identified, and the typists' task made easier.

8.11 TYPING POOLS

Typing pools were once rather dingy rooms where the 'poor relations' among the typists sat and performed a variety of dull, monotonous tasks using old machines, which had usually been handed down from the 'private secretaries' who were not above leaving the more routine or less interesting jobs to members of the pool. The poor working conditions were reflected in the poor pay and prospects of the pool typist. Today firms accept the need for efficiency and increasingly the pools are being replaced with what one newspaper called 'puddles' – small, well-equipped rooms where technologists rather than typists use high technology to produce a vast range of work and services. With the advent of more automatic machines the process is bound to accelerate and the pool typist will undertake more and more tasks once considered to be the province of the private secretary or the print room. There is no doubt that fewer typists will be employed in the pools but those who remain will be expected to operate very expensive and sophisticated machinery – and the extra training involved coupled with the extra responsibility is bound to be reflected in better working conditions and pay. It is highly probable that in the near future the function of the typist as such will be taken over by the computer operator, who will use a microcomputer to produce any typing required – as one of several functions provided by the machine (see also Section 10.1).

QUESTIONS

1. Prepare a list of the points to be taken into account when cleaning:

a manual machine;
a single-element electric machine.

2. What are the advantages and disadvantages of word-processors over standard typewriters.

THE PURCHASE AND SALE
OF GOODS

Most business organisations exist in order to make a profit. To do this they provide either a range of goods or a range of services, manufacture goods to sell, or advise on methods of selling goods, for example. In order to ensure that a business works efficiently, records of all transactions must be kept. The way in which these records are kept will, to a large extent, depend on the size of the business and/or the kind of activity it undertakes. In a small business, such as a sole trader's, all the records may be kept by the office secretary while in a large company the records may be kept by literally dozens of people working in many clearly defined departments; purchasing, sales, accounts and advertising for example. While a person working in a small business may see the whole of a particular transaction and all the documents involved, a person working in a large organisation may only see a single document concerned with one part of a transaction. The number and style of documents used by any one business organisation will vary but the list below contains the usual documents.

9.1 DOCUMENTS USED IN A BUSINESS TRANSACTION – HOME TRADE ONLY

Choosing what to buy
Firms and individuals purchase goods for a number of reasons and in order to make a decision as to what to buy will seek information from a number of sources. The usual source of information is from advertisements and firms regularly advertise goods in a number of ways.

9.2 SELLING GOODS

Representatives, also called *Sales Representatives* or *Travellers*, form a personal link between a firm and its customers and it is the job of a representative to *inform* potential customers what his firm has to offer, *give advice* about problems a customer might have and *sell goods*. A representative usually has a particular area or *territory* in which to work; the territory may be part of a large city or a number of towns. How often a representa-

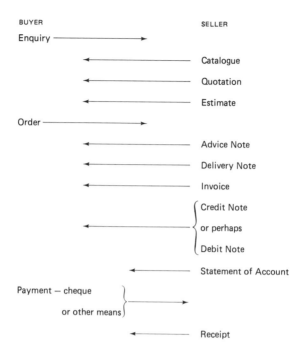

BUYER   SELLER

Enquiry ⟶

⟵ Catalogue

⟵ Quotation

⟵ Estimate

Order ⟶

⟵ Advice Note

⟵ Delivery Note

⟵ Invoice

⟵ { Credit Note / or perhaps / Debit Note }

⟵ Statement of Account

Payment — cheque / or other means } ⟶

⟵ Receipt

tive calls on a particular firm will depend on what he is selling; some calls may be made on a weekly basis, others monthly, while he may call elsewhere on an irregular basis – when he has a new product to sell or when a customer has a particular query. Most representatives keep records of calls made on a *calling card* or in *a diary*. Orders may be taken in an *order book* or on *order sheets* which list all the products a firm has to offer and has space for the name and address (or code number) of the customer, the date of the order and the number of each item required.

The advertising department of a firm is responsible for placing advertisements and for producing advertising material or campaigns. A large firm may employ its own advertising department while others may employ the services of an *advertising agency* which has specialists in the advertising field who can advise firms, place advertising for them and produce advertising campaigns. Advertisements may be placed in the *press* – newspapers, magazines or trade journals for example; *television, radio*, on *posters*, in *cinemas*, on the sides of *buses or vans* or advertising may be undertaken by means of *direct mailing* (sending customers details of the products through the post), or by employing people to push material through letter boxes, by sending *free samples*, by giving *demonstrations* in large stores or at *trade fairs* or *exhibitions*, or simply, by organising shop *window displays*.

An inquiry is a request for information and it may be made *in writing* or by means of a *verbal request* – to a person face to face or over a telephone – and is made by a potential customer to a potential supplier.

Some firms and organisations advertise the fact that they want goods or services by means of *a tender* and invite potential suppliers to give details of what they can provide, when they can provide it and at what price. The advertiser will select a supplier on the basis of information supplied; price may be the chief consideration or it may be delivery dates or quality.

The reply to an inquiry is usually one of the following:

A **catalogue** may be sent giving details of the products available. Each item may be described or even illustrated and a reference number given to identify each item. *A reference number* will identify each product exactly and should always be quoted when ordering goods. Sometimes a catalogue will contain details of the price of each item but, because of the cost of reprinting, *price-lists* are printed separately to show the price of each item. If tax is to be charged on a particular item, details of the tax payable will be given; the price should state if it is tax paid, that is to say that the tax is included in the price, or that the tax is extra – for example, price £10.00 plus VAT at the standard rate.

ACTIVITY

Find out what the current rate of VAT is. What would be the price of the following goods after adding VAT at the current rate?

1. £20   4. £7.50
2. £25   5. £0.80
3. £156   6. £15.50

A **quotation** is a reply to an inquiry and is usually given when a catalogue or price-list does not apply. A quotation may be given in writing or by word of mouth.

9.3 THE SALE OF GOODS – QUOTATION OF PRICES OR TRADE TERMS

When a firm quotes (or states) a price at which it is prepared to supply goods or services it often says what the price includes. The following is a list of the more commonly used terms in the home trade.

C.O.D. means Cash on Delivery – the supplier will expect the buyer to pay cash for the goods when they are delivered.

c.w.o. means cash with order – the supplier expects the goods to be paid for at the time the order is placed.

E. & O.E. is a term usually associated with invoices and means Errors and Omissions Excepted – if the seller makes an error in adding up the price of goods he reserves the right to correct his error.

f.o.r. or free on rail – the price of goods loaded on to a rail wagon; the buyer pays all costs from that point.

Examples of an inquiry and a quotation

John Betts & Sons Ltd
20 Hockley Hill
BIRMINGHAM
B34 9ER

Ref JB/TG

20 September xxxx

Aston & Taylor Ltd
2 Rickman Drive
SLOUGH
SL1 4AW

Dear Sirs

We have just purchased new premises at the above address and are looking for a company to supply us with plastic, cast iron and bronze valve fittings.

Will you please send us full details of the products you have to offer together with details of the discounts you offer. We can supply trade references if required.

Yours faithfully

Jack Benton
Purchasing Manager

ASTON & TAYLOR LTD
2 RICKMAN DRIVE
SLOUGH
SL1 4AW

Ref TA/RC

27 September xxxx

John Betts & Sons Ltd
20 Hockley Hill
BIRMINGHAM
B34 9ER

For the attention of the Purchasing Manager

Dear Sirs

We thank you for your recent communication and have pleasure in enclosing our latest Valves Price List which also includes list prices of our entire range.

Our Standard Discount Sheet is also enclosed but if you are prepared to place regular large orders with us we are prepared to negotiate further discounts. On hearing your special demands Mr Eric Jenkins, Sales Director, will contact you to discuss discounts.

All our Sales Offices have supplies of our current Price Lists and should you require further copies please apply to them for your requirements. A list of our Sales Offices in your area is enclosed for your convenience.

Yours faithfully
ASTON & TAYLOR LTD

Terry Aston
General Sales Manager

Encs

ex works - the price of goods as they leave the factory or works of the supplier. The buyer pays all costs from that point.

Ready delivery - the goods are in stock and can be despatched as soon as the order is received.

Prompt delivery - delivery within a few days of receipt of an order.

Forward delivery - delivery at some time in the future.

For acceptance within X days - the offer is open only for the number of days stated.

Five per cent X days means that a discount of 5 per cent (the amount could be anything) will be allowed if the goods are paid for within the number of days stated. After that time the allowance will be lost.

P/C - Prices Current - used basically when dealing with raw materials and it states that the prices charged will be those at the time of delivery.

Carriage paid - the seller will pay delivery charges.

Gross weight - the weight of the article and its container.

Tare - the weight of the container holding goods.

Net weight or net contents - the weight of the contents, or the number of the contents, only.

Carriage forward - sometimes given as **Carr. Fwd** - means that the buyer must pay transport costs.

Prompt cash - goods must be paid for within one or two days of delivery.

Cash discount - an allowance given to the buyer for payment within a fixed period. Cash discount is usually given to encourage prompt payment of bills.

Trade discount - an allowance given within a trade to allow a margin of profit when goods are resold.

Net cash - the amount due after all deductions and allowances have been made. It can also mean the amount payable when no deductions are allowed - that is to say, that the price given is the price for prompt payment without deduction. Usually the phrase is completed by adding a time limit - for example, Net cash 7 days.

9.4 ORDERING GOODS

When a buyer is satisfied with the reply, or replies, to his inquiry he will order goods. **An order**, which is a request for goods to be supplied, can be made *in writing*, usually on an order form (see Figure 9.1), it can be *word of mouth*, a face-to-face request or a telephone call, or it can be by *implication* (the offer of a suitable coin to a person selling a newspaper would be taken as a request for a newspaper without the buyer saying (anything). Verbal orders are usually supported by written confirmation at a later date and in the commercial world it is usual to place orders in writing on a prepared order form. When orders are made out it is usual to send the top, or original, copy to the supplier and keep one or more copies for the records department of the buying firm. In some firms the order takes the form of *a requisition* - an internal request for goods to be purchased (or drawn from stock if the goods are owned by the firm). In some large firms more than one copy of an order may be kept; copies might be sent to the buying department, stores (for stock-control purposes), accounts (to enable a check to be made on the eventual invoice) and the department which will receive the goods.

Fig 9.1 *an order form*

ORDER   Order No _____

TO: (Supplier)	DELIVERY ADDRESS:

Quantity	Description of Goods	Ref or Cat No	Price £	Total £

The execution of orders

If a seller is dealing with a buyer for the first time he may seek some assurance that the seller can pay for goods, particularly if credit is asked for. A seller may ask for one or more *trade references* or *a bank reference*. The former is a statement from one or more firms of repute supporting the buyer's standing; the latter is a statement from a bank as to the buyer's creditworthiness. If a potential buyer offers trade references a seller may make *status inquiries* – seek assurance from reputable sources as to the ability of the buyer to pay. Some business undertakings specialise in investigating the creditworthiness of large numbers of firms and keep records to show what has happened in the past. When a seller is satisfied about the buyer's ability to pay he will undertake to meet the order.

The way in which orders are dealt with depends on the system used by the seller and it can vary considerably. The following is fairly typical of what can, and does, happen:

1. The orders are date-stamped to show when they were received.
2. Orders are checked to see that they do not contain errors (incorrect reference numbers, for example) or ambiguities (points which are not clear – paint ordered, for example, with no indication as to colour).
3. The *Credit Department* may have to approve the order – especially if the buyer is not known.
4. The invoice section prepares the documents which the seller will send to the buyer. As the invoice is prepared it is usual to prepare other related documents at the same time – using packs of forms and carbon paper or packs of No Carbon Required forms. The packs may consist of:

The invoice – which will eventually charge the seller for the goods. An invoice will state what has been supplied, any allowances, the price of the goods, any tax due and the terms of the sale.

An office copy – or a copy for the accounts department of the seller.

A warehouse copy – telling the warehouse to collect and pack the goods for despatch.

An advice note – sometimes sent to buyers of goods informing them that an order has been received and indicating when and how they will be sent.

A delivery note – a list of the goods sent which is included with the goods so that the buyer can check to see exactly what has been sent. It is usual for there to be two copies of the delivery note – both have to be signed by the buyer of goods as they are delivered and one is given to the person delivering the goods while the other is kept by the buyer. If it is not possible to check goods against a delivery note it is usual to sign the note to the effect that the goods have not been checked. In this case any shortages must be notified as soon as possible – usually within seven days.

Only the invoice and copy invoice will show the price of goods – the carbons on the other forms may be cut away so as not to show prices or the price columns may be printed over so that the price does not show.

5. The order is packed and the goods are sent.

9.5 RECEIVING GOODS

As indicated earlier, a buyer might be sent an *advice note* informing him when he can expect his order to be met. Advice notes are not as common as they used to be but if they are used they may also state how the goods will be dispatched, by rail or by van (common carrier or own vans, etc.), and when the goods will be sent. This tells the buyer when to expect delivery.

When goods are delivered the buyer will be given a *delivery note*. The note may be included in the consignment itself, it serves as a check of what is supposed to be in the consignment, or it may be handed to the buyer by the person delivering the goods for signing as proof of delivery. As indicated earlier it is usual to check goods against the delivery note and to sign as to the correctness of the delivery. One copy of the note may be kept by the buyer and the other by the person delivering the goods. It if is impossible, because of pressure of time or because of the size of the delivery, to check goods against the delivery note the person receiving the goods must sign the note to the effect 'Goods received but not checked' and inform the seller as soon as possible of any damaged goods or any shortages (or excess goods – goods supplied but not ordered), usually within seven days.

(a) Pro forma invoice

If the goods are ordered on approval – that is, the buyer wants to inspect them before deciding whether to purchase them – the goods may be sent with a pro forma invoice (for form's sake). This invoice shows what the charges would be, if the buyer decides to keep the goods or order them as usual.

If a seller decides that goods must be paid for in advance he may send a pro forma invoice to a customer first and ask for payment before delivery. When goods are sent abroad a pro forma invoice may be accepted, by the customs authorities, as a declaration of the value of goods and be used for calculating any duty payable.

(b) Invoice

An invoice is the document which tells a purchaser of goods what he has to pay (see Figure 9.2). It lists the goods sent; the price of each item; the total due for all the goods sent; indicates what, if any, trade discount has been allowed; what deduction, if any, there will be for prompt payment and shows what tax (VAT), if any, has to be added or has been added.

All invoices are numbered and the number provides a quick and easy reference to the transaction in the books of both buyer and seller of the goods. Invoices cannot be changed – any corrections are made using either a debit note or a credit note. *When preparing an invoice* it is usual to list each item sent, the price of each item and the total charge. For example if the following goods were sent the invoice would be made up as follows:

Sent: 10 tea trays @ £5.00 each
100 assorted tea mugs @ £1.25 each

Fig 9.2 *a sales invoice*

INVOICE

NIXDORF PRODUCTS LTD
ARDEN INDUSTRIAL ESTATE
GALGATE
LANCASTER
LA2 OPR

Telephones Lancaster 34354-9

Invoice No _____

Date of order _____

Tax point/date _____

VAT REG NO 100 5672 25

Sold to

Quantity	Description	Rate	£	p

Goods

Discount

Sub-total

Tax

Net Total £

INVOICED	£
10 Tea trays @ £5.00	50.00
100 Assorted tea mugs @ £1.25	125.00
	£175.00

Once the items have been listed and priced any trade discount is deducted. If, in this example, trade discount at the rate of 25 per cent is allowed the calculation will be made as follows:

		£
10	Tea trays @ £5.00	50.00
100	Assorted tea mugs @ £1.25	125.00
		175.00
Deduct: Trade discount @ 25 per cent		43.75
	Amount due	£131.25

If the seller is allowing some cash discount for prompt payment the invoice will state the terms – 5 per cent Cash monthly a/c. This means that, in this example, if the buyer pays for the goods within a month a further 5 per cent can be deducted from the bill. This means that the buyer will have to pay £131.25 *less* 5 per cent (£6.56). £131.25 – £6.56 is £124.69. *Note*: invoices are worked out to the nearest penny.

9.6 VAT

Value added tax is a tax on some spending. Any business with a turnover above a certain sum (the amount changes from time to time as the Government wishes) must be registered with the Customs and Excise authorities for the collection of VAT. (This means that a small turnover of less than the required turnover does not have to collect VAT.) All businesses and individuals have to pay VAT – those businesses registered to collect it are allowed to claim back any VAT paid by them. Businesses and individuals not registered are not allowed to claim back any VAT paid by them. A firm collecting VAT claims back VAT paid by sending only the balance, after taking what it has paid on goods from what it has collected on those goods, to the Customs and Excise authorities. VAT is collected at each stage of production. When a business sells goods it must add VAT to the value of the goods – it pays that amount to the authorities less the amount of VAT it paid when it purchased those goods. Certain goods and services are *exempt* from VAT (no VAT is charged on them) while others are *zero rated* – which means that VAT is at nil per cent so that no VAT is charged on them.

How VAT is collected
For the purpose of illustrating how VAT is collected a rate of 15 per cent is assumed. It is suggested that students check to see what the current rate is and, if need be, make the necessary adjustments.

1. A business sells wood, nails and varnish to a manufacturer to make toy trains. The materials cost £50.00. The business selling the materials must add on VAT at the appropriate rate (in this example 15 per cent is assumed). The goods are invoiced:

	£
Materials for making toy trains	50.00
Add: VAT @ 15 per cent	7.50
	£57.50

The business pays the £7.50 VAT collected to the Customs and Excise (taxman).

2. The manufacturer buys the materials for £50.00 + £7.50 VAT and makes the toy trains. He sells them to a wholesaler for £80.00 plus VAT @ 15 per cent. The goods are invoiced:

	£
Toy trains	80.00
Add: VAT @ 15 per cent	12.00
	£92.00

The manufacturer pays £12.00 VAT to the taxman *less* the £7.50 he paid when he purchased the materials – so he pays the taxman £4.50.

3. The wholesaler sells the toy trains to a retailer for £120.00 and adds on VAT @ 15 per cent. The goods are invoiced:

	£
Toy trains	120.00
Add: VAT @ 15 per cent	18.00
	£138.00

The wholesaler pays £18.00 VAT to the taxman *less* the £12.00 he paid when he purchased the toy trains – so he pays the taxman £6.00.

4. You buy the goods from the retailer for £160.00 and are charged 15 per cent VAT. The goods are invoiced:

	£
Toy trains	160.00
Add: VAT @ 15 per cent	24.00
	£184.00

The retailer pays the taxman the £24.00 VAT *less* the £18.00 he paid when he purchased the goods from the wholesaler – £6.00. As you are not registered for VAT you cannot claim back the VAT you have paid. The £24.00 VAT that you pay has been made up as follows:

From the supplier	£7.50
From the manufacturer	£4.50
From the wholesaler	£6.00
From the retailer	£6.00

VAT must be calculated after deducting trade discount and any cash discount allowed.

Example

	£
Goods	100.00
Less	
Trade discount @ 30 per cent	30.00
	70.00
Less	
Cash discount @ 5 per cent	3.50
	66.50
Add	
VAT @ 15 per cent	9.97
	£ 76.47

Tax point
The tax point is the point in time when VAT is chargeable and is either the date the goods were delivered or the date the goods were invoiced. Invoices must state the VAT registration number of the firm collecting VAT and the tax point. They usually also state the order number to which they refer, for ease of reference, and the delivery note number – in case of discrepancies between the invoice and the delivery note.

9.7 DEBIT NOTE

A debit note is used to correct an invoice when either an item has been omitted or undercharged, or when a customer fails to return returnable containers not charged for on the invoice. A debit note is, in effect, an additional invoice.

9.8 CREDIT NOTE

A credit note is the reverse of a debit note – it is sent to correct an invoice when goods have been overcharged and is often printed in red (see Figure 9.3).

The amounts given on debit or credit notes are taken into account when preparing the invoice which is adjusted upwards or downwards accordingly. If no further trading takes place between two firms the adjustment will be made by means of a cheque or other form of payment. It is usually accepted that it is the duty of a seller of goods to correct an overcharge or an undercharge on an invoice. A customer who notices that an invoice requires correcting should notify a supplier at once. The receipt of either a debit or a credit note should be acknowledged as soon as possible.

Fig 9.3 *a credit note*

CREDIT NOTE

NIXDORF PRODUCTS LTD
ARDEN INDUSTRIAL ESTATE
GALGATE
LANCASTER
LA2 OPR

Credit Note No _____

Date _____

Customer

Date	Details	£	p

Note! Both debit and credit notes should contain the VAT registration number of the supplier.

9.9 STATEMENTS

From time to time, usually every month, a supplier sends a record of all transactions between him and a customer in the form of a statement. This record provides, in date order, all items sold in the period covered, all payments made and any debit or credit notes sent. The last item on the statement shows the amount due to the seller at the time of making it out and serves as a reminder to the purchaser as to what he still owes, assuming that payment has not been made in the time between the statement being made and received by the customer (see Figure 9.4).

Fig 9.4 *a statement*

STATEMENT

REF NO

NIXDORF PRODUCTS LTD
ARDEN INDUSTRIAL ESTATE
GALGATE
LANCASTER
LA2 OPR

Customer

Date

Terms Less 5% Cash Monthly a/c

Date	Ref No	Item	Debit	Credit	Balance

E & OE

THE LAST AMOUNT
IN THE END COLUMN
IS THE SUM DUE

If a customer receiving a statement thinks that it is an incorrect record of the transactions he will notify the supplier at once – quoting the reference number(s) of the document(s) concerned. Should the complaint be justified any adjustment will be made by issuing either a debit note or a credit note and the transaction will appear on the next statement.

When accounts are overdue a copy of the statement will be sent to the customer and on it will appear some request for payment – 'This account is overdue – prompt payment will be appreciated.' Each time a copy is sent requesting payment some indication will be given as to the number of times payment has been requested. If payment is still not paid after two or three statements the supplier will have to take legal steps to obtain his money. Some firms charge interest on money owed so that a customer not making payment within a reasonable period of time may forfeit any cash discount allowed and be charged interest on the balance.

9.10 PAYMENT

Payment for goods may be made by any of the methods described in Sections 9.14 and 12.1–10.

9.11 RECEIPT

If a customer asks for a receipt to prove that he has paid for goods he will ask the supplier to send one. Cheques and Giro accounts are proof of payment and do not usually require a receipt. Receipts are usually numbered and copies kept for reference purposes.

9.12 BUSINESS ACCOUNTS

The main business of any trading concern is the buying and selling of goods. Firms need to know what they owe to other firms and what they are owed by firms. Since the number of transactions involved will be very numerous the task of recording them may have to be spread over many people. Goods or services not sold for cash are said to be sold on *credit* and all credit sales require documentation. Details of cash sales are kept in the *cash book*. Details of credit sales are kept in a *sales book* and *sales account*. Details of purchases are kept in a *purchases book* and a *purchases account*. A *ledger* is composed of a number of accounts. Transactions recorded in accounts are recorded on the *double-entry* principle. Each account has two sides – a *debit side* (Dr), which is a list of sums owed by a firm (kept on the left-hand side of the account) – and a *credit side* (Cr), which is a list of sums owed to a firm (kept on the right-hand side of the account). Accounts in the United States are entered the other way round – credits on the left and debits on the right. The difference between the two sides of an account show whether the firm named at the head is a debtor or a creditor at any time. If the total of the debit side exceeds the credit side the firm is a debtor – it owes money. If the total of the credit side exceeds the debit side the firm is a creditor – it is owed money.

Any entry into a ledger will be matched by an entry in another account – called a *book of prime entry* (the sales book, cash book and purchases book are books of prime entry). A seller of goods will make out an invoice for all credit sales and keep a record of them in a sales book. This book will list, in numerical order, all invoices and each entry will represent an item of credit – money owed to the seller by the persons named under each entry. Any items returned will be recorded in a *sales returns book* – each amount returned will represent money owed by the seller. The *cash book* will list all amounts paid to the seller by those who have purchased goods. From these books of prime entry a seller of goods is able to produce *sales ledgers* for each customer. A sales ledger is an extract from the books of prime entry showing what has been sold to a customer on the one hand and what has been received from the customer (in the form of payments and returns) on the other. From the sales ledger the monthly *statement of account* can be made. The statement of account sent to a customer is the same as the information shown in the sales ledger – the only difference being one of form – and both can be made at the same time.

The value of the sales book is that it shows a firm what has been sold over a period of time – the total of the sales book will show the total sales over a period of time. If a firm uses a machine (such as *a computer*) to prepare its accounts it can be programmed to extract the details required for each customer and print out the sales ledger and statement of account at any time this information is required. There is no need to wait until the end of the month to extract this information – a computer could produce it very quickly at any time. If *machine accounting* is not used a firm will have to keep books of account and entries and abstractions will have to be made by hand – probably using mechanical aids such as an adding listing machine or, more probably, an electronic calculator. A small firm would keep its accounts either in bound books, loose-leaf books or on cards; a large firm would use a computer and other mechanical aids. *Mechanised accounts* are not produced in the form given here, but the principle is the same. Mechanised accounts are not produced with debit and credit entries side by side but in adjacent columns with further columns showing the balance owing. A further advantage of *using a computer* to keep accounts is the fact that as items are sold it can keep track of the *stock position* and advise when further supplies should be ordered. It is also able to keep track of all amounts received and paid out so that the current cash position can be given whenever required. Each time money is paid out or is received a computer can calculate the resulting balance at high speed. A computer can also be programmed with the credit limits for each customer and warn when these limits have been reached – in this way a firm can keep a grip on its bad debts situation. As items are received by a firm details can be fed into a computer which can be programmed to warn of possible overstocking – and any cash problems in settling debts.

9.13 BUYING AND SELLING OVERSEAS

When a transaction involves foreign trade, trade between two or more countries, prices may be quoted as follows:

f.a.s. - free alongside ship - the price of the goods delivered to the docks waiting to be loaded on to a ship. The cost of loading the goods is met by the buyer.

f.o.b. - free on board or the price of the goods loaded on to a ship. The quotation usually states the port at which the goods will be loaded.

c. & f. - cost and freight - the cost of the goods delivered to a particular port. The quotation usually states the port to which the goods are to be sent.

c.i.f. - cost, insurance and freight or the price of the goods delivered to a port (which is usually named) and the payment of the insurance costs. **c.i.f. & e.** is the same as c.i.f. but includes 'exchange' - a charge for fluctuating exchange rates or, sometimes, a charge to cover banker's charges.

franco or free indicates the price of the goods delivered to the buyer's warehouse and this includes all costs.

If goods are quoted **In Bond** it means that the goods are to be delivered to a bonded warehouse. The cost of taking the goods out of a bonded warehouse - including any customs duties - is met by the buyer of the goods.

The following documents are used in foreign trade:

A **bill of lading** is an official receipt given by the captain of a ship for goods loaded for transport. Bills of lading are usually prepared in sets of three; one copy is sent to the person purchasing the goods, one copy is kept by the person selling the goods and the third copy is kept by the captain of the vessel carrying the goods. The bill of lading which is sent to the person receiving the goods is usually sent together with a **freight invoice** - an invoice listing what has been sent and the price of each item plus any other relevant charges such as commission and insurance (where they apply). A bill of lading is a document of title to the goods, it acknowledges receipt of goods by a captain of the vessel carrying them and it is evidence of the terms of the contract for carrying the goods between the shipper and the ship-owner. A bill of lading may be signed *clean*, indicating that the goods were in good condition when loaded, or *foul* or *claused*, indicating that the goods were damaged in some way at the time of loading. A **ship's manifest** is the total of all the bills of lading plus particulars of all cargo, stores and articles liable for duty payments carried on a vessel. It is prepared and signed by the captain for presenting to port and customs officials who may require it.

An **insurance certificate** is usually required when exporting goods - most goods are insured against a number of risks.

If goods are duty payable and it is not practical, because they might be damaged for example, for the customs officials of the country receiving them to examine them a **consular invoice** may be made out. This is an invoice certified by a consular official of the country receiving goods stating that the goods are as stated on the invoice. Any duty payable is charged against the invoiced price – usually the FOB price plus shipping charges. In some countries *ad valorem* import duties (customs duties charged on the value of goods as opposed to a duty levied on the quantity of goods) are charged and importers must present a consular invoice – to assist in the production of correct returns by the importing country. A consular invoice does not prevent any goods being examined should the customs officials require to examine them. In some cases a **certificate of origin** may be required as proof of place of origin, growth or manufacture of goods being exported. This is to ensure that the correct tariffs are levied on goods and that no evasion takes place by means of routing goods through countries enjoying a preferential tariff. There are many other documents used in foreign trade – the above are the most commonly used.

9.14 OVERSEAS PAYMENT

Overseas payment may be made by means of a bill of exchange. Bills of exchange can be used for payment within a country (they are then called *inland bills of exchange*). Bills used for foreign payments are called *overseas bills of exchange*. **A bill of exchange** is an unconditional order in writing, addressed by one person to another, signed by the person giving it, requiring the person to whom it is addressed to pay on demand or at a fixed or determinable future time a certain sum of money or to the order of a specified person, or to bearer. *The parties* to a bill of exchange are *the drawer*, the person addressing the order (making it out); *the drawee* – the person to whom the order is addressed and who indicates his *acceptance* of the bill by signing it across the face of the bill, and the *payee* or *endorser* – any other person who may sign the bill (usually on the back).

9.15 THE DISTRIBUTION OF GOODS

The transporting of goods is becoming increasingly expensive and failure to select the most economical method can reduce profits or price goods out of the market. The selection of method will depend on the nature of the goods themselves. Are they small, or large? Are they urgently required? Are they perishable? Are they liable to explode or catch fire? How far have they to go? Are they to go to an address near a railway station, port or an airport?

Local deliveries will probably be sent by the firm's own delivery vehicles, if it has them. If the firm's own transport is to be used care must be taken to ensure that goods are dropped off in an orderly fashion and the driver is not constantly forced to go back on his tracks. A round should be planned and goods loaded accordingly, with those to be dropped first loaded last. If a firm does not have its own transport it will hire a local carrier, usually on a contract basis if delivery is on a regular basis.

Long-distance deliveries may be sent by firms specialising in nationwide deliveries or, if the destination is on a main railway line, rail transport will be used. If large quantities of small goods have to be sent *a container* may be sent to the firm to be loaded and the full container loaded on to a trailer or hitched to a vehicle. *Liner trains* provide a fast rail service on a regular timetable between centres – British Rail will give details.

Mail order business will rely on the Post Office Parcel service or the services provided by British Rail, or the numerous parcel delivery firms. Regular bulk dispatches can attract preferential rates.

Overseas goods must be sent by sea and/or air. As a rule air transport is used for high-value goods or goods which are urgently required. Sea transport is cheap by comparison for those destinations where it can be used and is especially useful for large, bulky goods which are not urgently required. Most goods go by a combination of sea and rail/road transport. Containers are particularly useful for large consignments of small- and medium-sized goods as there is not the problem of loading and unloading at railway stations and docks.

Specialist goods such as liquids require tankers while some foods may require refrigeration.

Before a firm sets up its own transport/delivery service it must take into account such factors as:

the cost of vehicles, depreciation and maintenance;
the wages of drivers;
insurance and general running costs, including road tax and garaging;
the nature and volume of goods to be carried;
the cost of hiring vehicles as opposed to buying them;
comparative costs of using available delivery services;
the amount of 'free' advertising it would obtain from using its own vehicles
    compared with using rented vehicles;
market trends – that is, the expansion or contraction of the volume of
    goods to be carried;
the possibility of carrying goods for other firms to offset general running
costs.

Air transport is particularly useful for sending high cost goods, including perishable goods, which are required in a hurry. Large bulky goods of low value are not suitable for transporting by air. *The documentation* required is a *consignment note*, also called an *air waybill. The consignor*, the person sending the goods, must make out the consignment note in three copies for the carrier, the consignee (person receiving the goods) and for himself. The first is signed by the consignor and kept by the carrier for making up *the manifest* which serves the same purpose as a ship's manifest. The second acts as a bill of lading – it is signed by the carrier and goes with the goods. The third is signed by the carrier and returned to the consignor. The main function of airlines is to carry goods from airport to airport and not to handle goods for collection and delivery. If a door-to-door service is required it is advisable to use the services of an agent.

Air charges are based on the weight of goods and so it is essential that goods should be adequately packed and stamped with the weight of the goods in kilograms. Some air charges are based on the weight of the consignment and its dimensions – in this case the dimensions must be stated. A separate consignment note is usually required for each package. Other documents required include the invoice or consular invoice, customs entry (if required) and any export licences which might apply.

Rail transport provides a fast service for long distances when the dispatch and delivery addresses are near to a railway station. Small items will be sent as railway parcels – see Red Star Service (Section 4.7) – or using the City Link service. Larger quantities which can be loaded into containers may be sent using the *freightliner* train service, which offers a fast through goods service on main lines, the trains running to a time-table which is published at regular intervals. If Freightliners Ltd are employed to collect the container only a *consignment note* is required. This is completed using three copies: the customer keeps the pink copy as a receipt; the yellow copy is used to charge for the service while the white copy is kept at the terminal from which the service is operated. If other road vehicles are used a *collection order* is required – there are two copies.

Road transport is a flexible means of transporting goods and offers a door-to-door service which can be used for the whole range of goods from the very large and bulky to the small and compact, irrespective of value. It is possible to make intermediate stops. To ensure full efficiency a return load is required – otherwise the vehicle must return empty. Road transport is not as fast as rail transport over long distances but it does avoid *trans-shipments* (loading and unloading from one means of transport to another). Containers help to prevent handling problems. Goods sent to EEC countries will be sent TIR, Transport International Routier, in sealed containers which are allowed to pass from one EEC country to another without customs inspection – the necessary documentation being accepted at customs posts. If goods are sent in the firm's own vehicles the only documentation required will be a delivery note but if goods are sent by another firm a *consignment note* may be used. The form of documentation used by private hauliers varies considerably but usually contains such informa-tion as: the name and address of consignor and consignee, a description of the goods, the number of packages, their weight and/or size, the date and space for signature by the driver, the consignor and consignee.

Transport by sea is the cheapest means of transporting goods but there is the problem of sending goods to the docks and loading them on to a vessel and then unloading them and delivering them. *Containers* help to solve these problems because they can be filled (also called '*stuffing*') any-where and not just at the docks. Containers filled at a factory can be col-lected by tractor (the propulsion unit used to haul containers by road) for hauling to the docks or taken to a freightliner terminal for transport to the docks by rail. Special container ships have been built to handle the containers, which are loaded and unloaded by special cranes. According to the International Standards Organisation a freight container should be of a permanent nature and capable of repeated use; specially designed for use by one or more modes of transport without intermediate reloading;

fitted with devices for ready handling and be designed for filling and emptying. An *LCL* load is a Less than Full container Load; a *FCL* is a Full Container Load. *The documentation required* includes the bill of lading, insurance certificate, freight invoice, standard shipping note, consular invoice, import licence and so on as required. If goods are not sent by container ship they will have to be loaded and unloaded from the ship by dockers after they have been taken to a port. Sea transport is often used to take goods round the coast of the United Kingdom since it is cheaper than using road or rail transport when the dispatch and delivery points are near suitable docks. *Cargo liners* are ships which ply direct routes carrying cargo on scheduled services and *tramp steamers* are cargo boats which do not keep to a scheduled route or timetable. *The information required* when sending goods by sea includes; the marks and numbers on the containers or packages; the numbers of packages and a description by which they can easily be identified; the gross weight (the weight of the goods and the container in which they are packed) in kilograms; the loading berth; the name of the sender; the port at which the goods will be unloaded – and the name of the ship.

Your local Chamber of Commerce will be able to provide you with full details of sending goods by sea.

QUESTIONS

1. Prepare a list of the documents commonly used in the home trade and write brief notes on each.
2. Prepare a list of the documents commonly used in the export trade and write brief notes on each.
3. What do the following abbreviations stand for? Write a sentence on each.

f.o.r.	E. & O.E.
P/C	c.w.o.
c.o.d.	c.i.f. & e.

4. What factors should be taken into account when deciding which method of transport a firm should use for (*a*) domestic orders and (*b*) overseas orders?

MECHANICAL AIDS

The purchase and sale of goods involves, among many operations such as record-keeping and stock-control, the making of calculations. Depending on the nature and size of the business a range of aids will be used. The exact nature of these aids will depend on such factors as the number of transactions involved, the complexity of the business, the cost of the aids and the purpose to which the aids can be put other than for one specific purpose - and the cost of training staff to use them.

A ready reckoner is still used by many small businesses where the volume of business, and hence the number of calculations, is small. *Pocket calculators* are cheap and simple to use and have a wide range of features other than adding, subtracting, multiplying, dividing, working out percentages, profit margins - and so on. It is impracticable to describe any one such calculator here because their cost and functions are constantly changing. Any office supplier will be able to provide full details of the many current models on offer - and almost all will have features far in excess of the demands of any one business.

Some means must be provided for keeping cash, particularly if goods are sold for cash at the point of sale. A small shop might keep a simple *till* in which notes and coins of various denominations are kept separate. A large unit will use an *electronic till* in which notes and coins are kept separate and the till remains locked between transactions or until the amount to be paid in is recorded, by pressing the appropriate keys. The range and facilities of electronic tills is extensive - some can be used to add up and total individual sales and dispense the correct change from the amount submitted (if required). Many keep a running total showing the total amount 'rung up' during any given period. The amount in the till at any one time should equal the amount recorded less any *float* - a sum of money kept in a till to enable the operator to give customers change. Some electronic tills will provide the customer with a list showing the amounts of individual items and the total for any particular transaction while others can be used by firms to record not only the amounts of each sale but the department from which they came - each department having a code. Large firms regularly empty tills during the day to prevent them becoming over-full. It is usual for tills to have a numerical keyboard with which to register information – but some businesses simply label keys with the item being sold and the assistant simply has to press the appropriate key. Some firms take advantage of the coding of goods from departments as part of their stock-control policy; *shrinkage* – a term used to describe stock losses – can be monitored by this method.

Most sales and purchases are on a credit basis – goods are not paid for at the time of the transaction but are paid for some time later. Both buyers and sellers of goods need to ensure that the amounts charged are correct and it is usual to 'double check' by going through the calculations made on the various documents used. There are several kinds of machines available for making calculations – mechanical and electrical (battery and/or mains operated). Manufacturers are constantly seeking to improve the efficiency and range of functions offered by their machines and students should note, by visiting firms and exhibitions, the latest innovations.

Non-recording machines (non-printing) are used in situations where the basic function is the checking of addition and multiplication. Some have full keyboards containing all the figures from zero to nine while others have half-keyboards with keys from one to five (large numbers are produced by dividing them so that nine would be entered as five and four – eight as four and four, etc.). As the machines are used for reckoning purposes only and do not print this does not matter. Increasingly these machines are being replaced by electronic calculators.

Adding–listing machines print calculations and are used for a wide range of functions such as checking till rolls, making calculations for invoices and other sales documents, adding pay rolls (including tax and other deductions), checking statements (bank and statements of purchases/sales), preparing books of analysis and the production of trial balance-sheets, etc. These machines, which provide a printed list of the various calculations are electronically operated, and thermal printers are used to produce the roll of calculations.

Coin-counting machines are used where large amounts of coins have to be handled. The machines will sort and count coins as well as bag them. *Banknote counting* machines save time when handling and counting banknotes – either when counting the takings for a given period or when paying-in to a bank. *Cheque-writing* machines are used by firms making large numbers of payments by cheque. The machines are used to enter the amounts on cheques in such a way as to prevent fraud while *cheque-signing machines* are used for printing signatures on cheques when large numbers are involved. Care must be taken to ensure that the plate(s) containing the signature(s) is locked away in a safe place when not in use.

Ledger-posting machines are used, when the volume of business is too great for the work to be undertaken by hand, to produce the ledgers for customers from the various documents used in business transactions – in particular the invoice.

Computers are used for keeping a wide range of information concerning both individual customers and such information as total sales, sales by departments, the stock position of items (including indicating when stock should be reordered) and indicating such matters as cash flows and the calculation of forecasts.

10.1 COMPUTERS

A computer is, basically, a vast series of switches coupled to storage devices and is a machine which, working at very high speeds, chooses between alternative courses of action. Early computers used valves as switches and were huge machines, often housed in temperature/humidity controlled buildings. The modern microcomputer uses what is known as a 'chip' – a wafer of silicon which has been manufactured, using the processes of deposition, etching and microphotography, to cause it to adopt the characteristics of many electrical components – and to perform their functions. The 'chips' are increasingly sophisticated and are constantly being reduced in size despite the fact that the number of functions built into them are constantly being increased. While the early use of computers was in the fields of science, today they are a business tool of rapidly increasing importance. See also Sections 5.13, 8.5, 9.12, 11.0, 14.11 and 16.2.

Computer systems are playing an ever-increasingly important part in the storage and processing of business records. There is a vast range of *microcomputer* systems available at prices which put them within the range of most small businesses which do not need the facilities offered by a fully integrated computer system housed in one location and connected to branches by the British Telecom services.

A microcomputer usually consists of a video display unit (VDU), often a 15-inch screen, a keyboard and the processor itself which is housed underneath the keyboard. The keys on the keyboard resemble those on a typewriter but there are additional ones. Some of the keys double as control keys for the microcomputer. Information is fed into the computer and displayed on the video screen, making it easy to see where amendments need to be made. The computer can be programmed to perform a wide range of operations either manually by an operator or automatically by loading prepared data. Information is stored either in what is called a *backing store* or what is called a *working store*. Information is usually transferred from the working store to the backing store so that it can be used at a later date when it can be put back from the backing store into the working store. Microcomputers use either tape cassettes or small discs, known as floppy discs, for backing storage. In microcomputers, as in larger computers, duplicates are made to avoid accidental loss of programs or data. A microcomputer has to be linked to a *printer* if information is required on paper. This is known as *hard copy*. Printers fall into two main categories at the time of writing – *dot matrix* and *daisy-wheel.* A dot matrix printer is capable of producing work at high speeds – over 200 characters a second – the quality of the printed material is not as good as that produced by the daisy-wheel system. This system works at a slower speed – around 50 characters a second – but can be used to produce a very high quality of work in a wide range of styles including proportional spacing. Both systems enable three or more copies to be taken at a time in a range of colours – the colour depending on the ink or ribbon being used. Many microcomputers can be linked to other systems or *peripheral devices*, such as *synthesisers*, and can transmit and receive information over postal or private links.

The size of microcomputer used by a firm will depend on the nature of the business and the kind of work handled but there is a vast range of programs available including:

Accounts – the continuous updating of accounts with orders placed. As invoices are received any over- or under-estimating on the original is allowed for and the exact financial position of the firm can be shown as required. The accounts handled can be for literally hundreds of customers and dozens of departments – depending on the power of the unit being used.

Address book – the names, addresses and telephone numbers of all customers, suppliers, etc., can be stored for use as required as, for example, in the preparation of mailing lists.

Bank balance programs enable personal cash-flow problems to be handled and can be used to indicate future expected balances using stored information relating to regular income and expenditure. A business can use such a program to keep it advised of current transactions and warned of potential future problems – such as the possibility of being overdrawn.

Critical-path analysis programs assist in forward planning of a wide range of projects and show starting dates and completion dates of elements within projects as well as warning of possible problems – such as delays in the supply of materials or components affecting future targets. A computer is able to give factual information in a logical fashion and is a useful tool in decision-making because it is able to make decisions without the 'interference' of human emotion.

Curreny converter programs enable foreign transactions to be undertaken with reduced risks because the computer can advise on exchange rates and warn or advise on the effects of fluctuations in exchange rates.

Debtors can be reviewed on a day-to-day basis since a computer can be programmed to 'test' the date of all invoices and produce letters reminding debtors that sums are outstanding with a series of 'chaser' letters – each one of increasing severity. Such a program is a useful tool in controlling cash-flow problems.

Discounted cash-flow programs help to advise on the value of future cash-flows given any interest rates which apply. **Forecast** programs present, often in a visual form such as a histogram, forecasts of future growth in such areas as purchases and sales. The forecasts can be on a daily, weekly, monthly or yearly basis.

Invoicing programs provide a wide range of information on the processing of invoices – such as validation, pricing, price adjustments, cancell-ation, discounts, VAT and other sundry charges.

Job evaluation is greatly assisted because the computer can conduct the necessary evaluation to establish pay structures and grades and can take into account weighting for such factors as eductaion, training, respons-ibility over men and machinery and working conditions for example. Such a program can be used not only to compare jobs within a department but within one or more firms and can assist the pricing policy of a manu-facturer or retail organisation.

Mailing lists can be constantly up-dated and material produced as and when required. This function is particularly useful to retail outlets with mail order customers.

Payroll programs can be used for all the functions of a wages department – keeping records of hours worked, pay rates, the calculation of gross and net salaries, the production of all the necessary documentation – including salary advice slips and cheques – and generally advise the mange-ment on all matters connected with the payment of wages and salaries. If employees are paid in cash a computer can print the wages advice slip for each and indicate what notes and coins are required to make up individual salaries – and the total amount of coins and notes required to make up all pay packets. Income tax, National Insurance and other deductions can be automatically handled.

Portfolio programs assist firms which invest in the stocks and shares of other companies – producing reports, the current values of investments, the returns on investments and so on.

Profit-and-loss programs take into account all stocks, stocks sold, returns, stock in manufacture, direct expenditure, expenses and salaries – and any other related factors – and greatly assist the production of profit-and-loss accounts.

Stock-control is greatly assisted by a computer. The stock position at any time can be printed out as required with such information as the total costing of all items in stock and stock reorder lists. Data can be stored under such headings as stock number, description, stock code, VAT rates (if more than one rate applies), quantity on order, quantity in stock, units of quantity, designation, minimum level, allocated stock, sale price, purchase price, stock group, sales for any given period and receipts for any given period.

This list is by no means a complete list of the programs and functions of even a small microcomputer and the range is constantly being expended. It is impossible to produce an up-to-date list of the functions available because the field of microcomputers is rapidly expanding and new pro-grams and functions are being marketed daily. Just as the price of elec-tronic calculators has been reduced to a level which would have been thought impossible only a few years ago so has the cost of computers. Units which were once housed in huge temperature/humidity controlled buildings are now available as desk models. Where once punched tape and huge rolls of magnetic tape were used to store information small plastic discs and miniature cassettes are now used. All microcomputers can be used as **word-processors** and so be used to supplement the typing requirements of any business. A word-processing program can be used with a microcomputer and printout unit to produce any kind of letter or document – including work which contains boxed display, flow charts and other diagrammatic information. **Standard letters** can be individually produced at a very high speed – and so save the time and cost of duplicating material.

Other functions include estate agent lists, travel guides and hotel guides, house-finding (for estate agents), text-editing, mortgage information, dealing with incoming and outgoing calls and other Telex Communications, percentage costing, restaurant-finding (to help restaurant users or firms who entertain potential customers or personnel), taxation information – and so on. You are advised to consult your local suppliers in order to keep up-to-date information on the range of machines available and their functions. There is no doubt that microcomputers will soon be as common as typewriters in offices – that is, if they do not take the place of typewriters and all calculating machines – not to mention their application in the field of filing (see Figure 10.1).

QUESTIONS

1. Write a paragraph on each of the following:

   electronic printing calculators
   electronic tills
   cheque-signing machines

2. What is a microcomputer and how does it work? How could such a machine be used to assist stock-control in a medium-sized firm?

Fig 10.1   *accounts produced by a computer – a COMMODORE Pet*

A/C	NAME	DR		CR	
101	SALES	£	.00	£	40982.77-
102	OPENING WIP	£	2000.00	£	.00
210	SALARIES & NI	£	5912.99	£	.00
220	TELEPHONE	£	686.40	£	.00
221	INSURANCE	£	25.30	£	.00
222	P P & S	£	261.45	£	.00
230	VEHICLE EXPENSES	£	2336.04	£	.00
240	GENERAL EXPENSES	£	735.84	£	.00
250	ACCOUNTANCY	£	.00	£	.00
255	HP INTEREST	£	213.43	£	.00
260	DIRECTORS REMUNERATION	£	9400.00	£	.00
265	AUDITORS REMUNERATION	£	200.00	£	.00
270	DEPN F & F	£	130.00	£	.00
271	DEPN PLANT & EQUIPMENT	£	85.21	£	.00
272	DEPN MOTOR VEHICLE	£	1121.56	£	.00
295	PROVISION - CORPORATION TAX	£	.00	£	13.86-
300	S/L CONTROL	£	19067.75	£	.00
310	BANK ACCOUNT NO 1	£	793.75	£	.00
315	PETTY CASH A/C 1	£	73.72	£	.00
320	CLOSING WIP	£	4000.00	£	.00
330	ASSET - COMPUTER	£	638.00	£	.00
331	DEPN TO DATE - COMPUTER	£	.00	£	186.00-
332	ASSET - PLANT & EQUIPMENT	£	446.21	£	.00
333	DEPN TO DATE - PLANT & EQUIP	£	.00	£	205.21-
334	ASSET - MOTOR VEHICLES	£	4817.56	£	.00
335	DEPN TO DATE - MOTOR VEHICLES	£	.00	£	1751.17-
400	B/L CONTROL	£	.00	£	1512.52-
410	HP CREDITORS	£	.00	£	1073.15-
420	SHARE CAPITAL	£	.00	£	500.00-
430	RESERVES	£	.00	£	3660.39-
440	DIRECTORS LOAN A/C - AB	£	.00	£	300.00-
441	DIRECTORS LOAN A/C - XY	£	.00	£	426.00-
450	VAT OUTPUTS 15%	£	.00	£	2487.10-
455	VAT INPUTS 15%	£	152.96	£	.00

ZERO PROOF :   .00

Trial Balance

STOCK CONTROL

Stock tends to mean different things in different situations. In a factory it can mean a supply of raw materials waiting to be processed or it can mean a quantity of part-finished goods, or yet again it can mean the quantity of finished goods waiting to be sold. In the office of the factory it could mean the supply of stationery and office materials. In a warehouse the word 'stock' means the goods waiting to be sold to retailers while in a shop the word means the goods waiting to be sold to customers. Stock can refer to the number of goods held or to the value of goods held. When a business man talks of *'turnover'* he means the total amount of goods he has sold in a period of time - usually a year. When he talks of 'turnover' he talks of the value of goods sold in that time. The *rate of turnover* refers to the number of times a business man sells his average value of stock. For example, if a business holds an average stock of £10 000 and has a rate of turnover of 12 the turnover for the year would be £10 000 × 12 - or £120 000.

11.1 KEEPING ADEQUATE STOCK

Apart from being the quantity of goods held in particular parts of a business stock represents money which is tied up in the business - money which cannot be used until goods have been sold. Just as it is important to ensure that there are sufficient goods to meet demand, customers will soon go away if you do not have goods to sell, it is equally important to ensure that you do not hold too many goods because this will tie up all your money and you might find that you cannot sell the goods you have in stock (they might go out of fashion, for example). Apart from these problems there is the problem of having the right balance of goods in stock so that production can go ahead without supply problems. A car manufacturer needs to ensure that he has all the components required to build cars in the right proportions at the right time - if he had only one wheel for every engine he would soon find that he was short of wheels for the cars he had made and would either have to stop production or store cars until he had the missing wheels.

11.2 STORAGE OF GOODS

The storing and handling of goods is known as *stock control*. There are several ways to store goods - much will depend on the nature of the goods themselves. Are they perishable? Are they affected by heat or damp? Are they inflammable? Are they compact or are they bulky? Some goods will require storage inside special buildings while others can be stored in the open.

11.3 STOCK RECORDS

No matter what method is used to control stock, all records have one thing in common - a separate record card or sheet is used for each item - even if all the records are kept in one place in a file or a ring binder. Stock records should show the following information:

1. The name or description of the item - together with a reference or catalogue number if possible.
2. Where the goods are stored.
3. The minimum amount of stock it is desirable to hold at any time - to ensure that supplies do not run out before fresh supplies can be obtained.
4. The maximum amount of stock to be held at any one time - to prevent overstocking and money being tied up unnecessarily.
5. The date each entry is made on the record.
6. When fresh stocks are accepted to the store.
7. When stocks are taken out of the store.
8. The balance after each movement of stocks into or out of the store.

In addition the sheet may contain details of the price of each item of stock, the address of the supplier and the date on which new stock was ordered - and how much was ordered.

If goods are for resale or the production of other goods it may be necessary to order stocks before the minimum figure to be held is reached - so as to ensure that new supplies arrive before stocks run out. This can present problems and such factors as unexpected demand or delay on the part of the supplier can lead to shortage.

(a) Keeping stock records
When goods arrive at a firm they are usually accompanied by a *delivery note* and the person accepting them must sign the note. If it is not possible to check goods against the note it should be signed 'Goods received but not checked'. Many delivery firms simply need to be informed of shortages within seven days of delivery. It is usual to list all goods received on a *Goods Received Register* after they have been received and checked. This register lists, in date order, all goods received - the number (or quantity), the supplier and a general description. Once the goods have been received individual items are entered on the individual stock record cards or sheets.

When individuals require supplies of goods they usually have to present a *Requisition Form* to the person responsible for the goods (see Figure 11.1).

Fig 11.1   *stores requisition*

```
STORES REQUISITION          Job No. _____

From _____
To _____
_____
QUANTITY | DESCRIPTION
         |
         |
         |
         |
         |
_____
Signed _____ Date _____
```

Very often two copies of the stores requisition are made; one is kept by the storekeeper and the other by the department drawing supplies. At any one time the amount of stock should represent:

the opening balance;
any entries into the stores;
any withdrawals from stores.

(b) Stock shortage
From time to time the number of items in stores are counted. Most firms have an *annual stocktaking* or *annual inventory*, a time once a year when all items in the firm (fixed assets and stock alike) are accounted for. Some stores, particularly those in the fashion trade, have several checks of stock – some check four times a year.

Any stock shortages will be the result of:

Poor stock control - care has not been taken to ensure that all items withdrawn have been recorded or care has not been taken to record all items received.

Shrinkage - a term used to describe pilfering or theft.

Wastage - possibly due to the deterioration of perishable stock. Any stock which is *written off*, listed as missing, should be recorded and the stock record amended so that it is in fresh balance.

When stock is taken of goods held it is usual to make two counts – one of the total number of individual items and the other of the value of the items held. Any *stock which is found to be obsolete* is usually disposed of in order to prevent it taking up valuable storage space. The storage of stock costs money and to store obsolete or outdated stock is simply adding to the loss on that stock. For this reason many shops in particular hold sales from time to time – to clear off old or obsolete ·stock.

(c) Visual control boards

One way of keeping a visual check on the stores position is by means of a visual control board and there are several kinds available. Most have spaces at the top and the side in which headings can be inserted – usually on cards. Markers are placed in slots, holes, channels or by means of magnets to show movements of stock into or out of the stores. The markers are usually in colour to show up the current position more easily.

In addition to stock-control, visual display boards can be used to show the progress of certain projects – the state of building a series of houses, for example – the progress made towards reaching targets (how often have you seen an appeals barometer showing how much has been received towards reaching a target?), the movement or whereabouts of staff within the firm or department (for example, where various personnel are on training courses or the holiday position) – and indeed any information which is likely to change (the daily/weekly/monthly sales of representatives or departments for example).

ACTIVITY

Design a stock-control card for supplies of A4 bank typing paper. Make ten entries to and from your stock.

(d) The bin system

As an aid to the orderly storage of certain items and to ensure that adequate supplies are constantly available one of two forms of bin system may be used (see Figure 11.2).

The one-bin system uses, as the title suggests, one bin or storage container. A mark is made on the bin and when stock in the bin reaches that line more supplies are ordered.

The two-bin system obviously uses two bins – the first is used from which to draw supplies and as soon as it is empty stock is ordered and goods drawn from the second. It is essential that supplies are drawn only from one bin at a time if the two-bin system is used and is to work accurately.

Fig 11.2 *illustration of the bin system*

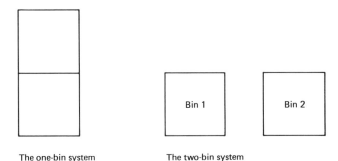

The one-bin system   The two-bin system

One-bin system
Stock is ordered when the line is reached.

Two-bin system
Stock is drawn from Bin 1 until it is empty, at which time fresh stock is ordered and goods drawn from Bin 2. As soon as Bin 2 is empty stock is again ordered – the stock ordered for Bin 1 should have arrived and hence be available for use.

(e) Computers and stock-control

As indicated in the last section, computers are playing an increasingly important part in many aspects of business organisation - and stock-control is one of these aspects. Small firms are now able to purchase sophisticated microcomputers either for programming themselves or for use with prepared programs which can be adapted to meet the individual needs of firms. Turn to Section 10.1 for the factors which are taken into account when preparing a computer program dealing with stock-control.

QUESTIONS

1. Write a sentence on each of the following:

turnover	shrinkage
stock-control	annual stocktaking
rate of turnover	stores requisition

2. What steps can a firm take to prevent shrinkage from its stores?

METHODS OF PAYMENT

All debts may be settled in *legal tender* - that is to say, any value of Bank of England notes, 50p coins to the value of £10, 5p and 10p coins to the value of £5 and bronze coins ($\frac{1}{2}$p, 1p and 2p) to the value of 20p. For reasons of security and the sheer problem of carrying large sums of coin about most transactions are made in other than legal tender. Strictly speaking a person can demand payment in legal tender (legally shopkeepers and others are not obliged in law to give change) or accept payment in other than legal tender. That they do so is for their own convenience and for the convenience of customers.

12.1 REGISTERED MAIL

If payment is demanded in legal tender and it is not possible to make the payment in person it is possible to send legal tender through the post by means of registered mail. The *Post Office Guide* gives full details of the service and while it is a method of making a payment, sending legal tender through the post is not a particularly cheap or convenient method - and so is rarely used.

Most payments, other than those in legal tender, are made through the Banks or the Post Office using one of the many services offered by each.

12.2 BANK SERVICES

The commercial banks, also known as **Joint-Stock Banks**, of which the Midland, Barclays, Lloyds and the National Westminster (NatWest) are the largest, offer a wide range of services for both the payment of debts and for the collection of money in addition to their other services. All banks offer a range of services for both the private individual and for the businessman, and the main purpose of this chapter is to discuss the latter. However, since many employees have bank accounts, so that they may be paid their salaries directly into an account if for nothing else, students should know a little of the services offered to the private individual.

12.3 BANK SERVICES FOR THE PRIVATE INDIVIDUAL

Savings accounts provide a safe place to keep savings and the service is offered by most banks. To open a savings account a person simply has to go to the bank of his/her choice and after giving such particulars as name and address has to pay in a small sum to open the account - and will be given a savings bank book. This book must be presented each time a deposit or withdrawal is made. Interest is paid on deposits.

Deposit accounts are very similar to savings accounts and have the same advantage that interest is paid on deposits. Wages or salaries can be paid into deposit accounts which have a possible disadvantage in that banks may make account-holders wait a short period for their money - although this is not usually the case.

Current accounts are the most common kind of bank account used by both the private individual and the businessman, and because of their importance they are described in some detail.

To open a current account an individual simply has to go to a bank and ask. He or she will be required to give his/her name and address and to provide one or more samples of his/her signature. Generally the bank will ask the individual to provide the names and addresses of two individuals who will act as referees - that is, give the bank an assurance as to the honesty/creditworthiness of the person opening the account. Once the simple formalities have been completed and an opening sum has been paid into the account, the account-holder is given a cheque book and usually a paying-in book. Some banks simply require the individual to fill in a form and take or post it to the local branch of the bank, together with an opening deposit, to open an account. Other banks may require the individual opening the account to be over a certain age. The easiest way to learn about opening any bank account is to visit a bank and ask. All banks are keen to offer services for students on the grounds that they will be future wage-earning adults - or even run their own businesses.

12.4 CURRENT ACCOUNT SERVICES

(a) The cheque

The most commonly used current account service is the cheque book. While interest is not paid on deposits held in current accounts, account-holders have the facility of the cheque book, which enables them to make any payments by means of a cheque - providing of course that they have sufficient funds in their accounts to meet the cheques they write. *A cheque* is basically an unconditional order in writing addressed to the manager of a named bank, telling him to pay a certain sum of money, written in words and figures, to a third party from the account of the person signing the order. Providing that the order is signed and dated correctly a cheque can literally be written on anything (although an extra charge may be made for clearing such a cheque) but for the convenience of the individual and the bank cheques are pre-printed and the account-holder simply has to fill in the details as required. When making payment by cheque the transaction is not completed until the money has been actually transferred from the account of the person making the payment (the drawee) to the account of the person receiving the payment (the payee). It usually takes three working days for cheques to be cleared so care must be taken to ensure that sufficient time is allowed for when making payments which are due on a particular day – such as insurance premiums. In such a case it is not sufficient to hand over a cheque on the due date – time must be given for the cheque to be cleared (see Figure 12.1).

Fig 12.1   *an open order cheque*

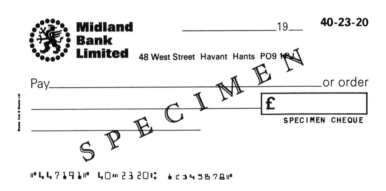

As can be seen from Figure 12.1, the basic information required on a cheque is:

the name and address of the bank;
the date;
space for the person to be paid to be written in;
space for the amount to be paid to be written in words and figures;
space for the account holder to sign.

The three sets of numbers at the bottom left-hand corner of the cheque are printed in magnetic ink and can be read by a computer – they are: the number of the cheque, the number given to the account-holder and the number given to the branch of the bank at which the account is kept.

A bearer cheque is one which has written on it 'Pay Bearer' – this means that anybody can take it to the bank to be cashed. Since this can lead to other people being paid than those intended (a lost cheque could be cashed by anybody), bearer cheques are not common.

An order cheque is a cheque which must be endorsed by the person named before it can be cashed. *Endorsing* a cheque means that the person named on the front signs his/her name on the back. It is an attempt at ensuring that the person for whom the cheque is intended obtains the money written on it. This is, again, not a safe way of paying a debt since anybody finding the cheque can endorse it with the name of the person intended. A person given an order cheque and who owes a similar amount to another person may endorse a cheque given to him/her - and pass it to another in settlement of the debt.

Crossed cheques are those which have two parallel lines drawn across their face - as in the following examples. The parallel lines do not have to be drawn across the full width of the cheque.

(b) Kinds of crossing

The effect of crossing a cheque is to place a limitation on the person receiving it for a number of reasons - safety and the prevention of fraud being the most common.

A general crossing may be made by drawing two parallel lines across the face of the cheque as in Figure 12.2 (example 1). Another general crossing is to draw the lines and to write '& Co.' between them - example 2. The effect of the crossings is to ensure that the cheque is paid into a bank account before money can be drawn from it. These crossings will not prevent a person who does not have a bank account from obtaininy money. It simply means that such a person will have to endorse the cheque and give it to another for the amount of the cheque and ask that person to pay the cheque to his/her account - and write out a cheque to themselves to obtain the money.

Not negotiable crossings - that is, cheques crossed with two parallel lines between which the words *'Not Negotiable'* have been written are still negotiable and can be passed to a third person for payment into his/her account. The only effect of this crossing is to cause any defect in the title of the holder to affect that of any subsequent holder. It acts as a warning to any person accepting the cheque that he/she may not get a good title (see Figure 12.2, example 3).

Cheques crossed with two parallel lines between which the words *'Account Payee'* (A/c Payee) have been written are normally to be paid into the account of the person named - but are in fact still negotiable and can be passed to another person (Figure 12.2, example 4).

Special crossings serve a number of purposes and not all involve drawing two parallel lines across the face of the cheque. The examples shown in Figure 12.3 are typical of special crossings. If, Example 1, the name of the bank is written across the face of a cheque, with or without the lines, it must be paid at the bank named. In Example 2 the branch of the bank is named and that cheque must be paid at the branch of the bank named. Either crossing may be used in conjunction with two parallel lines and the words 'Not Negotiable' or 'Account Payee' - Example 3 and 4. When an amount is specified between the parallel lines it is done so as to prevent possible alterations to the cheque - *a limit* of £50 means what it says - Example 5.

Fig 12.2   *cheque crossings*

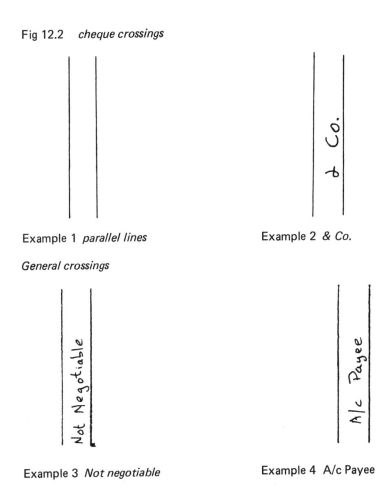

Example 1 *parallel lines*   Example 2 *& Co.*

General crossings

Example 3 *Not negotiable*   Example 4 A/c Payee

Not negotiable crossings

Not-transferable cheques are those crossed with the words 'Pay *X* only' and name the person to be paid or the words 'Not transferable' written across them with the words 'or order' or 'bearer' crossed out. A cheque crossed in either of these ways is not transferable to another person (see Figure 12.4).

(c) Parties to a cheque

The person who writes a cheque, the account-holder, is called *the drawer.* The person to whom the payment is being made is called *the payee.* The bank ordered to make the payment, the one holding the money, is called *the drawee.*

146

Fig 12.3 *special crossings*

| Example 1 | Example 2 | Example 3 |

Lloyds Bank Ltd

Midland Bank Chester

Lloyds Bank Ltd Not Negotiable

| Example 4 | Example 5 |

Midland Bank Ltd Chester A/c Payee

Under Fifty Pounds

(d) Obtaining cash from a crossed cheque
Many firms and individuals have their cheques ready printed with the crossed lines. In order to obtain cash from his/her current account an individual simply has to write 'Pay Cash' between the parallel lines and initial or sign his/her name in full. Some banks require a cheque altered in this way to be endorsed before making payment.

(e) Using a current account
It is essential that all the details are accurately filled in and any person receiving a cheque should examine it to see that:

the date is a current date, not one in the future, and is not more than six months in the past. A cheque with a date more than six months old is called a *stale cheque*. A cheque with some future date written

Fig 12.4   *not-transferable cheques*

Pay X (John Scott) – in this
example only

Not transferable

on it is called a *post-dated cheque* and cannot be cashed until that date
is reached. One purpose of post-dating a cheque is to delay payment.
A cheque written with a date in the past is called an *ante-dated cheque*
and it is perfectly acceptable so long as the date does not make it a stale
cheque. Banks will not cash stale cheques;
the person to be paid is named;
the amount to be paid is written in words and figures and the amounts
are the same;
the cheque is signed.

An individual writing a cheque should keep a record of the number
of each cheque written, when each cheque is written, to whom each
was paid and the amounts. Most cheques are issued in books and each
cheque has *a counterfoil* on which the details are recorded. Any mistakes
made when writing a cheque should be crossed out and initialled before
the correct information is inserted. Cheques should be written in ink
or ballpoint (felt-tipped) pen (not pencil or using one of the ink pencils
which enable corrections to be made by using a soft rubber providing
that the correction is made within 24 hours).

A **joint account** is one which is opened in two names and very often
both signatures are required before the cheques are acceptable. In order
to prevent fraud many companies require all cheques to have two signatures – the second one is called a *counter-signature*. Married couples
may have a joint account – husband and wife sharing the same account,
though their cheques do not generally require both signatures.

(f) Bank statements
At regular intervals, usually about every three months, banks send copies
of their records to individual account-holders. These records list all payments into and out of a current account and enable both individuals
and firms to see and check what has been going on. If there is a letter

'C' after the balance it means that the account is in credit – the bank owes the account-holder the balance. The letter 'D' after an entry means that the account is in debt – and that the account-holder owes the bank money. Some banks use *Cr* and *Dr* to denote credit and debit items.

Each debit entry shows that money has gone out of the account – if it has gone by cheque the cheque number will be shown. If the amount has gone out by standing order (see later) it means that money has been paid to the concern or individual named. All credit entries show that money has been paid into the account. An account-holder should check to see that all the cheques paid out have actually been paid into the account, if not any credit balance will be false; that the cheques paid out correspond with the amounts listed on the counterfoils (in case of fraud or error); and that all credit entries are correct.

Fig 12.5 *bank statement*

```
                                        CENTRAL BANK LTD
Miss Pamela Wickham                     34 High Street
18 Kidderminster Road                   BEWDLEY
BEWDLEY                                 Worcs      DY12 2UJ
Worcs      DY8 7JU
```

Statement of Account

19xx	SHEET 098 ACCOUNT NO 89210	Debit	Credit	Balance	Credit C Debit D
May 2	Balance Brought Forward			145.00	C
May 8	Midshires Building Society	50.00		95.00	C
May 8	745601	60.00		35.00	C
May 9	Sundries		150.00	185.00	C
May 10	745600	45.00		140.00	C
May 12	Life Insurance	10.00		130.00	C
May 15	745602	50.00		80.00	C
May 16	745603	90.00		10.00	D
May 18	Sundries		150.00	140.00	C

ACTIVITY

Answer the following questions using Figure 12.5.

1. Who is the owner of the account and what is his/her account number?
2. Where is the account held?
3. How much money was there in the account on 2 May?
4. Can you suggest what the entry for 8 May means?
5. Can you suggest why some of the cheques do not appear in the correct order?
6. What would have happened if cheque number 745600 had been paid in on 8 May?
7. What happened on 9 May?
8. What does the letter 'D' on 16 May mean?

(g) Paying in (sometimes called Bank Giro credit)

In order to make it easy for individuals and firms to pay money into current accounts banks provide current account-holders with paying-in slips - often books of them (see Figure 12.6).

A paying-in slip is simply a form to be filled in. The form must be dated with the date the transaction takes place; the bank at which the account is held must be filled in, as must the name of the account-holder and the number of the account. The person paying in money (cash, cheques or postal orders or a combination of these) has to sign the slip after filling in the details on both the slip itself and on the counterfoil. The columns on the right of the slip (£20 notes, £10 notes, £5 notes, £1 notes, 50p, silver and bronze) show where the value of each item has to be entered and the total amount of cash being paid in. The entry for Cheques & P.O.s shows the total value of cheques and postal orders, etc., being paid in - each item is listed on the back (reverse) side of the slip and the number is entered in the box - lower left-hand side. (S & I - Scottish and Irish notes.)

If Mary Walters was paying Mark Yates - Midland Bank, Tinacre Drive, Wolverhampton, account number 012984: 2 £20 notes; 3 £10 notes; 5 £5 notes; 3 coins of 50p; 5 coins of 5p and 3 of 10p as well as 15 coins of 2p and 4 of 1p in addition to a cheque for £5.50 and another for £10.00 she would enter the amounts as follows:

£20 notes	40.00
£10 notes	30.00
£1 notes	5.00
50 p	1.50
Silver	0.55
Bronze	0.34
Total cash	77.39
Cheques	15.50
	£92.89

She would list the cheques on the back of the slip and enter 2 in the box.

(h) Standing orders

To save time and the problem of remembering when regular bills - such as subscriptions to societies - have to be made, firms and individuals may instruct their banks to make the regular payments for them. These regular payments, which may be weekly, monthly or annually, are called Standing Orders. To start a Standing Order either write to the bank telling them the amount to be paid; the name of the account to be paid and how often the sum is to be paid (annually until further notice; 52 weekly payments, etc.,) - or fill in a Standing Order form - or go to your bank and give them the information (you will be asked to sign the Order).

150

Fig 12.6   *paying-in slip*

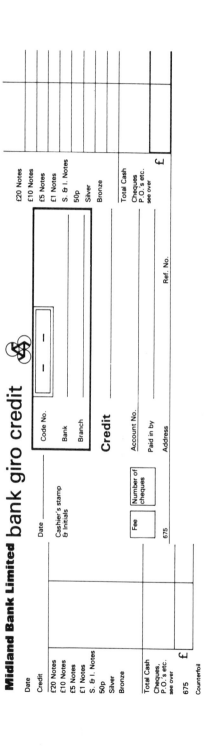

To cancel a Standing Order, or to change either the amount or the interval of payment, simply inform the bank. Unless the account-holder keeps a certain sum of money in the account banks may charge a small fee for this service. Standing Orders can only be made from a current account and on some statements they are indicated by the letters 'SO'. On the statements issued by some banks Standing Orders are not indicated by the letters SO; the payment is indicated by naming the firm/organisation credited.

(i) Direct debiting

When regular payments have to be made from a current account, but unlike the Standing Order the amount is not known in advance, an account-holder may agree to allow the payee (the person to whom money is owed) to request the bank to make the payment. Very often the payee sends the account-holder (the payer) an invoice and, unless the amount is questioned within a certain period of time, requests the payment from the bank. Before any direct debits can be made, the account-holder must give the appropriate authorisation. The method can be used for paying fixed amounts at fixed dates or irregular amounts at irregular dates.

(j) Credit transfer (Bank Giro)

The credit transfer service, or Bank Giro as it is sometimes called, should not be confused with Post Office Giro or Girobank - see later. Credit transfer enables an account-holder to pay several people with one cheque. A list of the creditors, people to whom money is to be paid, is sent to the bank together with one cheque for the total amount. The bank arranges for credit slips to be sent to the various banks of the creditors - each must have agreed to be paid in this way. This service can be used by an employer wishing to pay his employees their wages or salaries. Many individuals use the service to pay their bills, telephone, gas and electricity, for example; indeed many bills are sent out with a credit transfer slip ready to be filled in. The service can also be used to pay money into the accounts of others - an individual must go to a bank and complete a credit transfer slip giving his name and address, the name of the payee (person to be paid), the payee's bank and branch, account number (if known), the date and the amount to be paid. Sometimes a small charge is made for this service - which saves the problem of writing and sending cheques. Payment can also be made this way using cash instead of cheques. Proof of payment is provided by the stamped counterfoil from the form. A mail order firm with agents in many parts of the country may issue its agents with credit transfer forms to enable them to pay cash to its account from any local bank.

(k) Cheque cards

Many people do not like accepting cheques from strangers - they have no proof that the person offering the cheque is the person named on it or that the individual has sufficient funds in his/her account to meet the cheque. There is always the possibility that the cheque might be stolen so, in order to make cheques more acceptable, banks offer current account-holders cheque cards. Some banks may require applicants for cheque cards to have kept their account in good order for six months or so first. A cheque card is proof to a person accepting a cheque that the bank will honour any cheque up to the amount of the card, usually about £50. The card must have the signature of the account-holder on it. People accepting cheques must compare the signature on the card and other details with those on the cheques to see that they match, note the number of the card on the back of the cheque – and make sure that the card has not expired (is not out of date). The number on the cheque card identifies the account-holder. Cheque cards can be used in many countries and are usually valid for a period of twelve months.

(l) Cash cards (Dispenser cards)

Current account-holders who want to withdraw money from their accounts when the banks are closed often use cash cards. Each card has a number superimposed upon it, usually in magnetic ink which can be read by a machine in a bank. The account-holder inserts the card into the cash dispenser machine, often found in the walls of banks, and enters his/her number on the keyboard. If the number is entered correctly the machine dispenses cash in notes, usually £10 or £20 – depending on the bank. If the number is entered incorrectly the machine will ask for the correct number – before keeping the card if the incorrect number is again entered. This is to prevent fraud. If a machine keeps a card the card-holder will be sent a replacement by his bank. Some banks issue a card which is returned to the card-holder by the dispensing machine while other banks use a machine which keeps the card each time it is used – the account-holder being sent a number of cards to use. The used cards are, in this case, returned with the next statement. The Midland *Autobank* is a system very similar to its cash card system, but the user is able to withdraw any sum (in whole pounds) up to an individually set limit each week. The user pushes keys to tell the machine how much money he/she requires after inserting his/her identification number.

(m) Bankers' drafts

A bankers' draft is an order addressed by one branch of a bank to its Head Office or to another branch (or is addressed by the Head Office to a branch). A person who owes another person or firm money may buy a bankers' draft from his bank and send it as payment. Bankers' drafts can be crossed like cheques.

(n) Dividend and interest warrants

Firms and organisations paying dividends or interest often use what is known as a warrant. These warrants are usually in a form which complies with the legal definition of a cheque.

12.5 OTHER BANK SERVICES

It is not the purpose of this chapter to discuss all bank services - or indeed to discuss all the methods of payment offered by banks. Students who wish to learn more about bank services and how they work should go to any bank and ask. Most banks offer a great deal of information about their services free of charge. The following services are worthy of further study:

letters of credit	market intelligence
cashing facilities	bank references
travellers' cheques	taxation
bills of exchange	budget accounts
foreign currency	documentary credits
night safe	change

12.6 GLOSSARY OF TERMS

Alterations   Any alterations on a cheque must be initialled or signed in full by the account-holder. Erasures invalidate a cheque.

R/D   The letters R/D on a cheque mean Refer to Drawer and mean that something is incorrect and requires the attention of the drawer. The letters are sometimes used instead of the letters N/F.

N/F   A cheque returned and marked N/F is one which cannot be paid because the account has no funds - in other words it has a nil balance or is overdrawn. The letters may indicate that the account has assets which have not yet been cleared - cheques may have been paid in but have not yet been cleared.

PR   A cheque returned with the letters PR should be re-presented. It has been paid into a bank for payment, but for some reason, the bank is unable to cash it. The usual reason is that the account has insufficient funds because a cheque which has been paid into the account has not yet been cleared. PR - Please Re-present.

R   The letter R written on a cheque by an account-holder indicates to the payee that a receipt is required. It is usually written on the same line as the amount of money in words. Normally cheques do not require a receipt - the counterfoil or statement is taken as being sufficient proof of payment.

Blank cheque   A blank cheque is one which is signed by the account-holder but the person receiving it is left to fill in the details. It is not wise to issue blank cheques because the receiver can fill in any details he/she wishes. A maximum figure above which the cheque may not be honoured is sometimes written at the very top or bottom of the cheque - or the cheque is crossed in such a way as to limit the amount.

Bank charges   Some banks make a charge for each entry on a current account statement unless the account-holder keeps a minimum sum in the account. Conditions and charges vary considerably - ask at your local bank for current charges.

Stopped cheque Should a cheque be given in error, or be stolen, the account-holder can order his/her bank to stop payment by telephoning or calling and giving the number of the cheque(s). Unless an order is given to stop payment a bank is obliged to make payment - providing that all the details are correct. The account-holder must confirm the stopping order in writing. A cheque endorsed with the number of a cheque card cannot be stopped.

ACTIVITY

Find out what is meant by a bank loan and a bank overdraft - your local bank will give you full details.

12.7 POST OFFICE SERVICES

(a) Stamps
Postage stamps may be used as a means of payment when the sum involved is small - the stamps used should be those up to the cost of the first- or second-class mail service. The Post Office will repurchase stamps used for payment - but it makes a charge for the service and will not accept amounts of under £1.00. Before deciding to use postage stamps as a means of payment it is advisable to consult the *Post Office Guide* and check current regulations.

(b) Postal orders
Postal orders are a useful means of making payments for small sums of money and can be purchased at most Post Offices. Check the *Post Office Guide* for the current regulations and denominations available.

A fee is charged on each postal order, the amount varies according to the value of the order, and this charge is known as *poundage*. Check the latest edition of the *Post Office Guide* for the current poundage at each of the values currently offered.

At the smaller Post Offices only postal orders of the values most in demand are kept in stock - all values are obtainable at short notice. If the value which is required is out of stock two or more orders may be issued to make up the value - in which case the fee payable on a single order only is charged.

The value of a postal order may be increased by affixing current postage stamps up to the value of $4\frac{1}{2}$ p - providing that not more than two stamps are used on a particular postal order. It is worth noting that banks may refuse to pay any odd $\frac{1}{2}$ p on postal orders.

(c) Completion of postal orders
The sender of a postal order must fill in, in ink or ballpoint pen (not pencil or one of the ink pencils which can be easily corrected within

24 hours of use) the name of the person to whom the amount is to be paid. It is also recommended that the name of the office of payment should be filled in. If the sender does not know the Post Office most convenient for payment to the payee, he should insert the name of the town or village in which the payee lives. Postal orders may be crossed for payment through a bank. *A counterfoil* is provided on every postal order so that the purchaser may keep a record of particulars of the order and the Post Office counter clerk will, if asked, stamp the counterfoil with the official office stamp at the time of purchase. The sender should keep the counterfoil and not send it with the order.

Postal orders may be presented at any Post Office for repayment or be paid into a bank account providing that the regulations are followed and providing that the postal order is not more than six months old – after that time an order must be referred to the nearest Post Office or the Head Postmaster in London to find out whether the order may still be paid.

Postal orders are not negotiable and only the rightful owners may cash them. If the sender has filled in the name of the payee, the owner may take legal action against any other person who negotiates it.

In addition to providing a useful means of making payments within the United Kingdom, postal orders may be used for making payments overseas in certain countries – the payment being made in the currency of the country of payment. The *Post Office Guide* will provide up-to-date information on the *Overseas Postal Order Service.*

(d) Inland telegraph payment orders
Should a payment be required urgently – the same day, for example – and the payee lives some way from the payer, the inland telegraph order service may be used. In effect the person making the payment goes to any Post Office offering the telegram service and makes the required payment at his local office. A telegram is sent to the payee informing him that payment has been made and on receipt of the telegram and proof of identity the sum will be paid over. The service is expensive but it is useful in an emergency or for sending money gifts – a message may be included in the telegraph order. A telegraph payment order is valid for three months – after which time it must be sent to the Giro and Remittance Service (ISB) for renewal.

(e) International payment orders
International Payment Orders may be sent to all countries, subject to the current Exchange Control Regulations (if any) – see the *Post Office Guide.* No single order can, at the time of writing, be sent for a sum exceeding £100.00 to most countries or for a sum including a fraction of 1p. Orders are purchased at any Post Office and the person making a payment must fill in the appropriate application form, fill in full details of the payee and make the required payment together with the appropriate fee. International Payment Orders may be crossed – in which

case repayment will be through a bank. Orders are handled by the Giro and Remittance Service, using the service which it considers to be the most convenient and speedy. Payment may be made in cash or through a bank and orders paid abroad are paid in the currency of the country of payment – subject to the regulations of that country. Orders are valid for periods of between a month and a year.

ACTIVITY

1. Use a current edition of the *Post Office Guide* to find the up-to-date rules and regulations concerning **International Payment Orders.**
2. How does the **International Rapid Payment Order** service work?

Note that International Payment Orders may be used both for *making payments abroad* and *receiving payments from abroad.*

(f) The National Giro (Girobank)

The National Giro provides a low-cost banking and money transfer service in which accounts are held at the National Giro, Bootle, Merseyside. All Post Offices hold application forms for personal accounts, and cards for business applications. The full conditions of service are contained in the National Giro handbook – a copy of which is available for reference at most Post Offices or free on request from the Accounts Manager. The *Post Office Guide* provides a great deal of information about the National Girobank. The principal facilities for account-holders are as follows:

Transfer/Deposit forms are used to make a payment to another Giro account or to make a deposit to the account of an individual by the individual himself. When someone opens a Girobank account he is given an account number and transfer/deposit forms and Girocheques printed with his account number, name and address as well as some envelopes which are printed with the address of the National Giro.

To make a payment to another Girobank account the holder must fill in: the number of the Girobank account to be credited; the amount to be paid (in words and figures); the date on which the form is filled in – and finally sign it. The transfer/deposit form is then posted to the National Giro centre using one of the envelopes provided (postage paid). A message can be sent on the back of the form.

To make a deposit to his own account an account-holder must fill in a transfer/deposit form and either take it together with the cash sum to be paid into his account to a Post Office handling Giro accounts or post it together with a cheque to the National Giro centre – again using one of the postage paid envelopes provided.

Standing orders can be made from a Girobank account by the National Giro providing the payment is to a Girobank account – standing orders cannot be paid to people/firms who do not have a Girobank account. To enable payment to be made an account-holder must fill in the appropriate form giving details of his account number, the account to be credited, when the payments are to be made and how much is to be paid. The National Girobank makes the required payments without further instructions – taking the required amount from the account of the person making the payment and crediting it to the account of the payee. No charge is made for the service – providing the account making the payment has a credit balance.

Automatic debit transfers can be made from a Giro account to another Giro account when the person owing money fills in the necessary authorisation form. The payee, or person requiring payment, sends notice of the amount due to the account holder with details of when the payment is to be made. Unless the account holder objects the payee informs the National Girobank of his account number, the number of the account making the payment, what is due and when it is due. On the agreed date the National Girobank makes the payment and sends details to the collecting firm.

Girocheques are used to make payments to people who do not have a Girobank account or to draw cash out of a Girobank account. A Girobank · cheque for £50.00 (at the time of writing) can be cashed every other business day from either of two nominated Post Offices. A **guarantee card** may be used by account-holders over the age of 18 to offer proof of identity to any person to whom payment is made, using a Girocheque. If the account-holder wishes to draw more than £50.00 from his account the Post Office to be used for the payment must be stated.

The Girobank guarantee card also enables the account-holder to draw up to £50.00 every other business day at any Post Office handling Girobank business.

Statements of account giving details of payments, receipts and fees are issued every time money is paid into a Girobank account. For business accounts statements are issued for any day on which there has been a transaction on the account and statements, on magnetic tape, can be provided for use by a computer.

Envelopes with first-class postage are provided for account transactions sent to the National Girobank – postage is free.

Personal loans are available to account-holders over the age of 18. Booklets are available at most Post Offices showing the current regulations and interest rates.

(g) People making payments without a Girobank account

People without a Girobank account can make cash payments to people/firms with Girobank accounts at Post Offices using a form provided by the account-holder or the standard Girobank inpayment form, G20. Inpayment forms provided by an account-holder must not be used for payments to another account-holder. A charge is payable at the counter for each inpayment except where the account-holder has provided an inpayment form which indicates that a lesser fee, or no fee, is payable. Payments must be made in cash and in whole pence. Cheques and other

158

instruments will not be accepted unless by prior arrangement. *Proof of payment* is provided by *the counterfoil* which should be filled and stamped at the time of making the payment - the Post Office clerk receiving the payment will stamp it. Some firms print their bills on Girobank inpayment forms, which should be taken to a Post Office together with the amount due - proof of payment is provided by the form itself duly stamped and returned by the clerk receiving the payment.

(h) Deposit of cash by agents
Firms which require branches or agents to make deposits to their accounts can, by arrangement with the Accounts Manager, arrange for the deposits to be made at any Post Office offering Girobank services. Special *paying-in slips* are used, they can be designed by the National Girobank to assist firms, and the slips have stubs to acknowledge deposits. The amounts deposited are credited to the Girobank account of the firm/business receiving/collecting the money on the day following the deposit at a Post Office and a statement is sent the following business day showing the amounts paid in. Agents do not pay the usual inpayment charge - the firm's fee is negotiated with the Post Office.

(i) Collection of rents
Special services are available for the collection of rents by Local Authorities and these include **rent inpayment service, rent voucher service** and **rent card scheme.** There is also a **deposit service** for rent collectors.

(j) International Giro
Payments can be arranged from Girobank accounts to any country, even if it does not have a Giro system itself, but particular speed is achieved if the country of payment does have a Giro service. Exchange-control regulations (if any) apply to all payments made to people or organisations - the payments can be made in sterling or the currency of the country in which the payment is to be made. Payments from abroad can also be received through the Girobank service in this country.

ACTIVITY

Use the *Post Office Guide* to find the following:
1. The cost of an inpayment by a person who does not have a Girobank account.
2. The current regulations concerning International Giro.

(k) Other Giro services
An ever-increasing range of services are being offered by the National Girobank and these include:

Automatic debit transfer service
Bridging loans

Fig 12.7   *international transfer form*

Budget accounts
Bureau de Change
Deposit accounts
Dividend payments to Girobank accounts
Investment through National Girobank
Personal loans
Rapid transfer for large amounts from Girobank accounts
Travellers' cheques and foreign currency

ACTIVITY

Visit your local Post Office and obtain the current leaflets outlining Girobank services. Use the information given to keep your notes up to date.

12.8 CREDIT CARDS

Goods and services may be obtained by using a credit card - there are several types in common use and the number of institutions offering them is rapidly growing. Some banks offer credit cards to their customers and to people who do not have bank accounts; Barclaycard and Access are typical examples, while several firms offer a credit card service - American Express and Diners Club are just two of them. To obtain a bank credit card a person simply has to fill in an application form and post it to the address indicated; to obtain a credit card from a firm a form has to be filled in and returned as indicated together with (usually) a fee to enrol and an annual subscription. In either case a credit card is issued which enables the user to spend up to an agreed sum each month or, as in the case of Access and Barclaycard, the total agreed sum at any one time. It is possible to borrow cash to the limit of an Access and Barclaycard and so use the cash to obtain a cash discount when making a purchase. Access cards are issued by the Midland Bank, NatWest and Lloyds while Barclaycards are issued by Barclays Bank and the Trustee Savings bank. A Barclaycard doubles as a cheque card as well as a credit card. Interest in this case is charged on a daily basis but any interest payable can sometimes be offset by discounts negotiated at the time of purchase of goods. Credit cards are embossed with the account number of the holder and have space for his/her signature. When goods or services are obtained using a credit card the holder has to present the card to the seller who makes out a bill in triplicate and embosses the copies with the credit card using a special sliding machine. The card-holder then signs the bills using a ballpoint pen. One copy of the bill is given to the card-holder for reference purposes, one copy is kept by the seller of the goods or services for his records while the third copy is sent to the bank or firm issuing the card. At the end of the month the bank or issuing firm sends payment to the seller of the goods or services - a discount is usually charged so that he receives slightly less than the face value of the bill. All the amounts listed against a particular holder's account are added together and details of them and the total amount due for the month is sent to him/her. American Express or Diners Club cards have to be settled each month - and in the strictest sense the holder is only given credit for a very limited period of time. When using Access or Barclaycard the account-holder can either make one payment to settle the bills for a particular month (and so avoid paying interest - except when cash has been borrowed against a card, in which case interest is charged for each day the loan is outstanding), or make the minimum repayment indicated on the bill and spread the repayments over a period of time. If the repayment period is extended interest is charged on the outstanding balance, but the card-holder can still use the card to purchase goods - providing the limit on the card is not exceeded.

The advantage to the card-holder of a credit card is that he/she does not have to carry sums of money about or to have a cheque book. All monthly bills can be settled with one cheque/payment - or in the case of Access and Barclaycard they can be spread over several months. Credit cards can be used for practically any transactions and they can, in agreed circumstances, be used overseas. By borrowing cash using a credit card the holder may be able to obtain a discount on purchases (usually fairly large) and so save considerably more than the interest paid on the loan. Individuals who are faced with sudden large items of expenditure are not faced with the problems of negotiating a bank loan or an overdraft - or entering a hire-purchase agreement. *The disadvantages* of credit cards are the fact that holders are tempted to spend more than they can afford and firms selling goods or services have to pay a discount to the credit card firm - and as a result cannot afford to offer discount to card holders.

Trading checks can be bought from companies such as Provident, Shopacheck or Refuge and used when making purchases. The value of each card is often much less than the credit cards previously discussed and repayments, plus interest, are made to an agent who calls regularly, usually weekly, or to a branch of the company. If a card is not being used it is still usual for interest to be charged on the value of the card - and not the amount actually spent. Many department stores offer **budget accounts** - for regular monthly payments customers are able to spend up to about 24 times the monthly payment. Interest is charged on outstanding balances, but no interest is paid on amounts in credit. Terms and conditions vary considerably and students should collect information on the facilities available locally. The interest charged by the various credit firms varies according to the general interest rate applying at any particular time.

The Trustee Savings Banks offer a wide range of services for people who want to save money as well as spend and borrow it. The banks now offer their own credit card - Trustcard - in addition to a growing range of facilities. Visit your local branch of the TSB to see the services currently offered and compare them with those offered by the Commercial Banks. Students who wish to make a complete study of the various banking services offered would be well advised to include a study of the **Co-operative Bank**.

12.9 POINTS TO NOTE

In selecting any method of making a payment consideration should be given to the following:

The amount to be paid.
The speed of payment required.
The acceptability of the method used.
The cost of the service to be used.

In practical terms many people use a combination of cash and one of the services previously described - bank services, Post Office/Girobank services or credit cards. When deciding whether to open a bank account or a Girobank account consideration might be given to opening hours and days of opening, the nearness of the bank/Post Office to place of work and home address and the general efficiency of each in processing customers - banks and the Post Office can be packed with customers at the very time (lunch hour) when many private account-holders need to use them. Individuals who are not primarily concerned with making payments through the banks/Post Office but prefer to have their wages/salary paid into some form of account and draw cash from it to make payments might consider one of the many **Building Society** accounts offered. Interest is paid on all deposits, opening hours are usually longer than the banks and there are considerable advantages to those who hope to become house-owners one day – and need to borrow money to do so. Any building society will give full details of its services.

12.10 THE FUTURE

The 'plastic money' revolution has begun and increasingly department stores and supermarkets are putting their tills under computer control. Banks and the retail trade are moving towards a system that would, in effect, produce the cashless, paperless sale. Goods can now be coded with bar codes which identify the price and type of goods as well as the individual store. As the goods pass over a laser beam the codes are read by the machine at the till which automatically itemises the bill and produces the total for the sale. The computer-cum-till then reads the customer's bank card and after the customer has keyed the computer with his/her own personal code (to prevent fraud) the required money is taken from the customer's account and is credited to the firm selling the goods. The firms selling goods do not have to give credit and their stock records are revised after every transaction. It is estimated that at present 95 per cent of all transactions are for cash and that half the working population is paid in cash – but there can be no doubt that the move to the cashless society has begun, if only in a small way. The benefits to future customers will be faster service, no mistakes at the till, a detailed receipt for all purchases – and the possibility of discounts for large purchases.

QUESTIONS

1. What is the difference between an order cheque and a crossed cheque? Name two general crossings, two not negotiable crossings and two not transferable crossings.
2. Write two sentences on each of the following:

   Stale cheque   Post-dated cheque
   Joint account   Bank statements
   Standing orders   Direct debiting
   Credit transfer   Cheque cards.

3. Explain fully how Girobank works.

PROJECT

Make a study of the services offered to the businessman and the individual by the Joint-Stock Banks, the Post Office, the Trustee Banks and the Co-operative Bank. Compare the costs of each service and write reports showing the 'best buy' in each service.

THE PETTY CASH

Small items of expenditure on goods or services are usually paid for out of petty cash and not out of general departmental/business accounts; the amounts are too small and numerous for normal accounts. It is usual for the petty cash to be supervised by a senior person in the office, the office supervisor or the personal secretary. The most commonly used method for organising/controlling petty cash is called the **imprest system**.

13.1 THE IMPREST SYSTEM

Under this system:

A sum of money is allocated to the person responsible for the petty cash - the sum being considered sufficient to meet the expected payments for a period of a week or a month.

Small items of expenditure such as postage, transport, stationery and cleaning are paid out of the sum allocated.

At the end of the period the person responsible for the petty cash receives a sum of money equal to the amounts paid out during the period - so that the petty cash is restored to its original balance. At any time the amount of petty cash available plus the sum of the receipts received for payments made should equal the amount of the original balance.

The petty cash is usually kept in a cash box and is locked in a safe place when not in use. When payments have to be made it is usual for the person in charge to authorise them - Figure 13.1 is typical of the document used by many companies. Sums not authorised in the normal way are usually recorded by keeping the receipts received from them; all sums spent should have either a petty cash voucher or a receipt to account for them.

Petty cash vouchers vary in style and the detail given, but in Figure 13.1 the voucher is numbered, states who is making the authorisation, what is to be purchased and the amount, the date on which the authorisation was made and who was given the money for the purchase.

Cash receipts also vary in style and the information given but usually contain such information as the name of the supplying firm, their VAT

Fig 13.1 *a petty cash voucher*

Petty Cash Voucher

Folio _____

Date _____ 19

For what required	AMOUNT £	p

Signature _____

Passed by _____

Fig 13.2 *cash receipt*

CASH RECEIPT   008332

Office Supplies Ltd
Essex Street

        VAT Reg No 100 0732 52

Date of supply .... 19..

Cash Sale

DESCRIPTION	£	
Total Goods		
VAT		
Amount Due		

Received by _____

registration number, the date, details of the sale and who sold the article (s) (see Figure 13.2).

Petty cash vouchers are normally issued before a purchase is made; they are all numbered so that they can be accounted for; receipts are given by sellers of goods at the time of sale and are handed to the person in charge of petty cash as proof of the purchase, and of the amount.

If details of all sums spent are kept under general headings and the details are recorded on a sheet of petty cash paper the exact position of the petty cash can be seen at any time – it is thus easy to analyse how the money is being spent (see Figure 13.3). The analysis columns of the petty cash sheet provide a quick and easy check on all spending and the totals for each period can be transferred to the individual accounts. Sometimes the items are entered on the petty cash analysis sheet as the money is spent; sometimes the entries are made at the end of the period.

The petty cash analysis sheet may be ruled in several ways – Figure 13.3 is typical. The sheet is divided into two parts, items headed *Dr* (Debit) meaning sums paid into the account, usually from the cashier, and *Cr* (Credit) meaning sums paid out of the petty cash. Items paid out of the account are recorded in date order, as they are spent, under two headings – a running total column which shows the amounts spent in date order and in individual columns which show amounts spent under specific headings.

People in charge of petty cash should use headings which are convenient for their particular situations. In Figure 13.3 the items of expenditure are postage, transport, stationery, office expenses and VAT. Each of the headings represents an account in the firm's ledger and at the end of the period, in this case a month, the total in the column is transferred to the ledger. It is usual to write the word 'To' before all items on the debit side, money received, and word 'By' before all items on the credit side, items paid out, although individual firms have their own systems. In Figure 13.3 all items have been authorised and while this may be the rule in some firms in others sums spent may have a combination of voucher numbers and receipts for items which did not have a voucher, the amount of postage may have been more than expected and the office junior may have paid for it out of her own pocket and obtained a receipt which she used to claim the amount back out of petty cash. The amounts in the 'Total paid out' column include VAT where this has been paid and the amount is recorded in a separate column.

At the end of the month the columns are totalled; the 'Total paid out' was £42.75 and this was made up as follows: Postage £15.00, Transport £3.25, Stationery £17.25, Office Expenses £7.25 and VAT £3.00. When columns are totalled it is usual to indicate that they are totals by ruling two parallel lines under them. In Figure 13.3, on 30 May the amount left in the petty cash was entered, £7.25, and added to the money spent, £42.75, to make the original entry of £50.00. On 1 June the balance was transferred from the 'Total paid out' column to the debit side of the account and the sum of £42.75 was paid to petty cash to restore the imprest or original balance. Note that the VAT is kept separate and is not added in twice.

Fig 13.3 *a page from petty cash*

DR CR

DATE	DETAILS	FOLIO	TOTAL RECEIVED £	DETAILS	VOUCHER NO.	TOTAL PAID OUT £	POSTAGE	TRANSPORT	STATIONERY	OFFICE EXPENSES	VAT
2 May	To cash	CB4	50.00								
3 May				By carbon paper	71	5.75			5.75		0.75
4 May				" stamps	72	10.00	10.00				
5 May				" taxi fare	73	2.50		2.50			
5 May				" window cleaning	74	1.50				1.50	
11 May				" envelopes	75	4.60			4.60		0.60
17 May				" bus fares	76	0.75		0.75			
18 May				" glue	77	2.30				2.30	0.30
22 May				" stamps	78	5.00	5.00				
22 May				" cleaning materials	79	3.45				3.45	0.45
28 May				" typing paper	80	6.90			6.90		0.90
						42.75	15.00	3.25	17.25	7.25	3.00
30 May			50.00	Balance b/d		7.25					
						50.00					
1 June	To balance b/d		7.25								
1 June	To cash		42.75								

ACTIVITY

1. Use a sheet of petty cash analysis paper to record the following entries:

1 October – received £40.00 from cashier
2 October – paid window cleaning £2.00 – voucher number 34
5 October – postage stamps – £3.50 – voucher number 35
7 October – by voucher number 36 stationery to the value of £4.60 – VAT £0.60
10 October – cleaning materials by voucher number 37 – £4.03 including £0.53 VAT
15 October – postage stamps – voucher number 38 – £4.00
18 October – fares by voucher number 39 – £2.35
21 October – typing supplies £2.87 including £0.87 VAT – voucher number 41

Total each column and restore the original balance on 1 November. What were the separate totals spent on postage stamps, stationery, travelling and VAT?

13.2 THE PETTY CASH NOT USING THE IMPREST SYSTEM

Some organisations do not use the imprest system to control the petty cash – instead the petty cash is given a sum when it is required and not on a regular basis as under the imprest system. When petty cash is operated on a *variable float* the agreed sum is not consistent and varies from month to month or week to week.

Fig 13.4   *a page from petty cash not using the imprest system*

Dr					Cr
	Date	Details	Voucher No	£	VAT
15.25	8 April	To balance b/d			
	8 April	By note books	145	2.88	0.38
	9 April	By cleaning	146	3.50	
	9 April	By postage stamps	147	1.25	
	10 April	By typing ribbons	148	4.03	0.61
	15 April	By balance c/d		3.59	
15.25				15.25	
3.59	16 April	To balance b/d		£	
20.00	16 April	To cash received			
	17 April	By typing paper	149	6.90	1.04
	19 April	By cleaning	150	3.75	
	20 April	By postage stamps	151	2.45	
	23 April	By balance c/d		10.49	
23.59				23.59	
10.49	23 April	To balance b/d			

In Figure 13.4 showing petty cash kept under a non-imprest system the original balance on 8 April was £15.25 and from this the following were purchased:

8 April – note books – voucher number 145 – £2.88 (including £0.38 VAT)

9 April – cleaning – voucher number 146 – £3.50

9 April – postage stamps – voucher number 147 – £1.25

10 April – typing ribbons – voucher number 148 – £4.03 (including £0.53 VAT)

On 15 April the balance in the petty cash was £3.59 and added to the total amounts spent equalled the original entry of £15.25. On 16 April the balance of £3.59 formed the opening entry and £20.00 was added. The amount in the petty cash thus varies from period to period and is not restored to a set figure.

QUESTIONS

1. Draft an illustrated set of notes which would explain to an office junior how the imprest system works.
2. Write an illustrated essay showing how the petty cash could be kept, using a system other than the imprest system.

FILING

Filing is a term used to describe a range of processes which are essential if most businesses are to work efficiently. Documentation is the backbone of most business undertakings and without quick and reliable methods of classifying material and then storing it in suitable forms, for data processing or easy retrieval, businesses would not be able to function with any degree of efficiency. Most business transactions involve the keeping of records and these records are usually kept in written or printed form - letters, minutes, memoranda, documents concerned with buying and selling, film records and, increasingly, on punched tape or cards, floppy discs and tapes. The preservation of business records creates problems; how to group them in some logical fashion, *classification*; how to keep them, *storage*; how to find them, *indexing*, once they have been stored should they be required - and increasingly how to extract facts from them - *data processing*.

14.1 THE REASONS FOR STORING CORRESPONDENCE AND RECORDS

1. **To preserve them** It may be that the material is still being worked on - orders being carried out, inquiries awaiting a reply - and so on, or it may be that the material has been processed and has to be stored for any possible future purpose - keeping invoices pending any possible query, keeping all the correspondence relating to a particular transaction, etc. Material should be stored in such a way as to be quick and easy to find should it be required. Increasing use is being made of microcomputers in the field of filing.
2. **To keep material tidy and clean** Material stored in a neat and tidy fashion is not only easier to handle - it also helps to preserve material and keep it safe.
3. **To keep material in a safe place** Records have value - that is why they are kept - and it is essential that they are kept safe from possible damage or loss.

Some material will not be required after a certain time; once a business transaction has been completed and a reasonable time has passed it will not be necessary to keep all the documents - only those such as statements which list the transactions which took place. Any filing system must have built into it some way of removing material which is no longer required. *A good file* is capable of being expanded or contracted if required and yet does not take up unnecessary space.

14.2 FILING TERMS

A file is, perhaps, best thought of as the container holding the material - a folder, a tray, a spike on which documents are kept, a clip holding several documents, a diary, a series of cards, a series of folders, a computer tape, etc.

An index is probably best thought of as the key to the file; the tool used to find material placed in a file. The best file in the world has little value if the index to it is poor. Once material is placed in a file it must be readily available.

A filing method is the way material is stored in a file - how the material is classified.

A filing system contains the files, no matter what form they take. The kind of container used will depend on the material being stored. Is it bulky? Is it just sheets of paper? Is it film? Is it tape? Is it harmed by heat or damp? These are just some of the questions which must be answered.

14.3 FILING - FIRST CONSIDERATIONS

Before any material is filed four basic questions must be answered:

1. What is it that is being kept? The material may be printed documents, general correspondence, telex tapes, dictation tapes, recordings of meetings, plans, drawings, books, film slides - and so on.
2. How can it be classified or put into some order so as to be easy to find when it is required? This will involve some *method* of filing.
3. Where is it to be stored? This will, in part, depend on the answer to the first question. If the material is bulky and takes up a great deal of space it will require one kind of container or *system* (remember that a library is a file) while if it is small or on tape it will require another kind of container (it may even be kept on a spool or in a cassette or a computer). Another factor to be taken into account when answering the question 'Where?' will be the question of whether the information is required in one particular place only (such as an office) or whether it is required by a number of offices. This will involve decisions about *departmental* filing systems or *centralised* filing systems.
4. How capable is the method, or system, to be used of being understood by a large number of people? If a method or system is difficult to use or follow only a few experts will be able to use the files and so general efficiency may be hindered. If a method or system is complicated but is

operated by experts who file and retrieve material for others then documents will be kept very safely and efficiently. The answer to this question lies in *indexing*.

The sections that follow set out to answer the many questions asked so far.

14.4 METHODS OF CLASSIFYING MATERIAL

Alphabetical filing
Alphabetical filing involves placing material into alphabetical order, the order in which letters appear in the alphabet. *Example*: Albert, Barry, Charles, David, Eric, Frank, George, Henry, Ian, John, Keith, Lionel, Maurice, Nevil, Orville and so on to X, Y and Z.

ACTIVITY

In order to obtain some experience of filing alphabetically, arrange the following correctly. Even if some of the words are strange to you do not worry – just concentrate on the first letter.

Radium	Uranium	Diamond
Gold	Silicon	Wood
Iron	Bismuth	Platinum
Tin	Calcium	Lead
Aluminium	Silver	Nickel
Zinc	Vanadium	Krypton
Magnesium	Neon	Oxygen

Once the material has been arranged into a general alphabetical order, words which begin with the same first letter must be arranged in order based on the second, third and fourth letters – and so on. *Example*:

Haas	Hagan	Jelf	Jesson
Habridge	Hahan	Jemson	Jetson
Hackett	Hain	Jenkins	Jevon
Hadcroft	Jeffs	Jepson	Jewsbury
Haffner	Jeggo	Jeremy	Jeynes

ACTIVITY

Arrange the following into the correct alphabetical order:

Tarus	Ray	Nix
Tavern	Read	Nicolson
Tarte	Rawlinson	Niven
Tattersall	Reader	Nicholls
Tate	Raven	Nightingale
Taylor	Rea	Niles
Thomas	Raybould	Nicholson

Rules for filing alphabetically
1. File according to the first letter of the name, or surname.
2. After the first letter file according to the letters which follow. (This is what you have just done.)
3. If, when filing names, the surname is the same, file according to initials. A surname with no initial comes before names with intials. *Example*:

Davies A F	Davies B T	Davies D F
Davies A G	Davies C	Davies E
Davies A I	Davies C A	Davies E A
Davies B E	Davies D D	Davies E B
Davies B M	Davies D E	

ACTIVITY

Arrange these names into the correct alphabetical order.

Attree H G	Baxter R H	Clarke T C
Attwood D C	Bayes L R	Clarke P
Attwell A	Baxter J M	Clarke V
Attree N H	Bayes G D	Clarke T J
Attrill S	Baxter W J	Clarke V B
Attwell T	Bayes D A	Clarke T K

4. 'Nothing' comes before 'something'. A surname by itself comes before a surname with an initial, as at rule 3, but a surname with an initial comes before a surname with a first, or Christian, name. *Example*:

Dale	Dale Arthur	Darby T
Dale B	Dale Barry A	Darby Edith
Dale B D	Darby	Darby Ray
Dale C	Darby R	Darby Joy K
Dale C G	Darby R S	

ACTIVITY

Arrange the following into alphabetical order.

Evans	Coates J L	Cliff Mary
Evans A W	Coates W P	Cliff N
Evans B W	Coates D	Cliff A C
Evans C A	Coates Arthur	Cliff Barbara
Evans David	Coates A	Cliff

5. Treat a prefix before a surname as part of the surname, La Trobe is filed under 'La', and treat names beginning with 'M"', 'Mc' and 'Mac' as if they were spelt Mac. *Example*:

La Barre	La Tienda	M'Alindin
La Bodega	La Trobe	MacAndrew
La Cutique	MacAdam	McAulay
La Mont	McAleer	Macaulay

ACTIVITY

Arrange the following into the correct alphabetical order.

O'Brien B K	O'Connor M	De Will M
O'Carroll P F	O'Brien M A	De Roas Ernest
O'Brien T E	De Bie H	De Lacy Simon
		De Ville P E

6. File names beginning 'St' or 'Saint' under Saint - unless the file has separate sections for Saint or St, in which case file accordingly.
7. 'Short' before 'long' - if all letters in a name are the same - arrange the shorter name in front of the longer. A surname by itself comes before the same surname which has an initial(s) or another name. *Example*:

Butler	Butler M P	Butler Charles
Butler M	Butler P	Butler David E

ACTIVITY

Arrange the following into the correct alphabetical order.

Wilson George M	Willoughby Andrew	Stinton
Willoughby	Stocks Robert	Stocks Wendy
Wilson	Stokes C	Stokes

8. Treat hyphenated names as though they were all part of the first word and ignore the hyphens; treat the whole as part of the alphabetical sequence. *Example*:

Davies-Llewellyn	Davies-Reese
Davies-Morgan	Davies-Williams
Davies-Parry	

9. File names consisting of initials before whole words. *Example*:

N A Haulage Ltd	N S Finance Ltd
N A Taxis Ltd	N V Motors Ltd
N M Pressings Ltd	

ACTIVITY

Arrange the following into the correct alphabetical order.

R P Motors Ltd	R A S Aerials Ltd	H S Electrical Ltd
R W L Leather Crafts Ltd	R B Motors Ltd	H M Coaches Ltd
R S R Textiles Ltd	H C M Engineering Ltd	H F Trust Ltd
		H T C Transport Ltd

10. Ignore 'The' and '& Co' when filing the names of firms and companies. *Example*:

Banner Textiles & Co Ltd

Bargain Shop Ltd The

Basra Trading & Co

Beaver Construction Co Ltd The

Bennett Manufacturing Co Ltd The

ACTIVITY

Arrange the following into the correct alphabetical order.

Forward Manufacturing Co Ltd The

Catos Engineering & Co Ltd

Forward Presswork & Co

Universal Plating Co Ltd

Merrell Casting Co Ltd The

Lambeth & Co Ltd

Roundale Construction Co Ltd The

Thomas A C & Co Ltd

Shayler & Co Ltd

Green Philip & Co Ltd

11. File government departments and ministries under the important word. *Example*:

Agriculture, Fisheries & Food
   Ministry of

Defence Ministry of

Environment Department of

Health & Social Security,
   Department of

Home Office The

12. Treat numbers in names as if they were spelt in full. *Example*:

5 Stars The (Five

4 Seasons The (Four)

4 Ways Garage (Four)

6 Ways Garage (Six)

66 Club The (Sixty-six)

10 Gallon Club The (Ten)

13. If several names are the same, such as a building society or a bank, file the names alphabetically by branches. If the town is the same file by streets. If town and street are the same, file by the number in the street – lowest first. *Example*:

Halifax Building Society, Birmingham, 26 Colmore Row

Halifax Building Society, Birmingham, 71 Colmore Row

Halifax Building Society, Bromsgrove, 122 High Street

Halifax Building Society, Brownhills, 25A High Street

ACTIVITY

Arrange the following into the correct alphabetical order.

Alliance Building Society, 13 Hagley Road, Stourbridge

Alliance Building Society, 51–53 High Street, Brierley Hill

Alliance Building Society, 87 Reddall Road, Old Hill

Alliance Building Society, 2 Bath Avenue, Dudley

Alliance Building Society, 89 Gate Street, York

14. Subdivide files for government departments into departments. *Example*:

Warwickshire County Council Education Department
Warwickshire County Council Fire Brigade
Warwickshire County Council Health Department
Warwickshire County Council Highways Department

15. When filing names of people with qualifications or titles ignore the qualifications or titles but note them (on the flap of a folder if the file is a folder or drawer). *Example*:

Owen OBE D F   Owen Kathleen (Mrs)
Owen Dr F J   Owen Michael BSc
Owen Sir John

Cross-referencing

Some documents can be filed under one name and yet be looked for under another. In such cases a cross-reference must be made – a note made in the file telling a person where the original file can be found. *Example*: Glover's Typewriters may be filed under *G* – Glover's Typewriters while at the same time under *T* – Typewriters Glover's – a card would be inserted saying Typewriters Glover's – see Glover's Typewriters.

Geographical filing

Sometimes it is more convenient to arrange names into alphabetical order according to their location and then to subdivide the location. If this is done the main guide card gives the geographical location, while subsidiary guide cards indicate towns or areas in that location. *Example*:

Africa	Kenya	Bamburi
		Eldoret
		Embakasi
		Kamiti
		Karen
	Nigeria	Akure
		Bare
		Benin City
		Calabar
		Lagos
Australia	Queensland	Bowen
		Cairns
		Cooktown
		Normanton
	Victoria	Ballarat
		Broken Hill
		Sydney
		Taree

ACTIVITY

Arrange the following into alphabetical order geographically:

London:	Vauxhall	Liverpool:	Childwall	Manchester:	Moston
	Mortlake		Aigburth		Ardwick
	Streatham		Sefton Park		West Gorton
	Fulham		Knowsley		Didsbury
	Brixton		Speke		Withington
	Deptford		Wavertree		Levenshulme
	Hanwell		Stoneycroft		Baguley

Numerical filing

In this method each file is given a number irrespective of the name of the person, company or area. The files are placed in consecutive order so that 996 comes before 997 which in turn comes before 998.

ACTIVITY

Arrange the following into numerical order – starting with the smallest number.

9845	2010	7773	2211
831	8945	642	556
8451	1976	10	9978
7340	23	99	1325
632	250	4208	390

Filing by numbers is normally very simple, especially if it is linked to a colour coding system where each colour represents a different category of material filed. In a very complex numerical system it might be advisable to keep some explanation of the system (or a 'key' to it) in a strip-index or a card index close by.

Chronological order

Chronological order is arranging material into date order, usually starting with the earliest date. Very often, as with numerical order, chronological order is combined with alphabetical order. For example correspondence under Central Motors could be subdivided by years – 1977, 1978, 1979, 1980 – and the years each be subdivided by months – January, February, March, April, May, etc.

ACTIVITY

Arrange the following into chronological order.

AD 1860	AD 1771	BC 742	BC 1239	AD 340	BC 49
AD 1206	AD 1826	AD 1671	AD 1170	BC 1400	AD 1980
AD 1883	AD 1723	BC 274	AD 1284	AD 706	BC 100
AD 849	AD 1779	AD 465	AD 1713	AD 890	AD 56

Terminal digit filing

Terminal digit filing is a variation on numerical filing but instead of files being arranged according to the first numbers they are arranged according to the last set(s) of figures. The numbers, which are grouped, are read from right to left and not, as usual, from left to right. **The two-digit-** system groups numbers in blocks of three. The last group of two digits are the number of the shelf, row or drawer, depending on the system being used. The central digits are the number of the folder and the first group show the sequence of the folder. A document numbered 39 89 21 would be filed on shelf, row or drawer 21, in folder 89 while it would be document 39 in that folder. **The triple-digit** system divides the numbers into two. The last three numbers on the right indicate the folder number while the first three numbers indicate the position of that folder. Document 478 106 would be found in folder number 106 while it would be number 478 in that folder.

The chief advantages of the terminal digit system are that files can be found quickly because long numbers are broken into smaller numbers; sorting is made easier; there is less risk of files being lost or misplaced and if files have to be taken away or extra files have to be added they do not affect the continuity of the system.

Decimal filing

Decimal filing enables numerical filing to be refined still further and so the exact location of material can be determined. The Dewey Classification, which is used in most libraries, is an example of decimal filing. Full details of this classification can be found in Dewey Decimal Classification and Relative Index   Numbers range from 000 to 999 and the general groupings are as follows:

000   Generalities
100   Philosophy and related disciplines
200   Religion
300   Social Sciences
400   Language
500   Pure sciences
600   Technology (Applied)
700   The Arts
800   Literature
900   General geography and history and their auxiliaries

Within each prime (whole number) there are subdivisions, each indicated either by prime numbers or decimal numbers. For example under the heading 000 Generalities the decimal numbers proceed as follows:

001   Knowledge and its extension
001.2   Scholarship and learning
001.3   Humanities
001.4   Methodology and research (this can be further subdivided)
001.42   Methodology
001.422   Statistical method
001.422 2 Collection
          Questionnaires and field work

The main advantage of a decimal system is the exact placement of material.

Alphabetical and numerical methods (Alpha-numeric systems)

In some files the alphabetical and numerical methods are combined. Material is first placed alphabetically and within the alphabetical placement a numerical order places material exactly. File D/24 would be placed under the general alphabetical order of D and it would be number 24 within the Ds. A file dealing with material relating to Ductile Steels would be filed under D and all the papers relating to Ductile Steels would be numbered from 1 to whatever number of papers there were. This method makes the location of particular documents easy; to find them a person has first to locate the letter of the alphabet and then the number required under that letter.

Classification by subject

Firms dealing with a range of subjects, for example an examining board dealing with Arithmetic, Biology, Chemistry and so on, might file material under subject headings in alphabetical order. Subdivisions may be used under the general subject headings; for example the examiners in Biology might be further placed in alphabetical order – Biology: Andrews M, Andrews P, Baker G, Barker M – and so on. Subjects may also be filed numerically, as in the Dewey System, or geographically. A firm dealing with London might subdivide its files according to products – Desks, Envelopes, Folders – and so on.

The method used for the placement of material will depend on what is being placed and many firms use more than one method. The important thing about any method must be to place material logically so that it can be placed with accuracy and this, in turn, will mean that it will be easy to locate once it has been filed – no matter what system is used to store the material.

14.5 INDEXING

Once material has been classified some form of indexing may be required to enable it to be found. Some methods of filing are *self-indexing*, a dictionary and a telephone directory do not require a separate index, for example. *Others give all the information required* on the actual index card, for example the record cards listing names and addresses and details of medical treatment given at a doctor's. *Indexes such as those used in libraries* or those used in conjunction with other numerical methods of classifying material *simply provide the key* to the material contained in the files.

Indexes which contain all the information required

While it is easy to give examples of methods of classifying material which are self-indexing, contain all the information required or provide the key to files, it is worth remembering that some indexes serve more than one function – and so a rigid classification of types is not advisable.

Card index

A card index consists of a series of cards on which the actual information is placed and the sections are indicated by guide cards which are usually arranged in alphabetical order. Some card indexes contain all the required information on the card, the names and addresses of customers or patients at a dentist's or a doctor's, or the members of a library, for example. Others are simply the means of finding material stored in other places.

ACTIVITY

Visit any library and study the card indexes found there. You will note that some indexes provide the key to where books are placed while others provide information relating to titles or to authors.

As you will have found from the activity above, index cards are approximately the size of postcards, 125 x 75 mm. A separate card is used for each item, title of a book, the name of an author, the name and address of a customer in the files of a business, etc. The cards can be kept in place by a steel rod or by a spring block at the back of the cards. Coloured cards may be used to assist location (see Figure 14.1).

Fig 14.1 *card index with guide card*

Card indexes can be used for a number of purposes with the following advantages:

1. The cards are easy to handle. **Guide cards** give a quick and easy guide to where individual cards may be found – alphabetical classification is the easiest to follow.

2. Information can be typed or written on to the cards.
3. The cards can serve a range of purposes; they might contain details of staff in a business, pupils/students at school/college, patients at a doctor's, dentist's or optician's, for example.
4. Coloured cards or coloured guide cards can further assist sorting and classification.
5. It is easy to remove unwanted cards or to add extra cards; if more information than will fit on one card is required a second can be added.
6. Should a card have to be taken away, a note can be left in the index giving details of when it was taken, by whom – and if required – for what purpose.
7. The boxes can be locked when not in use – a security precaution.

Rotary index
Card indexes can be stored in rotating wheel cabinets – or stands (see Figure 14.2). The information is recorded on cards using a whole card for each entry or recording an entry per line of card – the information being typed or written on the cards. The index is subdivided using guide cards and has the advantage of being able to hold a great number of card/entries in a limited space. To obtain information the wheel is simply rotated and cards can be removed for use elsewhere – an absence card being inserted to show where a card has been taken to and who has taken it – if required.

Fig 14.2 *a rotary index*

Visible book index
This is similar to a card index except that the index is kept in a book; the edges of the pages are cut away to provide an alphabetical or numerical

index. The simplest form of book index is an address book or a telephone book.

Loose-leaf index books

Loose-leaf index books are kept by some firms. The pages are kept in a file which can be added to or taken from as required. The disadvantages of such an index are the fact that pages can be pulled out easily and the fact that others can insert or remove pages without security. For this reason many index books contain a mechanism which can be locked to prevent unauthorised persons tampering with them.

Visible card index

In a visible card index system the cards overlap and a strip on the edge of each remains visible. Information can be typed or written on the cards which can be looked at by lifting back the other cards which overlap. The cards are usually kept flat in trays and the trays are kept in cabinets – usually made of steel – which can be locked (see Figure 14.3).

Fig 14.3 *a visible card index*

Each tray holds up to 70 cards which can be controlled by use of coloured signals which slide along the visible edge to the required position. If, for example, the index is being used for stock-control purposes the coloured signals can be slid across each card listing a particular item of stock to show the current stock position of that item. The edge of each tray contains information as to what is in each tray. Partially extended trays can be used to support higher ones at a convenient angle for writing on cards. Cards which need to be removed and carried about can easily be removed and carried in binders (see Figure 14.4).

Fig 14.4 *Twinlock Datatray binder*

Strip index
While a visible card index gives the appearance of a number of strips at the edges of sheets/cards a strip index is, in fact, a series of strips. Single strips up to 7 mm. ($\frac{1}{4}$") and up to 315 mm. ($12\frac{1}{2}$") long are mounted into a panel, often made of plastic, which, in turn, can be mounted on to a variety of fixtures (see Figure 14.5).

An easel binder produced by Twinlock provides the versatility of a portable binder and desk unit in one free-standing outfit – it contains five index panels.

A wall/desk unit is dual-purpose for either desk use or wall-mounting. Units can easily be extended by adding special extension units; each unit holds up to ten plastic panels and the Twinlock unit can be extended in multiples of ten.

Rotary stands are designed for big capacity and the Twinlock rotary stand is available with one of three fitments to hold 25, 50 or 100 panels to provide fast access even with up to 20 000 records.

Fig **14.5** *title inserts*

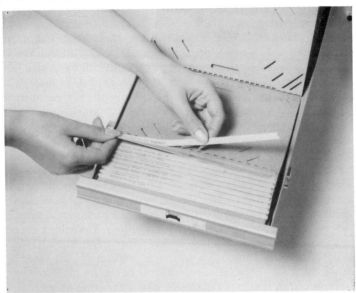

Fig **14.6** *box file roundabout – Expandex*

Each line of a strip index contains information and the system can be used to store such information as telephone numbers, names, account numbers and addresses in current use. The information is available without the need to search through sheets of paper, cards or books and individual references, each on its own strip, can be located easily and quickly. Information can be placed on the strips using a typewriter or by writing prior to insertion into the holder; additions or subtractions can be made without affecting the continuity of the records. To assist the finding of material, strips can be colour coded; the plastic covering prevents material from damage and dirt.

Punched cards (edge-punched cards)

Sometimes there is a need to be able to sort information quickly and efficiently yet at low cost in terms of equipment. One way of doing this is to store information on cards, the edges of which are punched at predetermined locations – each location indicating a particular piece of information such as age, sex and individual qualifications. The cards are stored in a suitable container such as a box or tray. When information is required a steel needle is passed through a particular position and the cards in that position either fall away (in some systems) or remain (as in others). The advantages of this system are its cheapness and the range of material which can be stored on each card. The main disadvantage is that of checking to ensure that the cards are punched in the correct places.

It can be seen from reading this section that the range of indexing systems is very wide and that many indexes are in fact complete filing systems in their own right. When deciding which system to use the following may be taken into consideration:

1. How much does it cost?
2. What information can it be used for?
3. Is it easy to operate?
4. Can material be easily added to the file or taken from it?
5. Is the material fixed in the file or can individual items be removed for use elsewhere?
6. How much space does it occupy?
7. Can it be locked when not in use?
8. Is it easy to write or type information in the index?
9. Can it be used for more than one purpose?
10. Can the index be moved about or is it fixed?

14.6 FILING EQUIPMENT – SYSTEMS

While reading the previous section on indexing it must have been clear that indexes need some container and that some indexing systems are centred about the actual equipment.

A **card index** usually requires either a metal or wooden box in which to store the cards – or a wheel as in the case of a rotary index.

A **strip index** requires some form of holder to keep the strips in position and to make them readily available.

A **visible card index** usually requires a metal cabinet or a folder of some description.

Punched edge cards require a box or other container while *loose sheets* require a file or binder to secure them in. *Telephone or address books* are usually kept in a desk drawer or on a shelf when not in use.

Box files

Box files are made of wood, metal or heavy cardboard and papers/booklets are fitted into the box either by a spring clip or a clip which passes through punched holes. If the clip method is used the sheets/booklets do not have to be punched. The clip method is usually called an *arch file*. The system enables all the papers/documents relating to one particular topic to be kept together. The boxes are indexed on the spine and can either be stored on shelves or on roundabouts – each of which can hold up to twenty-four files on each tier and six tiers can be used in each stack; the height of each stack is determined by convenience of reach more than other factors (see Figure 14.6).

Expanding files

Expanding or *concertina files* (see Figure 14.7) are a number of wallets with gusseted pockets connected together. The divisions are indexed and papers are stored in the pockets. The whole file can be fastened, usually with a strap, and is useful for storing small quantities of information (such as documents at home listing details of rent/mortgage, gas, water, electricity bills and rates, for example) or papers required for immediate use. The file can be stored on a shelf or locked away in a drawer when not in use.

Fig 14.7 *an expanding file*

Plan filing

Plans and drawings are usually stored flat in drawers or upright in cabinets which contain compartments with dividers to enable them to be stored without buckling. Indexing is usually done by means of indexing strips.

Lateral filing

Lateral filing is a system of storing material on shelves, in cupboards or on racks. The material can be stored side by side, like books on a shelf, but usually it is suspended from rails in storage units in folders. The folders are hung separately so that they can easily be removed although the material may be placed in inserts so that it can be removed without taking out the whole file. Lateral files are very economical in use of space, units can be stacked from floor to ceiling, and they can be easily indexed on the spine rather like a book. Colours can be used to indicate sections, and folders are available to take a wide range of paper sizes.

The main advantages of a lateral file are:

1. It is a very economical use of space - there is no need to open drawers.
2. A large number of files can be seen at any one time.
3. A range of paper sizes can be accommodated.
4. If cabinets or cupboards are used they can be locked when not in use.
5. It is less likely that cabinets will tip over if they are carelessly used.

The main disadvantages are:

1. The open files can easily become dusty.
2. Although the files can be stacked high the actual height may create problems in finding the required material or taking it out of the files.
3. Although it is easy to label files it is not so easy to read them because they are hung vertically.

Suspension files

In a suspension file the folders or pockets are suspended vertically from runners which are fitted inside cabinet drawers. The files are hung so that they are held clear of the bottom of the drawer and can be indexed by means of tabs which stand clear or indexing strips which lie flat. Either kind of indexing is done on tabs or labels which are supplied in perforated lengths so that they can be typed or written on. Plastic covers keep the index tabs or strips clean. Modern storage cabinets allow suspension files to be kept in cabinets in one or two rows per chassis - the files are suspended on nylon runners and can be pulled out when required or they can be linked in a continuous concertina which keeps them permanently in sequence and prevents loss of paper between folders. A file can be removed from a concertina by opening it and extra files can be inserted. Modern plastic covers are angled with a lens to make reading of labels easy and tab inserts can take up to three lines of information. The inserts are offered in a range of up to ten colours to facilitate indexing and location. Folders will take a range of paper sizes. Whether the concertina type of holder or

Fig 14.8 *a lateral file*

the individual type is used, material is not, as a general rule, placed directly into the file. Instead it is placed in a folder which, in turn, is placed inside the file and this means that care must be taken to label quite clearly both the insert and the file to ensure that the correct insert is placed in the correct file.

Suspension files are also used to store ink duplicating stencils and spirit masters – a special cabinet is generally used and care must be taken to label correctly. Suspension files can be housed in fireproof cabinets, in drawers in desks, in trolleys, in cupboards and in personal files for use at home. A suspension file on *a trolley* enables it to be taken to where it is required; *a desk file* enables the person sitting at a particular desk to have all the information at hand. No matter what 'vehicle' is used for the suspension file, the material is kept clean and tidy and is protected from wear and tear because it is kept inside a folder which, in turn, is kept inside a file.

Suspension files can be used for both lateral and vertical filing.

Vertical filing
In a vertical file papers are stored in files which are arranged upright. Files can be stored in a cabinet, on a shelf, in racks or in drawers. Indexing can be by strips or labels on the top edge.

The main advantages of a vertical file are:

1. Papers can be removed and inserted without removing the file.
2. Labels on files can be easily read because they are the 'right way' round.
3. Material is stored in a compact fashion.

190

Fig. 14.9 *suspension files:*

A: *individual folders in a suspension file –
illustration shows a range of folders*

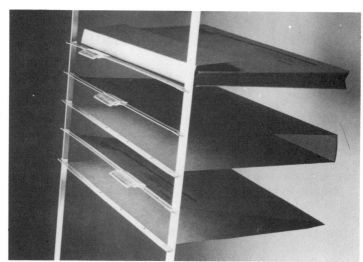

B: *linked folders in a suspension file*

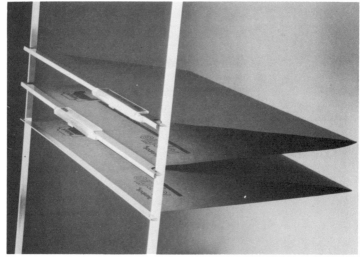

4. If cabinets or drawers are used there is protection from dust and loss, especially if they can be locked when not in use.

The main disadvantages are:

1. If drawers are used the system takes up a great deal of space - each drawer will occupy twice the space when fully extended.
2. If drawers are used in filing cabinets care must be taken to ensure that only one is opened at a time - particularly at the top of a cabinet - in case the whole cabinet falls forward under the weight. *Many cabinets can be plugged into a wall as a safety precaution* - always providing the cabinet is stacked against a suitable wall.
3. Cabinets can be expensive.
4. Only one person at a time can have reasonable access to a filing cabinet.

Pending files
Any papers/documents awaiting filing may be kept in any one of a number of different types of file - lateral, vertical, box, etc. The storage may be in any of the ways described under classification provided that it is clear and pending files should be cleared, by filing in permanent quarters, as soon as possible.

Multi-Stor shelf filing
The Twinlock Multi-Stor shelf filing system enables a wide range of material to be stored in a number of ways, lateral, suspension, box/lever arch and tapes, in the same cabinet - thus saving space and making best use of each method in one housing.

Computer sheets
The increasing use of computer printouts has led to the development of methods of indexing and storing the continuous sheets which are produced. One method is to fasten the sheets into a binder and lock them or fasten them in so that the binder can be indexed and suspended inside a cabinet. Sheets can be fastened inside a ring binder, stored in a daily storage binder or inserted into printout slings for storage inside suspension units. Sheets kept in folders can be indexed with self-adhesive strips with title inserts (so that there is no need to break open the binder to insert the index); binders can also be indexed with self-adhesive strips with inserts.

14.7 MICROFILMING

Microfilming is a filing process, using photographic methods, developed to copy all kinds of material in reduced form for storing until required. When material is required it must be read on special machines which enlarge the reduced image to readable proportions. The chief advantage of the system is that storage space is dramatically reduced - up to 28 000 A4 sheets can be reduced and stored on a single roll of film. The film used is either 35 mm. (as used in many cameras) or 16 mm. (as used in some home movie cameras). Should copies of originals be required at any time, full-sized copies can be made from the reduced images stored in the system.

Steps in the microfilming process

1. The material is photographed using *a microfilmer*. A wide range of sizes of document can be photographed and reduced; documents 114 × 160 cm. (45 × 63 in.) can be taken in the Kodak Recordak Micro-file machine Model MRG-1. Even a simple machine will photograph a document in under two seconds; a complex one will handle over 600 cheque-sized documents a minute. Single sheets can be photographed, parts of sheets can be photographed and even both sides of a sheet in a book can be photographed at the same time. If a duplicate copy is required, for security reasons in case the original is lost, this can be made at the same time that the original is taken. The photographing is on 16- or 35-mm. film although specialist sizes are also used and originally the photographs are on a continuous roll.

2. The film is developed. Like the photographing, this can be done on equipment owned by individual firms or by specialist firms.

3. The processed film is read to ensure accuracy and ensure that errors have not been made in processing.

4. The film is stored. This can be done in several ways:

   (*a*) The film can be stored on a *continuous roll.*

   (*b*) The film can be stored in *microfilm jackets* which are made from two clear, thin polyester films welded together to form channels. Strips of film are inserted into these channels to create a micro-film file.

   (*c*) The film can be stored in microfilm *aperture cards* which are based on the same principle as the jackets but with the advantage that the cards can be written on. Aperture cards are index-type cards which have an aperture (opening) in which microfilm channels are housed.

   (*d*) The film is stored in the form of a *microfiche* which houses over 200 separate document images in an area 150 × 100 mm. (6 × 4 in.).

5. The material is retrieved when required and read on a *microfilm reader.* There is a vast range of readers, each with varying degrees of versatility but the basic principle is to enlarge the film to readable proportions on a screen.

The advantages of microfilming

1. Great savings of space and weight – there is no need to keep all originals although many firms in fact do so – but they can be stored away from main offices.

2. Copies of material can be sent cheaply through the post.

3. Material is always in the correct sequence – it has to be placed in the correct sequence before filming.

4. Reproductions the same size, or even enlarged size, of originals can be made if required.

5. Film can be stored in fire proof containers.

The main disadvantage is the cost – although this can in any case be offset against the normal storage space required – while it is vital that the checking of the photographing is of the highest standards. Only large organisations can afford the equipment and if they wish to use the system they will have to purchase the equipment or take material to a specialist firm offering the service.

14.8 PUNCHED TAPE AND CARD

A great deal of information can be stored on punched tape or punched card for use in computers. The tape or card is produced by *keypunch operators* and checked by *verifiers*. The tape or card can be fed into a computer which can read cards at up to 1 000 per minute and take out and analyse material for presentation in various forms such as computer print-out sheets. Cards can be stored in boxes in cabinets while tapes can be stored on rolls in containers.

14.9 FILING – SOME GENERAL HINTS AND TERMS

1. Choose the most suitable method for classifying material; this will depend on the nature of the material itself.
2. Select a suitable method for indexing the material; again this will depend on the nature of the material itself and how it is to be stored.
3. Select a suitable method of storing the material and bear in mind such factors as:
   the cost of the units;
   expansion or contraction of the material to be stored;
   the problem of removing redundant material;
   the amount of space taken by the storage units;
   the security offered by the storage units in terms of loss of material and as protection from dirt and damage;
   the safety of the units in terms of handling (top drawers will make filing cabinets unstable if pulled out together) and terms of fire/damp risk;
   the nature of the material to be housed;
   the method of classification and indexing to be used;
   how often the material will be required.
4. Decide *where* the material will be stored; centrally or departments, in individual files or files to be used by many people.
5. File neatly and methodically. *Sort material* before filing – you may want to hold it in a *pending file* and group it so that when you come to file it all the material required in a particular place is at hand and you do not have to go backwards and forwards as you file.
6. Straighten material so that it fits squarely into a file and does not protrude. Select containers of a suitable size for the material to be filed.
7. Make sure that material is cross-referenced to assist location.

8. Remove clips from material to be filed, slips of paper can easily attach themselves to clips; staple sheets together instead.
9. If possible file daily or at frequent intervals to avoid a pile up of material.
10. File material within a file in date order so that it appears in the correct sequence in the file.
11. If a file is removed for any purpose ensure that an *absence card* or a *marker card* is placed in the file indicating by whom, when and why the material was taken.
12. Do not remove individual papers from a file unless it is absolutely necessary. If it is, ensure that a note is placed in the file indicating what it is that has been removed and by whom.
13. Set up a system of removing files/material which is:
    (*a*) not in normal use – store it where it can be found but keep it away from files which are in normal use;
    (*b*) no longer required. Material which is no longer required should be removed from files and destroyed. (See later note.)
14. Lock files when they are not in use.
15. Use colour if it assists location, classification or indexing.

Treasury tags are used to fasten material in files – the material has to be punched before the tags can be threaded through them to fasten the material.

A shredding machine should be used to destroy documents which are no longer required. There is a range of machines available from electrically operated machines to hand-operated machines and any documents which might possibly be confidential should be passed through a shredding machine for disposal or use as packing material.

Absent files are folders which have been removed from a file. As indicated earlier, an absence card or marker should be inserted.

14.10 REMINDER SYSTEMS – TICKLER FILES

Many documents have to be followed up – the matter they concern may involve long periods of time and it is essential that points are not lost. Letters require a reply, accounts need chasing, patients need reminding and so on. A desk diary or an appointments diary will serve as a reminder system – a diary is a date index!

A tickler file or follow-up file consists of twelve guide cards each set for a month, January to December. Each month has a card for each day in the month – for speed in setting up a tickler file thirty-one cards (the length of the longest month) can be used for each month. The action to be taken is listed on the cards in the correct place in the file and the person responsible must check daily to see what is outstanding for *each day and the following day. An appointments diary* should be checked a week in advance in addition.

Sometimes material in hand is stored in a **pending file**.

Transfer boxes are used to transport and hold material being removed from an active file to be stored.

A dead file is one used to house material which is old and possibly of little current value. The material is kept in case there is a need to refer to it but, because it is not in current use, it is kept away from files in normal use. Dead files are normally housed in store-rooms or store cupboards and a note of the file numbers is kept in the current file so that the material can quickly be located if required.

ACTIVITY

From what you have read in this section on filing, draw up a table listing points for and against departmental and centralised filing.

14.11 COMPUTERISED FILING

The advent of the printed circuit and the silicon chip made it possible to produce computers quickly and cheaply. Instead of requiring a computer which occupies some hundreds of square metres, housed in a temperature/humidity-controlled building, it is now possible to obtain a desk model which can perform the same functions and operate in a great range of working conditions. The field of the microcomputer is one of the fastest growing fields of human endeavour.

It is now possible to program a microcomputer with literally any kind of information and to use this information in a large number of ways – as stored information awaiting recall (the information can be shown on a visual display unit (VDU) or be printed either in its original form or any convenient form); as the basis for statistical extraction (information stored in a computer can be processed very quickly and facts can be extracted from it by the microcomputer); a central store can be used as a collecting-point for a number of departments which can feed the central store as material comes to hand or extract from the centre to meet particular requirements – the central store may be housed in the same complex or be kept literally hundreds of miles away. As indicated in Section 10 on Mechanical Aids microcomputers have many applications and further applications are given in Section 23 on Sources of Information. Organisations can either purchase programs for use in their own particular situations or can use trained staff to program their own computers using discs or tapes on which to store the information. It is essential that a careful check is made to ensure the accuracy of any information fed into any computer because once it is stored in a computer memory it is difficult to correct and the computer will treat all information held as fact. It is also essential to develop programs which are protected against misuse or accidental loss. Most computers have duplicate records to protect against 'Murphy's Law' – if anything can go wrong it will – a rather cynical approach to a very real problem.

Computers should be seen as both a filing system and a method and as one of a number of available options. It is not possible, at the time of writing, to store pictures in computers and their best application is the storage of the written/printed word. The fact that information is stored in a computer is not proof of authenticity – and the original source of much information must be kept to prove the legality of the material. To this extent much information fed into computers requires additional filing and storage in case originals are required. The greatest assets of computers in filing are their ability to recall facts very quickly; to process these facts to meet particular demands: arranging them into alphabetical, numerical, geographical, chronological order, etc., or to sort through them to extract information (when compiling statistics of purchases, sales, returns, losses, damaged goods, profits, losses, etc.); to act as a central store for a number of feeder-points; to act as a transmission source to a number of receiver-points and to transmit information over practically any distance at very high speed – computers can 'talk to each other' at speeds which are greatly in excess of any human capability. There are many applications of computers in the field of filing but, as in many aspects of activity, the machine is only as good as its user – even if a computer can have reminder systems built into it to assist the user.

QUESTIONS

1. Produce a set of rules from which an office junior could operate a filing system based on the alphabet.
2. Write an essay discussing the advantages and disadvantages of a centralized filing system to a large firm.
3. Write a paragraph on each of the following:

   Geographical filing   Numerical filing
   Terminal digit filing   Decimal filing

4. Write an essay on microfilming describing all the processes.
5. What are the advantages and disadvantages of using a microcomputer for filing?

MEETINGS

15.1 KINDS OF MEETINGS

Meetings are basically of two kinds – informal and formal.

Informal meetings are meetings which may be called at short notice either by means of a note or simply by word of mouth. They are often called to discuss matters which arise suddenly, for example, a representative has called to demonstrate a new piece of office equipment and the office supervisior calls a meeting to discuss staff views on it. Informal meetings do not usually have an agenda and it is not usual to keep a record of what happened at the meeting.

Formal meetings are usually held after the persons entitled to attend have been notified in writing some time before the meeting; there may be a rule which says how much notice has to be given before a meeting can take place. The notice is usually accompanied by an agenda.

Most formal associations, whether they are a club or a large company, have an elected committee to represent the views of members and to make decisions concerning the association or company. Most committees consist of a *Chairman*, who conducts the meeting, usually to an agreed set of rules called standing orders (see later); *a Secretary*, who takes notes of what is discussed at the meeting in order that a record may be kept and who is responsible for the organisation of the meeting (see the duties of a secretary at a meeting); *a Treasurer*, who is responsible for the financial affairs of the body (an Accountant is responsible in the case of a company); other elected officials – people elected to specific posts such as Personnel Director in a company or First Team captain in a club – and *general committee members*. In the case of a company the general committee members would be directors of the company.

Formal bodies usually have **annual general meetings**; meetings held once a year to elect the officials and committee, to receive reports and give members an oportunity to speak as well as elect the officials and committee. In clubs it is usual for each member to have one vote while at company meetings the voting shareholders are allowed to vote according to the number of voting shares they hold; a person holding 150 voting shares will have 150 votes. A shareholder who cannot attend an annual general meeting may *vote by proxy* – authorise another to vote for him. Once elected the committee may meet at **general committee meetings** where day-to-day affairs are discussed while **subcommittee meetings** will be meetings consisting of members of a general committee who have been given a particular task to perform which does not require the attention of all the committee members; in the case of a club it may be to arrange a social function while in the case of a company it may be to look into the possibilities of developing a new export market. An **extraordinary general meeting** may be called to discuss matters which cannot wait until the next annual general meeting; in the case of a club the committee may resign suddenly for some reason or a company may suddenly find itself in financial difficulties. A **special committee meeting** may be called to discuss matters which cannot wait unit the next regular meeting.

An agenda is usually included with the notice informing members of the meeting and tells them where the meeting will be held, when it will be held and at what time. It is usually signed by the secretary calling the meeting. An *honorary secretary* is normally a person who performs the function of a secretary in an honorary capacity – in other words without pay. A *general secretary* may be responsible for calling meetings and keeping a record of what takes place at the meeting (keeping minutes) or may simply deal with correspondence – leaving the note-taking to a *minutes secretary*.

The agenda for an annual general meeting differs from an ordinary agenda in two ways. Copies are sent to all members who are entitled to attend – all club members in the case of a club or the partners in a partnership or shareholders in a limited company. There is some difference in the type of business conducted – at the annual general meeting, for example, the directors may be elected.

The usual order for an agenda, which is prepared by the secretary in consultation with the chairman, is:

apologies for absence;
minutes of the last meeting;
matters arising from the minutes;
various reports from officials;
matters which members have indicated to the secretary that they wish to be discussed;
any other business (time given to allow members to raise points about which they have failed to notify the secretary prior to the drawing up of the agenda);
the date, time and place of the next meeting.

Examples of agendas

Fig 15.1 *notice of meeting and agenda for a hockey club*

Wanderers Hockey Club
Western Road

2 October 19xx

The next General Committee meeting of The
Wanderers Hockey Club will be held at the
Club House, Western Road, at 1930 hrs on
Monday 12 October.

A G E N D A

1. Apologies
2. Minutes of the last meeting
3. Matters arising from the minutes:
    (a) drive for new members
    (b) arrangements for the Dinner/Dance
4. Secretary's report
5. Treasurer's report
6. Selection Committee report
7. Entertainments Committee report
8. Any other business
9. Date, time and place of the next meeting

Dorothy Rowley
Honorary Secretary

Fig 15.2 *notice of Annual General Meeting of a large company*

NOTICE IS HEREBY GIVEN that the TENTH ANNUAL GENERAL MEETING of the Company will be held at The Dorchester Hotel, Park Lane, London on Tuesday 14 May 19xx, at 11.00 am to transact the following business.

Resolutions will be proposed

1   To approve and adopt the accounts for the year ended 31 December 19xx, together with the reports thereon of the directors and auditors, (Resolution No 1).

2   To re-elect the following directors, who have been appointed to the Board of Directors under Article 88.

   Robert J Hunt   (Resolution 2a).
   Frank Oldfield (Resolution 2b).
   Harold Yates   (Resolution 2c).

3   To re-appoint the auditors, Barlow & Maddocks, and authorise the directors to fix their remuneration. (Resolution No 3).

A Special Resolution will be proposed

4   That the name of the Company be changed to 'International Fabrications Limited'. (Resolution No 4).

   By order of the Board

   R W Newson
   Secretary
   3 April 19xx

ACTIVITY

1. Carefully read the previous two documents and answer the following.
   (*a*) What is the date, time and place of: (i) the hockey club meeting;
                                                 (ii) the company meeting?
   (*b*) Who called the company meeting?
   (*c*) What matters have arisen from the minutes of the last meeting of the hockey club?
   (*d*) What is the second item to be dealt with at the company meeting?

15.2 HOLDING A MEETING

Before a meeting can start, the Chairman, or Secretary, must check to see if there is **a quorum**, that is a minimum number of people required to be present before a meeting can take place. Many official bodies have a minimum number written into their rules. If the Chairman is unable to attend, either the official Deputy Chairman becomes the Chairman or members elect one, to act for that meeting, from the members present. While members are settling down an **attendance register** may be passed round for those present to sign; alternatively the Secretary may make a note of those present.

   The Chairman is responsible for conducting the meeting and it is his, or her, job to ensure that all remarks are made *through a chair* – in other words speakers must address their remarks to the Chairman; in the case of a man being in charge they generally address him as *Mr Chairman* while if a woman is in charge they generally address her as *Madam Chairman*. The Chairman introduces each item on the agenda in turn and is assisted by the Secretary, who may prepare a **Chairman's Agenda** – an agenda which contains added information to assist the Chairman in his or her conduct of the meeting. The Chairman's agenda for the hockey club general meeting may look like the one in this example.

Fig 15.3   *chairman's agenda for hockey club meeting*

AGENDA

1. Apologies	Apology received from Miss Yates – she has had to go away on a course
2. Minutes of the last meeting	All members have been sent copies
3. Matters arising (a) drive for new playing members (b) arrangements for Annual Dinner/Dance	Mrs Williams to report Miss Robertson and Mrs Hopkins to report
4. Secretary's report	Miss Rowley
5. Treasurer's report	Mrs Williams
6. Selection Committee report	Chairman of selection – Miss Yates – is away, Miss Wearing to report
7. Entertainments Committee report	Mrs Hopkins
8. Any other business	Complaint from groundsman
9. Date, time and place of next meeting	Should be the second Monday in November

In case members have failed to bring their agenda with them the Secretary often produces spare copies and lays them out before the meeting beings.

The Chairman may ask for apologies for absence before starting the meeting or may take the minutes first. **The minutes**, which are a brief record of what took place at the last meeting and are produced by the Secretary to provide a reminder to those at the current meeting and provide a record of all decisions taken, may be read out. Sometimes the minutes may be taken *as read*; members may have been sent copies and it is assumed that they have read and approved them. If a member disagrees with the minutes he, or she, can raise an objection. If the meeting agrees with the objection the minutes may be amended. Minutes may be kept in a special *minutes book* or be typed and inserted in a *loose-leaf book*.

Minutes should be accurate, brief and clear. They should be written in the third person: 'Miss Rowley reported that she had received . . .', and in the past tense. As a meeting progresses the Secretary should make a note of all the discussion and keep a record of all resolutions, the names of the proposer and seconder and all decisions reached. If votes are taken the figures may be included. It is usual for the Secretary to produce *a draft* set of minutes as soon after the meeting as possible, while events are fresh in the mind, and show them to the Chairman before producing the actual set of minutes for the meeting. It is essential that the minutes accurately reflect what took place at a particular meeting and record all decisions taken for future reference. The minutes should be produced in the order in which events took place at the meeting, even if the meeting did not accurately follow the prepared agenda. A set of minutes for the meeting of the hockey club can be seen at Figure 15.4. For more formal meetings it is usual to number all items, often beginning the numbering at the first meeting and then continuing the series through subsequent meetings, e.g. 1, 1.1, 1.12, 2, 2.1 – or else changing the numbering each years, e.g. 80.1 . . . 80.83 . . . 81.1 . . . 81.77, and for an index to the minutes to be kept at the back of the minutes book or the loose-leaf file.

If the members present at the meeting agree with the minutes the Chairman signs and dates them before the Secretary files them for future reference. As each item arises the Chairman asks members to speak. If several members wish to speak at the same time the Chairman will decide who should speak in turn; if members speak among themselves the Chairman may call the meeting *to order* – or order members to speak '*to the chair*'.

A member may wish to propose **a motion** – make a *formal proposition* or suggestion. If after the member has proposed a motion another member agrees, he, or she, may *second the motion* – speak in support of it. As a rule unless a motion is seconded no further discussion takes place but if seconded discussion takes place on the suggestion. Another member may not agree with the motion and so propose **an amendment** or alteration. If the amendment is seconded the amendment must be discussed and voted upon before further action can take place. If the amendment is approved it becomes a *substantive motion* – it becomes part of the original motion. After all the amendments have been voted upon in turn, and those agreed upon become part of the substantive motion, the substantive motion is put to the meeting for a vote. If an amendment is *not carried*, fails to win support, the motion is put to the meeting. If a motion wins a majority of the votes it becomes binding on the institution. If the voting is equal, there is no majority, the Chairman may have the **casting vote**, decide the issue by his, or her, vote. This vote may be in addition to the vote cast for or against the motion – but more often the Chairman does not vote unless a casting vote is required. The rules of the association should give a ruling on this point. A motion which is carried is sometimes called a **resolution**.

Voting at meetings may be undertaken in a number of ways; by *show of hands*, when members raise their hands for or against while *a teller* counts the votes; by *secret ballot* – members vote for or against a motion on a piece of paper, marked in advance to prevent 'extra' papers being put in the ballot box. If *a poll* is taken members write their names on the voting papers. If members vote by voice, *by acclamation*, it is possible that an unfair picture of the voting emerges. Very often at union meetings members vote *by card* – officials vote by card and each card represents the number of members represented by the official. Some associations permit members to vote *'by post'* or by appointing another person to vote for them – *a proxy* vote. It is usual for all proxy votes to be sent to the Secretary before a meeting.

If, after considerable discussion, it appears that progress is not being made on a particular motion a member may ask the chairman to *put the question* – propose that a vote be taken on the matter under discussion. It is usual to give the original proposer of a motion the *right to reply* – make a final statement in support of the motion. If the meeting rejects that *'the question now be put'* further discussion takes place. Before a vote is taken the Chairman usually states what is actually being voted upon. If a meeting feels that it cannot decide an issue, usually a report from a sub-committee, it may *refer the matter back* – ask the other body to consider the matter further and make other (or clearer) proposals. If it is decided at a meeting that only a few members are required to look into a particular point **a subcommittee** may be appointed by the full committee to undertake the task, and report back to the main committee. If a committee feels that it lacks the expertise required to make a decision or to act in a certain way it may *co-opt* a member or members – ask a person or persons to join the body, a general committee or a subcommittee. It is usual for each subcommittee to elect its own Chairman, who will report to the general committee. An **ad hoc committee** is a committee set up for one particular purpose – arranging a social event, for example, in the absence of an entertainments committee.

Once all the items on an agenda have been dealt with the Chairman closes the meeting after arranging the date, time and place of the next meeting if possible. If it is impossible to deal with all items on the agenda the Chairman may *carry over* items, leave them to be included on the agenda at the next meeting, or *adjourn* the meeting – postpone further discussion to a later time or date. At public meetings it is common for a *vote of thanks* to be offered to one or more officials for the way they have fulfilled their official capacities at the meeting.

15.3 OTHER MEETING TERMS

attendance book	– the same as an attendance register.
closure	– a motion put forward to end discussion on a matter before a meeting; the same as 'the question now be put' or 'put the question'.

dropped motion	– one which does not find a seconder or fails to be voted upon because the meeting is closed before a vote is taken.
en bloc	– the passing of one resolution to take the place of several resolutions, as in the election of a committee; electing a committee en bloc.
ex officio	– by virtue of office. This means that a person may be a member of a committee by virtue of his, or her, office and is not elected to that office. A committee Chairman may automatically be a member of all subcommittees by virtue of his, or her, office.
going into committee	– a meeting may split up into various subcommittees to discuss various points.
going into division	– members of a committee may physically split up to vote – as in the House of Commons.
in camera	– a meeting which is not open to the public. It may not be in the general interest that all matters at a meeting are discussed in public.
lie on the table	– a committee may decide not to act on an issue.
majority	– the larger number of members for or against a motion.
memorandum	– some committees may be presented with a document giving details of a matter under discussion. This may be useful if the matter is complex.
nem. con	– passing a resolution or motion with no members voting against; this may mean that some members have *abstained* – or refrained from voting.
next business	– some members may wish to delay a decision on a particular issue and request that the next item on the agenda be discussed.
no confidence	– members at a meeting may disagree with the conduct of the chairman and a vote of no confidence may be passed. If a majority agree the Chairman must step down and the deputy chairman, or one legally elected by the committee in the absence of a deputy, takes the chair.
point of order	– a question from a member of the committee that what is happening is illegal – taking a vote on a motion before it is seconded or before an amendment has been voted upon.
postponement	– delaying a meeting to a later date; bad weather may prevent members from attending and it is known that a quorum will not be present, for example.
resolution	– a decision taken by a majority of the members present at a meeting voting on a motion.

rider	–	an addition to a resolution or a motion. A rider must be. proposed, seconded and voted upon (and agreed) in the same way as a motion.
scrutineer	–	one who counts votes at a meeting.
standing orders	–	the rules by which an orgsniation conducts its meetings. The standing orders are usually part of *the constitution* of the body; the rules by which it is governed.
terms of reference	–	the framework under which a particular body or subcommittee works.
unanimously	–	a decision taken by all members present; all the members may vote for a motion – in which case it is adopted unanimously.

15.4 THE DUTIES OF A COMMITTEE SECRETARY

Before a meeting
1. Prepare the agenda for the meeting – usually with the chairman. Send copies to all members entitled to attend the meeting – usually with the notice reminding them that the meeting will take place. (It is advisable to run off spare copies of the agenda in case members attend the meeting without their copies.)
2. Duplicate copies of the minutes to send out with the notice and agenda of the meeting – if members are sent advanced copies of the minutes. If not, the minutes may be read out at the meeting or copies be given out before the meeting begins. Send copies of any supplementary documents with the minutes and agenda.
3. Prepare the Chairman's agenda; this may be left until the actual day of the meeting to ensure that it is as up to date as possible.
4. Ensure that a room is available for the meeting; it must be large enough to accommodate all the members.
5. If the meeting is a public one or the constitution of the body requires it, issue a notice of the meeting via the press – taking care to see that the required amount of notice is given.
6. Obtain all the necessary documents or statements from members who cannot attend the meeting but who have to make a report – or are known to have strong feelings on a particular matter.
7. Make sure that you have the following ready for the meeting.

writing paper, for yourself and members, and writing instruments;
spare copies of the agenda;
minutes of the last meeting – as well as previous minutes in case you have to refer to them at the meeting;
all the relevant documents required at the meeting – correspondence, reports and so on;
the attendance register, if one is used, or the attendance book;
any books or sources of reference – the constitution or standing orders, a register of members (if one is kept) and a diary (to help arranging the date of the next meeting, for example).

On the day of the meeting

1. Arrive early:

     make sure that the room is correctly set out with enough chairs;

     signpost the meeting, especially if members are unsure where it is to be held in a particular meeting place – a hotel for example (in which case inform the receptionist/commissionaire about the meeting – what the meeting is and where it is being held);

     see that members have supplies of 'essentials' such as writing paper, spare agendas, ash trays (if smoking is allowed); arrange a supply of water and drinking glasses; check the ventilation and heating;

     make a final check of your chief's file for any notes he may have left or for any items you both may have overlooked.

2. Note in your file (and your chief's) the relevant places where you will find items required during the meeting.

3. See that the Chairman is informed of last-minute matters and is given his/her agenda and relevant information.

During the meeting

1. Ensure that a record is made of those attending – see that all sign the attendance register if one is used.

2. Read the minutes, if required, and read any apologies if apologies are taken before the minutes are taken.

3. Assist the Chairman as each item on the agenda arises.

4. Record details of the discussion as it takes place. Note all propositions, the proposers and seconders and so on.

5. Take note of any particular points you, or your chief, are required to act upon by the Chairman or the committee.

After the meeting

1. Make sure that all relevant documents are accounted for before you leave.

2. Prepare a draft of the minutes for the attention of the Chairman – before reproducing them for the next meeting.

3. Deal with any matters you were asked to attend to at the meeting – such as writing letters, etc.

4. File all papers, and/or the minutes, for future reference.

5. Remind your chief, or the chairman, of any points for his/her attention.

Minutes

Minutes usually begin with a list of the members present at the meeting, in alphabetical order, with the officials listed first. Those given below are a typical example of those taken for a club – note the style of layout.

Fig 15.4 *page of minutes for the hockey club (linked to the agenda illustrated in Fig 15.3)*

THE WANDERERS HOCKEY CLUB

Meeting No 234

Minutes of the General Committee meeting of The Wanderers Hockey Club held in the Club House at 1930 hrs on Monday 12 October 19xx.

Present:	Miss M Anderson (Chairman) Miss D Rowley (Hon Sec) Mrs W Williams (Treasurer) Mrs S Hopkins Miss D Taylor Miss V Robertson Miss A Wearing
Apologies	An apology was received from Miss Y Yates.
Minutes	The minutes of the meeting held on 11 September, having been circulated to the members, were taken as read and approved and signed by the Chairman.
Matters arising	Mrs Williams reported that as a result of an advertisement in the local evening newspaper and the efforts of the playing members in particular, eight new players had joined the club. Mrs Hopkins and Miss Robertson presented a memorandum showing their proposals. After considerable discussion it was unanimously agreed to accept the proposals in full. A vote of thanks was proposed by Miss Anderson, seconded by Miss Rowley and agreed by acclamation.
Secretary's report	Miss Rowley reported that she had received a letter of complaint from one of the members, Mrs S Langham, about the state of the Club House. After a statement from the Chairman it was agreed to leave the matter on the table. The secretary was instructed to acknowledge receipt of the complaint.
Treasurer's report	Mrs Williams circulated a statement showing the current financial position. She pointed out that the rates were due to be paid and that there was an electricity bill outstanding.
Selection Committee report	In the absence of the Chairman of the selection committee, Miss Yates, the deputy Chairman reported. She said that one third team game had had to be called off because of lack of players but hoped that with the advent of new players this would be the last time this happened. Results so far confirmed earlier suggestions that the club would be in for a hard time - but it was encouraging to find that three of the new members were of very high quality.
Entertainments Committee report	Mrs Hopkins reported that the committee had arranged a very full programme of events and that a calendar would be published.
Any other business	The Chairman reported that following a conversation with the groundsman it appeared that he was not happy with the marking machine which was worn out. It was agreed to purchase a new one.
Next meeting	It was agreed to hold the next meeting on 14 November at 1930 hrs in the Club House.

Chairman

12 October 19xx

ACTIVITY

1. Study the minutes of the hockey club and answer the following.
   (a) Who is the Chairman? How would you address the chairman if you were a member of the committee?
   (b) What action was taken on the memorandum presented by Mrs Hopkins and Miss Robertson. What does 'accepted by acclamation' mean?
   (c) Can you suggest why the letter from Mrs Langham was allowed to 'lie on the table?'
   (d) Why do you think Mrs Williams presented a written financial statement?
   (e) What is the minimum number of copies of the minutes that the Secretary should produce?

QUESTIONS

1. Write brief notes on each of the following:

   Notice of meeting   Agenda
   Mintues   Annual general meeting

2. What are the duties of a Minutes Secretary before, during and after a meeting?

APPOINTMENTS

The smooth running of the world of commerce is assisted greatly by meetings between individuals and it is the job of the receptionist and secretary to see that such meetings are arranged with the minimum of fuss so that the principals can meet in an atmosphere free from worry about minor details.

16.1 THE DESK DIARY

Just as individuals keep a diary to remind themselves about important dates and events, those engaged in business must keep diaries to remind them of events both in the past and in the future. The desk diary is generally used to remind both employer and secretary/receptionist of important dates and events. In the desk diary will be kept details of appointments made in the future and probably some note as to what happened when past appointments were kept. These diaries are, in effect, a filing record kept in date order. An executive usually keeps a diary on or in his desk and in this he enters any information required to keep him advised of important matters as they arise. At the same time a secretary will keep a similar diary and check her diary against that of her employer – it helps if both keep the same kind of diary. Some secretaries find it useful to keep two diaries, one of dates, the other noting what has to be done to prepare for the appointments in the first. It is usual to have a page for each day and to note appointments in time order – leaving space for notes between appointments.

Making appointments
Before making any appointments an executive, secretary or receptionist should consult the diary to make sure that there is not a clash (more than one appointment at the same time), that the person involved is not being expected to carry too heavy a load and has time to recover from the last appointment, is not forced to rush one appointment to keep another and to make sure that the person involved is, in fact, available – he may be away from the firm at that time. All parties should check both their own

desk diaries and those of others before accepting appointments. It is advisable to enter appointments in pencil so that corrections can be made by erasing rather than crossing out. Appointments should be made in time order for each date with sufficient space left for the later insertion of notes. If the appointments are in different places, make sure that the person has time to travel from one to another. Always confirm appointments made by telephone in writing.

Keeping appointments

If the person at your firm is being met by visitors it is usual to advise reception that 'Mr/Mrs X from *ABE* Ltd is expected to see Mr/Mrs Y at Z hrs'. When the visitor arrives he/she should report to reception. Many visitors have *visiting cards*, a card on which is printed their name, the company they represent, their telephone number and their address (or that of their firm). This card may be presented to reception, to save having to give the information verbally, or be given to any person who may require a reminder of the information contained.

Very often the receptionist keeps a record of all visitors in a *reception register*. This provides a valuable record of all visitors and includes such information as the date, time, name of the visitor, his company, his rank or title, his address and/or telephone number and sometimes the name of the person visited.

Some receptionists keep a card index and note details of visitors on cards which can be used for future reference.

Greeting visitors

When a visitor arrives he should be greeted in a friendly manner and asked for his particulars before a check is made to confirm his appointment. Check to see if the person to be seen is available and if he is, arrange for the visitor to be taken to him – or be given directions. If the visitor has to wait for any reason offer him a seat, some refreshments and some reading material. Should a caller arrive who is not expected, the receptionist must find out the purpose of the visit in a friendly manner and check to see if the person required is available. If they are not, a substitute person, a deputy or a secretary, should be offered or, if necessary, an appointment should be offered at a later date. In some organisations it is a rule that no appointments will be offered unless advance notice is given – in which case the receptionist must be firm but polite. Unwanted callers must be handled with tact, politely but firmly. No visitor should be left with the impression that the person he wishes to see is on the premises but is refusing to see him, even if this is, in fact, the case. A secretary or receptionist must always take care to screen people from unwanted visitors and not give information as to their whereabouts at any particular time.

Reminder systems

Many receptionists and secretaries keep a card index to remind them of coming appointments. An index is made up of cards for every day of the month and each month is indicated by an index card. Every day a check is made on the card for that day to see what action must be taken to prepare for the following day – or, in some cases, for events some time in the future.

Year planners are sometimes used for planning appointments. They are often made of plastic and contain space for every day of the year. Appointments and events are entered so that they can be seen at a glance. Sometimes colour codes are used to indicate particular important dates/ events. The events for a year can be recorded on one board in this way. *A perpetual year planner* enables plans to be made on a rolling basis – the information can be added indefinitely and the planner does not have to be renewed at the end of the calendar year.

A microcomputer can be programmed to act as a year planner. Details of names, addresses, telephone numbers and dates of appointments are fed into the machine, which can be then used as a one-, two- or three-year diary, address book and appointments itinerary. Reminders of future appointments in time/day/week/month order are indicated either on the visual display unit or as a printed note. The same program can be used to address labels for business letters and print reminders to staff. As fresh details are available – new names, addresses and appointments, etc. – they are fed into the program, which shows if appointments planned overlap any already made or are likely to cause difficulties – because there is insufficient time between them, for example. A microcomputer can be used to print appointments cards – see the next paragraph. As well as reminding of future events the program can also be used as a reminder of past appointments – and any decisions reached.

Appointments card

Many secretaries type a list of the appointments for the coming day on a single sheet and leave it on the executive's desk so that he/she can see at a glance who has to be seen and at what time. A special code against the appointment may be used to signify that papers are necessary for that appointment. If the appointments are away from your firm it is usual to prepare an appointments itinerary to assist the person who has to keep them.

Appointments itinerary

An appointments itinerary is a list of times, people and addresses of firms which have to be kept during a day. It is usual to type an appointments itinerary on one single sheet or card which can be kept in an inside pocket – A6 paper is the most convenient size (see Figure 16.1)

16.2 TRAVEL ITINERARY

If a person has to travel to several destinations over a period of days it is usual to prepare a travel itinerary which shows where that person will be staying and given some idea of the route to be taken or the method of

Fig 16.1 *an appointments itinerary*

ITINERARY

Mr Mark Rogers

23 July

0900   Mrs Wendy Jenkins, Whitehead Bros, High Street.

1045   Mr Clive Hammonds, Charles Bolton Ltd, Trinity Road.

1230   Mr Arthur Hawkins, TI Group Services Ltd, Mount Hotel,
        Regent Road.

1430   Miss Fay Robins, Bacol Industries Ltd, Industrial
        Estate.

1600   Mr Peter Newman, Galena Ltd, Cleveland Street.

transport to be used – own car, train or by air. Separate daily itineraries
will be prepared for each day.

Preparing itineraries

When preparing itineraries always use paper of suitable size on which to
type them – daily itineraries should be typed on A6 paper while travel
itineraries should be kept to A4 paper. Make a note of special instructions
to assist the person keeping the appointments – if necessary give travel
directions after using an *A to Z* or a timetable. If the transport is by train
or by air, check to see that up-to-date timetables are used and verify the
times with a travel agent or the rail/air company. Note if a town has more
than one railway station – or if an airport is some way away from the town
at which accommodation has been arranged – and note accordingly. Give
full details of all reservations made – hotels, sleeping accommodation on
trains, buffet facilities, connections and taxis reserved. List relevant
telephone numbers. Always make sure that the person has time to make
connections and to get from one place to another so that they are not
rushed.

A microcomputer can be used as an added tool in the preparation of a
travel itinerary. *Route planners* are available as programs and can suggest
the most efficient route – given your address and destinations while *hotel
and restaurant finders* can assist in the planning of accommodation.
Information provided by *Prestel, Ceefax* and *Oracle* (see Section 23.5) can
further assist the production of travel itineraries.

Failure to keep appointments

If a person fails to keep an appointment for any reason always write and
apologise for any inconvenience caused. If it is known in advance that an
appointment cannot be made for any reason contact the person with

whom the appointment has been made as soon as possible, offer apologies and try to arrange another suitable date and time. It may be possible to offer a substitute person if the original is unable to keep an appointment.

QUESTIONS

1. How might a microcomputer be used for the following?

   In keeping appointments.
   In planning itineraries for a day.
   In planning itineraries over a number of days in several countries.

2. Write a paragraph on each of the following.

   The desk diary   Making appointments
   Itineraries   Reminder systems

OFFICE STATIONERY

Each department or section of any large organisation uses a wide range of stationery and all office workers should know the range and uses of available supplies and be able to distinguish between the various grades used.

17.1 PAPER

Most office work involves the use of paper and there are many sizes and grades available. Sizes and grades should be chosen to match the work being undertaken.

Paper sizes

Paper sizes are quoted either in metric units or imperial units.

Metric sizes are based on those recommended by the International Organisation for Standardisation (ISO) and of the three designations, A, B and C it is the A and C sizes which are most commonly used in offices. International Paper Sizes (IPS) are based on metric dimensions. A sizes are used for office paper, B sizes are used for larger sheets (as might be used for poster work) while C sizes are used for envelopes. The largest A size (A0) is roughly one square metre (841 x 1189 mm.) and each succeeding number, A1, A2, A3, A4, A5, A6 and A7, is half the previous size so that A1 is exactly half A0 – 594 x 841 mm. When quoting paper sizes the first measurement mentioned is the width of the paper.

Designation	Size (mm.)
A0	841 x 1189
A1	594 x 841
A2	420 x 594
A3	297 x 420
A4	210 x 297
A5	148 x 210
A6	105 x 148
A7	74 x 105

Because of the demand for a paper size between A4 and A5 (basically for letter-writing) a size called $\frac{2}{3}$A4 is now commonly used and it measures 210 x 198 mm.

A7 is the smallest size normally used in offices although the smallest size available is A10 (26 × 37 mm.).

Imperial paper sizes are no longer commonly used but because most computers use a typeface which prints ten letters to every inch (pica size) there is a continuing demand for them.

Designation	Size (mm.)	Size (inches)	
Brief	330 × 410	13 × 16	
Draft	254 × 410	10 × 16	
Foolscap	205 × 330	8 × 13	Also known as fcp
Quarto	205 × 254	8 × 10	Also known as 4to
Sixmo	205 × 165	8 × $6\frac{1}{2}$	Also known as 6mo
Octavo	127 × 205	5 × 8	Also known as 8vo
Memo	205 × 127	8 × 5	Octavo 'the other way round'

Paper is usually supplied in *quires* (24 sheets) or *reams* (480 sheets) although typewriting paper is supplied in reams of 500 sheets.

17.2 ENVELOPE SIZES

Metric envelopes, the C range, are designed to be used with A-size paper.

The most commonly used C-size envelopes

Designation	Size (mm.)	Uses
C3	324 × 458	Takes A3 paper flat
C4	229 × 324	Takes A4 paper flat
C5	162 × 229	Takes A5 paper flat or A4 paper folded once
C6	114 × 162	Takes A6 paper flat or A5 paper folded once or A4 folded twice
C5/6 (DL)	110 × 220	Takes A4 paper folded twice into three or A 5 folded once or $\frac{2}{3}$A4 folded once

The most commonly used British Standard envelope sizes

Designation	Size (mm.)	Uses
B4	250 × 353	Legal documents, company reports and accounts, calendars, examination papers
B5	176 × 250	Reply envelopes, catalogues, brochures, half foolscap material
B6	125 × 176	General commercial correspondence, computer punch cards, dividend warrants, greetings cards

Care must be taken to ensure that metric sizes of paper are used with metric sizes of envelopes and that metric and imperial paper and envelopes are not mixed.

Post Office preferred sizes (POP) sizes

To fall within the Post Office range envelopes should not be smaller than 90 × 140 mm. ($3\frac{1}{2}$ × $5\frac{1}{2}$ inches) or larger than 120 × 235 mm. ($4\frac{3}{4}$ × $9\frac{1}{4}$ inches). The ISO C5/6 and C6 envelope sizes fall within this range.

Weights of paper

Typewriting paper is usually referred to as bond, bank or airmail; each name suggests a weight of paper – the heavier the paper the better the quality as a rule. The name, or weight, given to paper does not, however, indicate what it is made from or the finish given to the paper – an absorbent one which will take and absorb ink or one which has a slightly sized, or glazed, surface. Manufacturers classify paper by descriptive titles – writing paper, tracing paper, blotting paper, carbon paper, duplicating paper, etc.

International sizes of paper are quoted in grams per square metre (g/m^2).

Bond paper is approximately 70 g/m^2 and is used for letter heads and top copies. A good-quality paper, intended to create a good impression, might be 110 g/m^2.

Bank paper is approximately 40 to 45 g/m^2 and is used for taking carbon copies.

Airmail paper is approximately 25 to 30 g/m^2.

Imperial sizes of paper are often quoted in terms of so many pounds weight per ream (480 or 500 sheets). Good-quality paper, used for top copies and letter heads, might weigh between 10 and 18 lb, (about the same weight as bond paper), bank paper might weigh between 7 and 10 lb, and airmail paper would be about 5 lb.

Typing paper and general writing paper is not very absorbent and has a slightly sized, or glazed, surface.

Duplicating paper is fairly absorbent so that ink applied to it dries quickly. An average grade of duplicating paper would be in the 60 to 70 g/m^2 range.

Carbon papers are also sold according to weight and as a rule the heavier the weight the more times the paper may be used. Very light, or thin, carbon paper is intended to be used once and then thrown away.

Envelopes are sold in grades according to the weight of paper used in their manufacture and the 1SO grades are normally used when describing weights. The strength of envelopes is important and a measure of the strength is called its *burst* – the pressure the material will withstand before it bursts. The standard measure is pounds per square inch (psi). The *opacity* – how much can be seen through – of envelopes is measured as a percentage.

Envelopes – general

Envelopes are divided, as a rule, into three classes.

Those which match notepaper or writing/typewriting paper.

Those used for commercial purposes – usually buff in colour.

Those used for packaging.

When describing writing envelope sizes the second dimension is the one which has the flap on it – for example, an envelope 80 × 150 mm. would have the flap on the 150 mm. side.

Banker envelopes are those with the opening and flap on the longer side. The deeper the cut, or throat, of an envelope the less it costs. A prestige envelope will have a shallow throat – and cost much more (see Figure 17.1)

Fig 17.1 *a high-cut envelope*

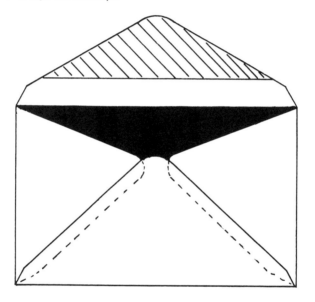

Pocket envelopes are those with the opening and flap on the shortest dimension and are normally used for commercial purposes. The flaps are of two basic shapes – square and round (see Figure 17.2).

Window envelopes are used to save time; the correspondence is folded in such a way that the inside name and address can be seen through the window (see Figure 17.3).

Gusset envelopes are those used for sending bulky enclosures and may be fastened by sealing, with a tuck-in pocket, with a metal fastener or a tension fastener (see Figure 17.4).

Fig 17.2 *a square-flap pocket envelope*

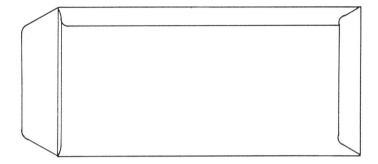

Fig 17.3 *window envelope with flap at the top*

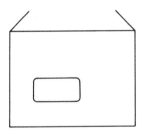

Fig 17.4 *a gusset envelope*

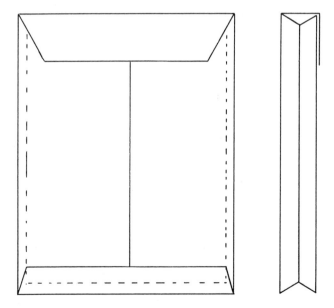

See also Figures 17.5 to 17.7 for the following styles of envelope: tuck-in style, metal fastener, and tension fastener.

Fig 17.5   *tuck-in style envelope, open and closed*

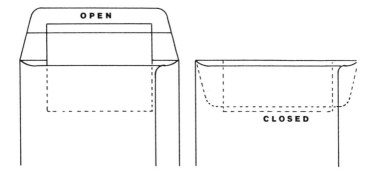

Fig 17.6   *envelope with metal fastener, open and closed*

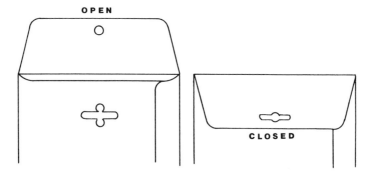

Fig 17.7   *envelope with tension fastener, open and closed*

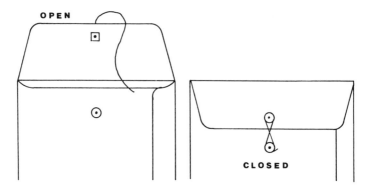

17.3 CARBON PAPER

Carbon paper is used for a number of purposes in the office – for taking copies of typed or handwritten documents or for producing spirit duplicating masters. This section is concerned only with the first use – Section 18 on duplicating deals with the latter.

Carbon paper is paper which has been coated with a mixture of waxes, pigments and oils. Carbon paper made in this way tends to smudge very easily, creases readily and is not stable in as much as the dye is not completely fast and comes off easily – particularly in warm weather. It must be kept flat, in a box or container of some kind and away from heat when not in use. If sheets of carbon paper are left in direct sunlight they will curl up as the waxes and dyes dry out. Carbon papers come in a range of colours – the most usual being blue or black.

Carbon films are rapidly taking the place of carbon papers and are not papers at all but, as their name suggests, are sheets of film coated with a sponge-like coating. This coating only releases ink under pressure – the point of a sharp instrument or the impact of the keys on a typewriter. When a typewriter key strikes the film it releases ink into the copying paper. Capillary action then allows ink to flow to the point of impact from surrounding parts of the copying film sheet – replacing the used area so that the film sheet is used to the maximum. These films are very flexible and have considerable advantages over the older carbon sheets which, apart from the disadvantages described above, do not have the advantage of the semi-fluid surface so that they are rapidly exhausted. The most modern films, such as those produced by Columbia International, have an anti-static backing to prevent sticking or clinging. They come in a range of colours.

The heavier the weight of films and papers, as a rule, the more ink they contain. While a heavier weight of film will last longer than a lighter one it is not possible to take as many copies at a time – because of the extra thickness.

Very thin carbon paper is often manufactured to be used once and then thrown away. It is sometimes called *'one-time' carbon paper* for this reason.

Sizes

Carbon papers and films are sold in several sizes and relate to both the metric and imperial measurements.

NCR or No-Carbon-Required paper is paper which is treated on one side, the 'back' or the side which is not to be written on, with a substance which produces a carbon-like image on a second or subsequent sheets when typed or written upon. NCR paper saves time in as much as it is often sold in packs and time is saved inserting carbon sheets in order to make copies. It has two possible disadvantages: the image tends to 'spread' when the paper becomes damp and care must be taken to ensure that only the required copies are taken. Any impact will go through several sheets and not just the one required.

Quantities

Papers and envelopes are usually sold in reams of 500 sheets as opposed to the normal 480-sheet ream of 20 quires. Carbon paper is often sold in packs of 50, 100 or 200 sheets. Sometimes envelopes are sold in dozens (units of 12) although a business tends to buy them by the box of 500.

Watermarks

A watermark is a mark made in some papers by manufacturers to distinguish their papers from those of other manufacturers. The marks are invisible when the papers are being used normally but can be seen if a sheet is held up to the light.

Colours

Paper is available in a range of colours and care should be taken to match writing/typewriting paper and envelopes if the correspondence is other than of a routine nature (when buff envelopes may be used for cheapness). Some papers are made using a quantity of *recycled paper* and while they are cheaper than papers produced without this material they are not as white. Paper made from recycled paper should be used with envelopes made from the same material. Carbon copies are often taken on papers of various colours – sometimes a particular colour is 'earmarked' for a particular person so that all copies for that person can easily be sorted.

QUESTIONS

1. Which envelopes should be used with the following paper sizes?

   $\frac{2}{3}$ A4   A4 flat
   A4 folded into 3   A5 folded into 2
   Foolscap   Quarto

2. What weight of paper is used for the following?

   Airmail letters
   Taking carbon copies
   Producing high-quality reports
   Normal business correspondence

3. What are the differences between carbon papers, carbon films and no carbon required papers. What are the advantages and disadvantages of each?

PROJECT

Produce a pack containing all the available sizes and weights of paper, carbon paper/film and envelopes – metric, imperial as well as poster sizes of paper. Label each item and produce a report on the suitability of the materials in your pack for particular tasks.

COPYING AND DUPLICATING

18.1 COPYING

The term 'copying' is probably best described as a process which results in an exact copy being taken of an original either for the purposes of keeping a record - as in the case of letters, orders, invoices, statements and plans/diagrams, etc. - or for the purposes of information - sending material to a number of persons either for comment, information - or their records.

Carbon copies

The most simple and economical method of taking an exact copy of an original is to take a carbon copy at the same time as the top copy is made. Carbon copies can be made using carbon paper or film or NCR paper (no-carbon-required paper).

As previously indicated, in Section 17.3 on Office Stationery, carbon paper is not the same as carbon film although it may be used for the same basic tasks. To obtain a carbon copy:

place a sheet of suitable paper, usually bank paper, flat on the desk;
place a sheet of carbon paper, or film, on top of this - face towards the sheet on the desk so that the back of the paper is facing towards you;
place the top copy on top of the back of the carbon sheet - the top copy is usually a good-quality paper.

Should more than one carbon copy be required, build up a sandwich of alternate layers of sheets of paper and carbon sheets. The greater the number of copies required the thinner the sheets of paper should be - and the carbon paper should be of a light grade. If a single copy is required then a better-quality carbon sheet may be used - and for economy use a heavy grade of carbon film. If the *copy is of a handwritten document,* make sure that the sandwich is placed on a hard, flat surface and that the writing instrument has a sharp, clear point; a ballpoint pen will produce good results while a felt-tip pen may not produce a carbon image at all.

Carbon copies made using a typewriter are taken in much the same way as handwritten carbon copies but care should be taken to observe the following:

make sure that the sandwich is put into the machine correctly - when typing the back of the carbon paper should be facing the typist;
use a machine with a hard platen - it will produce better copies than a machine with a soft platen;
use grades of carbon paper and plain sheets appropriate to the number of copies required;
use a sharp, clear typeface: a broad flat face will produce poor copies;
when erasing, make sure that corrections are made to the copies as well as the top copy - see Sections 8.1 and 8.2 on typewriters;
tap the keys sharply with an even pressure.

The number of copies it is possible to take at any one time will depend on some, or all, of the following factors:

the grade of carbon paper/film used and how much it has been previously used; the thickness of the paper used for the copies;
the surface on which the material was placed at the time the copies were being made;
the point of the writing instrument or the style of the typeface;
the pressure used while writing or typing - when using a manual machine the keys must be struck harder than when making just one copy while when using an electric machine it may be possible to alter the pressure with which the keys strike the page. (Remember that a silk ribbon will produce better carbon copies than a cotton ribbon, because it is thinner, and that a carbon film ribbon, as used in electric machines, will produce an even better image.)
As a general rule seven or eight copies is about the average - after that the copies are often unreadable.

No-carbon-required paper, as the name implies, is a method of taking carbon-like copies without carbon paper/film. The back of the top, or front of the copy, sheets are treated so that when pressure is applied a carbon-like image is formed on the copy sheets. When taking copies using NCR paper observe the same basic principles as for taking ordinary carbon copies - but if using *packs of documents* take care to place a hard surface between copies being taken and the rest of the pack. If this is not done the image may be imposed through several sheets in the pack.

Once-used carbon paper is thin carbon paper used once and then thrown away. It is usual to type advice notes, delivery notes, copy invoices and invoices at the same time using pre-printed packs of the various documents (see Section 9 on the purchase and sale of goods). When using packs of this nature care must be taken when erasing because the packs are usually fastened at the top. If corrections have to be made the typist must wind the pack as though out of the machine in order to make the correction.

18.2 OFFICE COPIERS

Should copies of an original document be required and it is not possible to take a carbon copy – a copy may be required of a document sent to a firm or the original document may not lend itself to being copied using carbon paper (it may be a technical diagram or a picture/photograph, for example) – other means must be used. There is a range of processes available and the method selected will depend on such factors as:

the number of copies required;
the size of the original;
the nature of the original – it may be black-and-white or colour;
the intended use of the copy, for filing (when it may be reduced) or for information;
the processes available in the firm.

18.3 ELECTROPHOTOGRAPHIC (ELECTROSTATIC) PROCESSES (PHOTOCOPYING)

There are two electrophotographic, or electrostatic for short, processes in common use. The processes use substances known as photoconductors which insulate (do not conduct an electrical charge) in the dark and conduct in the light. The processes used are known as the direct process and the indirect process.

The direct process uses paper which has been specially treated with a photoconductive coating (usually zinc oxide). In the copier this paper is given an electrostatic charge and is then exposed to a light source. Where light reaches the paper the charge disappears, but where it is not exposed, corresponding to the text of the original being copied, the charge remains. After exposure an invisible charged image of the original is retained on the copy paper. This invisible charge attracts extremely fine counter-charged (usually black) particles forming part of either a powder developer or a liquid developer in which the particles are dispersed. Liquid developers are sometimes called *toners* and manufacturers speak of *liquid tone transfer* copiers. After passing through the developer the image of the original appears on the copy paper – rather like iron particles being attracted by a magnet – and this image is fixed to the paper by heat to provide a permanent copy of the original.

The indirect process uses a system in which the function of the photoconductive coating of the copying paper is taken over by a coating in the unit. A charged image formed on this is made visible with coloured particles which are transferred to a sheet of ordinary paper (hence the description 'indirect'). This ordinary sheet is made into a permanent copy by heating. Such copiers are also known as *plain-paper copiers*.

The direct process is sometimes called the *Electrofax process* and the indirect process is sometimes called the *Xerographic process*, manufacturers talk of *xerography*. The direct process is sometimes known as a *wet process* if a liquid toner is used - while a reference to a *dry process* can be a reference to the direct process using a powder developer or to the plain paper, indirect process. To the casual observer there is little difference between the various machines offered and the terms 'electrostatic' or 'xerographic' are very similar.

Operation of photo copiers (direct and indirect)
The exact mode of operation of all the machines currently available varies slightly from machine to machine and manufacturer to manufacturer - the capabilities of each machine vary and each office must select the machine or machines best suited to its particular situation or situations. The basic operation is to place the material to be copied face down on the top of the machine - single sheets or a page from a book or magazine. The machine is switched on and the control indicating the number of copies required is pressed. The copy or copies emerge from the machine within seconds.

Some machines will produce copies on both sides of the sheet; others will produce copies on one side only. Some machines will take a range of paper sizes; others will take one size only. More sophisticated machines can reduce the size of originals or can collate up to fifty different documents which have been copied. Several models currently available take rolls of paper of varying widths and automatically cut off the length

Fig 18.1   *dry and liquid toner processes*

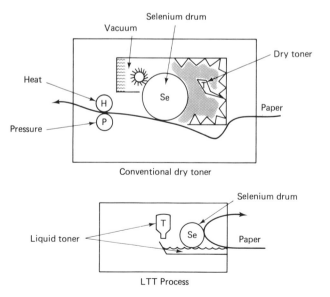

Conventional dry toner

LTT Process

of the material being copied. Some machines produce copies which are slightly damp; others produce perfectly dry copies, and while the direct process produces copies which are white the indirect process can be used to produce copies on any colour of paper - although the black image may not contrast so well with all colours of paper.

Before using a liquid tone transfer machine each day the operator should check the quantity of toner and developer and top up as required as well as check to see that the machine has sufficient paper. The *paper trays, or cassettes* as they are sometimes called, should be replenished as required.

There is a range of plain-paper copiers available to meet the various needs of business organisations and, depending on the machine purchased, the following facilities are available:

single sheets or copies produced from a roll of A3- or A4-sized paper (a single roll will give 700 A4, 400 B4 or 350 A3 copies);
automatic or manual feed;
copies on one side or both sides of the sheet;
copies from letters, memos, charts, printouts, invoices, contracts, ledger sheets, technical diagrams, three-dimensional objects and coloured originals;
copies on white or coloured paper and on translucent material - as in the production of overhead projector film;
reduction of original material.

The speeds at which copies are produced depend on the size of the original - smaller documents are produced quicker than large ones, but the speeds are the same as those for LTT (liquid tone transfer) machines.

Before using a plain-paper copier each day the operator should check the quantity of toner in the machines and then check to see that the paper tray has sufficient paper of the size required for the first copying to be undertaken.

No matter what machine is purchased, all photocopiers are very quick and reliable - needing the minimum of servicing. They are extremely simple to operate and can be used for a wide range of applications - including the production of offset litho plates. Model selection will depend on a range of factors which may include:

the amount of copying to be done each day/month;
the speed at which copies are required;
the size of documents to be copied;
the nature of the material to be copied;
the colour of paper to be used for copying and its nature - material may be required on translucent material such as used in overhead projectors;
the number of copies a machine can be programmed to produce at any one time;
copying from one original or several;

collation of documents by hand or by machine;
copies on one side of the page or both;
copies the same size or reduced;
copies taken on offset litho plates.

18.4 HEAT PROCESSES

Firms not requiring the volume of copying which the photo copiers are capable of producing may use a heat process (sometimes called *Thermography*). There are several kinds of heat-processing machines available.

Heat transfer (Thermographic)
In this process a copy paper which is sensitive to heat is used. The document to be copied must have a carbon base for its image - carbon in the ink or pencil drawings. Infra-red rays cause heat to darken the image to produce a direct positive form on the copy paper. The system is quick, cheap and simple to operate. The disadvantage of the system is the fact that it will not reproduce all colours and the fact that copies tend to fade and may not be very clear. Apart from the ease of use the other advantages of the system are that it:

produces masters for spirit duplicating;
produces thermal stencils for ink duplicating;
produces transparencies for overhead projectors;
produces dry copies;
can be used to apply plastic reinforcing laminate film to documents passed through the machine.

18.5 DUAL-SPECTRUM

The dual-spectrum process produces a paper negative first. The original and the sensitised side of special paper are exposed to a light source. As the light passes through the original the darkened areas stop light reaching the sensitised paper - while those areas of the original which are blank allow light through. In this way a negative is produced. The negative is then used with other sensitised paper and passed through the machine to produce a finished copy which is, in many ways, similar to a photograph. The process takes time because the negative has to be produced before the final copy but the method has the advantage that any colours can be copied. Copies are dry as they leave the machine.

18.6 TRANSFER PROCESSES

Typical of the transfer processes is the *diffusion transfer* process which is used by a wide range of low-cost machines. The diffusion transfer process is similar to the dual-spectrum process except that the final copies are slightly damp as they leave the machine. As in the dual-spectrum process, the original is exposed to a light source with a piece of light-sensitive paper. The exposed light-sensitive paper, together with a sheet of special paper, is then passed through a chemical solution to produce a positive image. The method is used for making small offset litho plates and for taking single copies but, like the dual-spectrum and thermographic processes, is usually limited to producing copies up to A4 in size.

The main disadvantage of the diffusion process, apart from the dampness of the copies and the time taken, is the cost per copy compared to the electrostatic copies. The main advantage is the low cost of the original equipment.

18.7 DIAZO (DYELINE)

Commercially marketed for the first time in the 1920s the diazo, or dyeline, process, as it is sometimes called, was one of the first methods used for copying originals. It is a process which still has wide applications – particularly in the copying of original drawings made on draughtsmans' paper.

Modern diazo copiers use an acetone film sheet which is coated with a writing/drawing surface (white) on one side and a diazo salt and coupler (colouring media) coating on the other. Any translucent material (one which the light can pass through) can be copied. The material to be copied is fed into the copier and comes into direct contact with the sensitised material. Both are exposed to an ultra-violet light source (a mercury vapour lamp). The darkened areas on the original prevent the light from reaching the sensitised film, which is then developed in an ammonia solution while the original is separated from it and emerges from the front of the copier. The copy, which emerges from the front of manual machines or from the rear of some automatic machines, appears with a sepia-coloured image on a white background or as black-on-white – depending on the coupler used in the preparation of the sensitised paper.

The advantages of the system are:

copies are as good as originals and can be written or drawn on;
originals can be added to or taken away from (by masking) before and after copies have been taken;
machines are simple and easy to use (the system has been developed over a long period of time and is very reliable);
the cost per copy is reasonable;
copies of large originals can be taken – up to A0 width;
attachments are available to fold large copies as they are produced for ease of handling;
machines are available to take copies of a large size range.

The disadvantages of the system are:

large machines require ducting to take away the ammonia fumes produced in the developing process;

copies can only be taken of one-sided translucent originals;

the originals must be in black or blue ink or pencil (although a limited range of other colours will copy the copies are not of an acceptable quality);

copies will darken if exposed to ultra violet light (particularly direct sunlight) and should, by choice, be kept in the dark or at the least in shade;

the speed of operation is not as high as more modern processes.

Machines are available in a wide range of sizes for all applications and are available as both manual and automatic options. While large machines must be installed in such a way as to ensure that the fumes are ducted to outside the building, small copiers (some of which can be desk- or wall-mounted) recycle the ammonia and do not require ducting. The latest automatic machines are fitted with rolls of paper of a range of widths so that the machine can select the width appropriate to the material being copied – automatic cutters ensure the correct length of each copy. Folders can be attached to modern machines to automatically fold copies to a size which is easy to handle. Copies which are to be folded and unfolded a great deal can be made on sensitised material containing fabric such as muslin or cotton to prevent damage. Large machines will copy at the rate of 16 feet per minute; small copiers operate at 8 feet per minute. Copies are usually produced dry and ready for use as they emerge from the machine – no matter what its size. The main applications of diazo copiers are in drawing offices although the process can be used to copy any black or blue translucent original material.

ACTIVITY

It is impossible to describe all the machines available here – in any case manufacturers are constantly developing existing models and bringing out new ones. Visit office equipment exhibitions of stockists and keep a file on the machines currently available. Keep a list of the names of the machines you collect and, more important, a record of the process each uses, electrostatic, heat transfer, diazo, etc. Most advertising literature contains details of the uses (applications) of machines, maximum and minimum sizes of documents, speed of operation and cost. Tabulate these facts so that you can compare the advantages and disadvantages of each machine – take care not to confuse manufacturer's claims with actual performance.

18.8 POINTS TO BEAR IN MIND WHEN CHOOSING AN OFFICE COPIER

1. What is the average cost per copy?
2. What is the cost of the equipment – and how much does it cost to operate?

(Some machines are cheap to buy, cheap to run but the materials required to produce individual copies are high compared with other machines which are, by comparison, expensive to buy, cheap to run but produce individual copies at very low cost. Sometimes the high initial cost can be more than met by the low cost per copy – while sometimes the high cost per copy is more than offset by the low initial purchase price.)

3. How quickly will the machine produce copies?
4. Will the machine make one copy at a time – or can it be set to produce several?
5. Will it copy black-and-white originals only or will it reproduce from a range of colours?
6. Will it copy double-sided documents?
7. Will it copy any original or only translucent originals?
8. Will the machine produce a range of sizes of documents – or only one?
9. Will the machine collate?
10. Will the machine feed automatically?
11. How long does the machine need to warm up – how long must it be switched on before it is used?
12. Can the machine be used for purposes other than copying – such as laminating?
13. Are the copies wet or dry?
14. How much space will the machine take up?
15. What kind of attention does the machine require – and how efficient is the after-sales service?
16. Can the machine be rented or hired?
17. How easy is the machine to operate – does the operator need any special training?

Some of the above points may apply to all situations – some will be irrelevant in many situations. When deciding which copier to choose, each case must be taken on its own and a list of requirements should be drawn up containing such things as the number of copies required, how often they are required, the kind of copies required, etc. Machines should be chosen which most exactly match the requirements listed.

18.9 DUPLICATING PROCESSES

In each of the three processes which follow – spirit, ink and offset – a master must first be produced and from it many copies may be taken. The chosen method will depend on a number of factors: the number of copies required, the number of colours required, the speed at which copies are produced and the cost per copy.

18.10 **SPIRIT DUPLICATING**

In this process a spirit, based on alcohol, is used to wash small amounts of dye from a prepared master. The master sheet is a specially china-clay-coated sheet of paper. The front side, which is written or typed on, has a matt finish, while the reverse side, which carries the carbon dye impression, is white and shiny. The process is known by such names as Banda, Fordigraph and Hecto carbon – but its true name is spirit duplicating – the other names are commercial ones.

Fig 18.2 *Banda 100 HAF spirit duplicating machine*

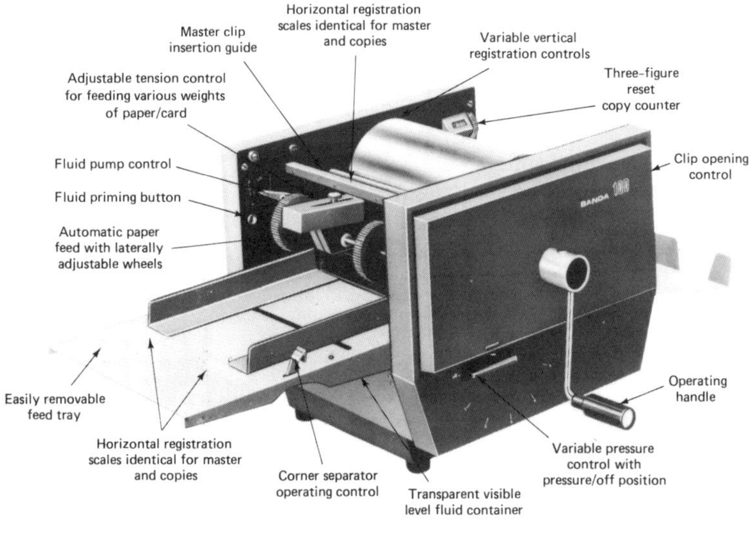

To prepare a spirit master
1. Place a sheet of spirit carbon paper flat on a desk, carbon side up.
2. Place a master sheet on top of the carbon sheet, shiny side towards the carbon.
3. Using a suitable instrument and a hard, flat surface write on the back of the master sheet. A ballpoint pen is an ideal instrument although a pencil will produce good results. If the material is being typed use a machine with a hard platen and a sharp, clear typeface. Tap the keys sharply to ensure that a good carbon impression is left on the reverse of the master sheet. The typewriter may be used with the ribbon engaged or with the machine on stencil. If the latter, take care when typing the 'o' key in particular because it is easy to cut a hole in the master. Use a good backing sheet if the platen is in poor condition.

When writing, drawing or typing to produce a master take care to leave a margin all round the sheet.

4. If an error is made the correction must be made on *the reverse* side of the master sheet. This may be done in several ways:

the image may be carefully scraped off with a sharp knife or a knife designed for the purpose;
a special eraser, made of putty rubber, may be used;
special correcting fluid may be painted over the error;
a fresh piece of master sheet may be stuck over the error.

Once the error has been removed/covered, fresh carbon must be used to make the required correction.

The carbon used for making spirit masters is made in several colours – Columbia International offer a range of five while Ozalid offer a range of seven – and each master may be made up using a range of colours – the master sheet being placed over a different coloured carbon each time a colour change is required. Some suppliers, like Columbia, supply packs consisting of a carbon sheet joined to a master sheet ready for production while rolls are available for use on continuous stationery machines such as typewriters or teleprinters.

Masters may also be produced using thermal office copiers or purchased ready-made for a variety of purposes. In addition to being produced by drawing, writing or typing they may be produced direct from computer printouts, electric billing machines and opaque or translucent originals.

Running off spirit masters

Once a master has been produced a spirit duplicating machine must be used to run off copies. The machines available range from simple machines to quite complex models. In principle each machine consists of a steel roller to which the master is fastened, a supply of spirit which dampens a felt pad and a feed roller. Machines may be electric or manual and most have a counter to show the number of copies run off.

1. Prime the felt pad either by pouring a quantity of spirit over it or by pumping the control lever several times. (Modern electric models have a push-button operation to do this.) Test the felt pad by hand-feeding a sheet of paper through the machine with the pressure control on 1. The sheet should be evenly dampened when the machine is ready for use.
2. Fasten the master sheet to the metal drum, carbon side up. This is done by opening the master clip on the machine. When using a manual machine; with the handle in the neutral position turn it to the left until the clip opens. When using some electric machines there is a key which has to be pressed to open the clip. Close the clip to fasten the master to the roller.
3. With the pressure control on 1 (the lightest pressure setting) hand-feed a sheet through the machine and check alignment and so on – making any adjustments required to top and bottom margins.

4. Load the feed tray with a sufficient supply of paper of a suitable size and quality - watermark upwards. The paper should be fairly absorbent, to take spirit, but of sufficient quality to dry quickly. Paper with a smooth surface is used.
5. Release the knob to lower the corner separators, having made sure that the paper is tight up to the corners of the separators.
6. Set the counter to 000 and run off the copies required. Some machines will automatically switch themselves off when the number is reached while with others the operator has to stop the machine manually.

The exact operation of each machine will depend on the model being used and the operator should study the manual supplied - or, better still, ask the supplier to demonstrate.

As the drum holding the master revolves, the master is moistened by the pad and a small quantity of dye is washed off the master on to the sheets as they are pressed against it. As the image fades more pressure must be imposed by altering the pressure control.

Once the required number of copies has been run off, the pressure control should be returned to 0 and the master removed from the machine by reversing the process used for fastening it in. The master can be stored for future use. Care must be taken to ensure that the master is not creased or subjected to more spirit than is required. The drum of the machine must be kept perfectly clean - otherwise copies will be spoilt, and worse still, masters may be damaged.

When cleaning electric machines make sure that the plug us pulled out first - do not simply switch the machine off. Remember that duplicating spirit is highly inflammable and must be stored away from heat and a naked light should never be placed near an open can. Use a well-ventilated room for running off spirit copies.

The advantages of the system are:

1. Comparatively quick and easy to operate. The range of machines available enables firms to chose machines suitable for their needs. The machines are cheap to run.
2. It can produce copies of a range of material, typed, handwritten, drawings, etc., in a range of colours.
3. It can produce copies on a range of material from lightweight paper to card - depending on the machine being used.
4. The initial cost of the equipment is low. The choice of machines available shows a wide range of price from the cheap, simple, hand-operated machines to more expensive, sophisticated electric machines.
5. A range of ready-made stencils is available.
6. A range of material can be run off - drawings, sales orders, purchase orders, works layouts, parts lists, dispatch documents, invoices, cards of various kinds (punched, needle-sorting, etc.), computer printouts, etc.
7. The master can be filed like any other piece of paper and copies taken later.

The disadvantages of the system are:

1. The quality of copy varies - as the master wears the quality fades.
2. A limited number of copies can be taken from each master - depending on the experience of the user the number might be as high as 250 or as low as 50.
3. Copies fade after a period of time - more quickly if exposed to sunlight than if kept in dark conditions.
4. The quality of work looks like carbon copy and is not as good as other methods such as ink duplicating or offset work.

Modern spirit duplicating machines offer a wide range of facilities including automatic numbering (a unit is available to add a line of up to 32 preset numbers on to the duplicated material), foot-pedal operation by a seated operator, automatic spacing and push-button selection of single, multiple or random lines. The sizes of copy (which is usually A4 or foolscap maximum on manual machines) ranges from 25 × 100 mm. to 430 × 343 mm. on some electric machines.

18.11 INK DUPLICATING

The process involves producing a master and using a machine to produce inked copies. In the ink duplicating process the masters are called *stencils*. Each stencil consists of a backing sheet with a perforated heading (the perforations vary according to the make of machine to be used) a carbon sheet which forms the middle of a sandwich between the backing sheet - and the actual stencil itself. The stencil is a specially prepared sheet with a wax finish. When this stencil is 'cut', holes are made in it, through which ink passes when it is fastened to an ink duplicating machine. The uncut waxed areas hold back ink - allowing it only to flow through the 'cuts' in the stencil.

Masters used in the ink duplicating process may be made:

by typing;
using a thermal-heat copier;
using an electronic stencil-cutter;
by hand.

Preparing a stencil by typing
1. Select a stencil suitable for the machine you are using. Special stencils are available for low-impact and single-element typewriters. If you are in doubt about the suitability of your stencils for your typewriter you should consult your supplier.
2. Insert the stencil into the typewriter with the backing sheet towards the platen. Use a hard platen if one is available and a machine with a clean, clear, sharp face. Sometimes, especially if the backing sheet is to be used for a copy of the stencil, an extra sheet (or a double-sided carbon sheet) of carbon paper is inserted into the pack - carbon

side towards the backing sheet. (The one fixed in the pack faces the typist.)

3. Set margins on the machine to correspond with the lines printed on the stencil. These indicate the areas in which typing must fit if copies are to be run off using the paper required. Stencils are usually available only in A4 and foolscap sizes – sizes smaller than these are indicated on the actual stencil.

4. Set the typewriter on S (for stencil) or the white spot (to indicate that the ribbon has been disengaged).

5. Type the required material. Take care to use sufficient pressure to cut the stencil but do not use too much – the letter 'o' in particular (as well as 'e' and 'a') is easily cut out. When typing on a manual machine the letters 'm' and 'w' need a slightly heavier pressure than other keys.

6. If an error is made wind the stencil slightly out of the machine so that a pencil or other object can be inserted between the stencil and the carbon sheet under it. Using white or pink correcting fluid paint out the error. Allow the liquid to dry completely before returning to the typing point and typing the correction.

Grafting

If a large correction is required it may be impractical to paint it out. Instead a hole is cut in the stencil to remove the error and the correction is typed on another stencil which is then cut to produce a piece slightly larger than the hole cut in the original. The new material is then 'glued' to the original using correcting fluid.

7. Smooth down any loose characters.

8. Carefully check the stencil for errors – the carbon beneath the stencil will show through the cut area to make reading easy. It is advisable to ask another typist to check the stencil at this point because once it is removed from the machine it may be difficult to reinsert and correct.

Before typing another stencil take care to clean the typeface with a stiff brush. A special transparent sheet is available for covering the stencil while it is being cut and this protects the typeface. Although single-element machines can be used for cutting ordinary stencils the heads are difficult to clean properly and it is advisable to use the correct stencils with such machines.

Preparing a stencil using a thermal-heat copier

Thermal stencils are specially prepared stencils and are prepared by passing them and the document to be copied through a thermal-heat copier. Thermal stencils can be added to by typing or writing while the document to be copied or cut into the stencil can be masked using ordinary bond paper.

Preparing a stencil using an electronic stencil-cutter

The machine used for this purpose is usually called an 'electronic stencil-cutter' or an 'electronic scanner' and is used for a range of work from copies of typed originals to copies of maps or photographs. The machine consists of a rotating cylinder on which the original to be copied and a specially coated stencil (supplied by the usual stockists) are placed side by side. As the cylinder rotates the original is scanned by a photo-electric cell which is synchronised with an electrode – a cutting stylus. The stylus travels backwards and forwards across the whole area of the stencil. As the photo-electric cell senses a dark area a series of tiny holes are cut into the stencil, the darker the area the more holes, so that the original is copied. A cut stencil is usually black in colour and is rather fragile – although with care it can be added to.

Preparing a stencil by hand

Place the stencil on a very hard surface – a sheet of steel or glass. Use a sharp-pointed object to write or draw on the stencil surface. Special tools, called *styli*, are available for the production of handwritten or drawn stencils which are specially prepared – they are double-coated as a rule. The base is usually white and the top is usually blue so that the person who is preparing the stencil can see what has been produced. It is possible to produce a range of work using the correct stylus – the main problem is taking care not to cut or tear the stencil. Once the stencil has been prepared it is ready for running off. Modern ink duplicators are either of the single-drum kind or the twin-drum kind.

Single-drum (cylinder) machines consist of a drum which is made of finely perforated metal covered with fabric. The drum contains ink, which is squeezed into it from a tube through a filler hole that is fastened with a screw cap. As the drum rotates ink spreads evenly through the fabric. Most single-drum machines are hand-operated and are used where the volume of duplicating is not very great.

Twin-drum machines consist of two drums or cylinders which are connected by fabric. This fabric, or carrier belt, is inked by a pressure roller and ink is pumped or sucked direct from the tube of ink attached to the machine. Twin-drum machines are generally electrically operated and the range available offers a great deal of variation of features.

The single-drum machine needs replenishing as the ink is used up – a filling will give 500 to 600 copies – and a stencil will produce up to 1 000 copies of any size up to foolscap. Twin-drum machines will produce over 7 000 copies an hour when electrically operated – the number of copies per stencil will depend on the quality of the stencil and between 35 000 and 6 000 copies should be obtained from a good-quality stencil.

Running off copies

The exact operation of any machine will depend on the nature of the machine itself. The instructions which follow are for a typical electrically

Fig 18.3 *single-drum ink duplicator*

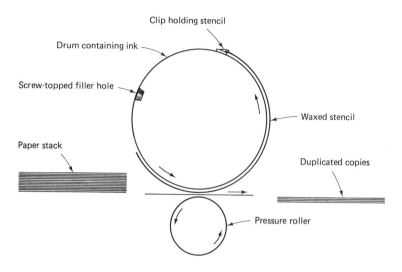

operated twin-drum machine and may differ in detail from other machines – such as a manually operated single-drum machine.

1. Lower the stacking tray.
2. Open the cylinder cover and anchor the head of the stencil on to the duplicator. Turn the handle slowly and let the stencil fall evenly on to the drum or cyclinder – taking care to smooth out any creases.
3. Tear off the backing sheet – it is usually perforated for this purpose.
4. Clip the bottom of the stencil under the tail flap. Close the cylinder cover.
5. Place the duplicating paper in the feed tray and adjust the feed guides as required. (It is advisable to loosen the sheets of paper from each other prior to placing them in the feed tray – if this is not done several sheets at a time will be fed into the machine, which will probably jam as a result.)
6. Raise the feed tray ready for duplicating. Switch the machine to the 'On' or 'Print' position.
7. Handfeed a sheet of paper through the machine to check the inking and alignment, etc. Make the required adjustments. Check the quality again using another sheet(s). (Alignment can be made side to side and top to bottom of the sheet.)
8. Set the counter for the number of copies required and switch on. The machine will automatically switch itself off when it reaches the required number.

If the machine is a manual one set the counter to zero and stop duplicating once the required number of copies has been run off.

Storing stencils

Remove the stencil from the machine by loosening the lower edge and turning the roller backwards. The backing sheet will stick to the stencil if it is held against it as the roller is slowly reversed and the flap holding the head is carefully lifted. The stencil can then be stored in a folder or book on which details of the stencil are recorded - subject, date, number of copies run off, etc. The folder can then be stored in a stencil box, a cabinet or a drawer. Stencils can also be stored on special suspension rails in filing cabinets or deep drawers. Sometimes stencils are dried first between sheets of newspaper or blotting paper.

Ink duplicating paper should normally be of 50 to 70 g/m^2 weight and should be absorbent - so that the ink will quickly dry. It is available in a range of colours. If a sized paper is being used the ink may not dry so readily and interleaving sheets of blotting paper, or some other absorbent paper, may have to be placed between the duplicated sheets while they dry. Most machines will accept thin card.

Care of ink duplicators

1. Always pull the plug out of electric machines before attempting to clean or repair them.
2. See that paper is still not passing through the machine when duplicating ceases. Remove spare duplicating paper and store it in its packet.
3. Remove scraps of paper and dust from the machine.
4. Remove surplus ink and leave the machine in a clean condition.
5. Always cover the machine when it is not in use. See that the plug is pulled out when the machine is not in use - it is not enough just to switch off the electricity.
6. Send for a mechanic if the problem is not obvious - attempts at do-it-yourself repairs often result in increasing the amount of damage.
7. Remember! Electric machines can be stopped at any time by pressing the red emergency stop button or moving the control lever to neutral. If in doubt pull out the plug. *Never* operate an electric duplicator with the cylinder uncovered - modern machines should not operate with the cylinder exposed.

General

Make sure that the stencil being used is the correct one for the task in hand. Although some stencils will fit several makes of machines it is advisable to use stencils with the correct head so that attachment to the drum is effective. While results of a kind can be obtained by using one grade of stencil for all tasks, best results are obtained by using the recommended grade for each task - long-run, short-run, handwriting, type-bar and single-element typewriters, thermal processing and electronic scanning. As with all machinery it is advisable to wear some form of protective clothing when operating ink duplicating machines and to keep long hair tucked away. Supplies should be kept in a safe place away from any potential fire risks.

The advantages of the system are:

1. Copies can be produced in two colours. This may mean emptying the machine of one colour ink, cleaning and replacing with a second colour - or using two machines each with a different colour. If two colours are used, separate stencils are prepared, one for each colour, and the duplicated material is run through each machine in turn. Care must be taken to ensure that the two colours do not overlap.
2. A large number of copies can be produced from each stencil - up to 5 000 as a rule; even larger numbers can be produced with care and good-quality stencils.
3. A wide range of material can be duplicated - hand and typed material, maps and photographs as well as drawings (full- and half-tone) and printed matter.
4. Good-quality reproduction and a high degree of uniformity of quality.
5. Cheap to run - paper is not expensive; the cost of ink per copy is very reasonable. Depending on the degree of sophistication of individual machines, the cost of purchasing them is not high compared to other similar methods.
6. It is easy to store stencils for future use.
7. The machines are relatively easy to operate.

The disadvantages of the system are:

1. Absorbent paper should be used - and this is not very good for writing on.
2. Problem of producing two colours.
3. Expensive if only a few copies are required - the cost of stencils is high if they are used for only a few copies.
4. Masters cannot be altered once they have been used.

18.12 OFFSET LITHO

The master for the offset litho (also called offset lithography) process may be either a paper plate, a plastic sheet or a metal plate, and can be prepared in the following ways:

using a typewriter fitted with a litho ribbon;
writing or drawing with special carbon paper or inks;
using an electronic scanner or a heat copying machine;
using electrostatic or photographic processes.

The image on the plate must be made of a greasy substance which will repel the water that covers the rest of the surface in the inking process. The master is fitted to a roller, dampened and put into contact with an inking roller. The ink is accepted by the greasy area, repelled by the water, and the image is offset in a negative form on to a rubber roller which, in turn, transfers the image in a positive form on to the copy paper.

Fig 18.4   *the basic principle of offset lithography*

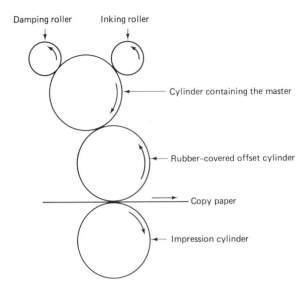

Damping roller   Inking roller

Cylinder containing the master

Rubber-covered offset cylinder

Copy paper

Impression cylinder

Producing masters on a typewriter
1. Use an offset ribbon.
2. Put the plate into the machine and type with just sufficient pressure to leave a clear impression on the plate. On no account should so much pressure be used that characters are pressed into the surface of the plate.
3. Use an offset eraser for making corrections. Take care not to scrape the surface of the plate and type the correction with the same pressure as the correct material.
4. Ensure that no greasy finger marks or dirt reaches the surface of the plate.

If the material is to be run off in colours, separate plates must be made for each colour and care taken to ensure that each colour does not overlap another. The duplicating paper must be run through the machine for each colour required.

Most lithography is of the offset kind – there is a process known as *direct lithography* and this involves producing a mirror image of the material to be duplicated (similar to that used in the spirit duplicating process). In most offices the offset method is used and modern machines are no larger than ink duplicators.

To use a typical offset machine:

clamp in the offset master;
set the machine to the number of copies required;

load the machine with paper – taking care to separate the sheets slightly to ensure easy feeding into the machine;

press the button to start the machine – which will automatically switch itself off when it has duplicated the required copies.

Modern machines are fully automatic and the etching unit for the masters (zinc-oxide, aluminium, paper or plastic) is an integral part – they do not have to be taken out of the machine when running off copies. The preselection of ink and water, the etching process, inking the master, offsetting the printing image, paper feed, washing of the inking mechanism and switching off are all fully programmed and follow each other once the machine is started. Copy positioning (vertical and lateral) is done manually. The inking units, essential for multi-colour printing, are easily exchanged.

The advantages of the system are:

1. High-quality work can be produced in a large range of colours – providing separate plates are produced for each colour. The machine must be absolutely clean before the second and subsequent colours are added.
2. Large quantities can be produced – up to 50 000 using metal plates or up to 10 000 copies from paper plates. The method is used for the production of newspapers and magazines as well as books – although the machines used are considerably larger than those found in normal offices. (This book has been printed using offset litho.)
3. Can be used for a wide range of applications – including the production of office forms, letter heads, circulars in large quantities, catalogues/price lists, fine line-drawings, photographs and tint lays. Because the plates can be stored easily there is no need to keep large stocks of duplicated material – copies can be run off to order.
4. Any material – handwriting, typewriting, diagrams, pictures, drawings, photographs, etc. – can be reproduced.
5. Good-quality paper can be used. A whole range of paper qualities can be used, ranging from thin bond paper to card. Machines are available to take paper in a range of sizes.
6. The method is cheap for the production of large numbers of copies.

The disadvantages of the system are:

1. The method is not economical for short runs, i.e. small numbers of copies.
2. Skilled operators are required for the more advanced applications – and they require training.
3. The initial cost of the machine can be high (machines can be hired).

18.13 COPYRIGHT

Before copying any document you are advised to check that it is not subject to any copyright. The author of any work, writing, painting, film, music, computer data, etc., holds the sole right to reproduce that work unless he/she gives authority to another. In the United Kingdom the period of copyright for books is the author's lifetime and fifty years after death. A writer may, for example, keep the copyright to a book or an article (in which case you must ask him/her for permission to reproduce all or part of a book or article and pay any fee required for the privilege of doing so) or may sell the copyright to a publisher or printer – in which case you must write to the printer or publisher of the article, be it in a book, newspaper or magazine, and ask for permission to reproduce it. Again, a fee may be required before permission is given. If you look in the front of any book you may see the world copyright symbol © – the letter 'c' inside a circle – and this indicates that the work is copyright. The name of the copyright-owner and – in printed matter – the date of publication follows the copyright symbol, which is followed by words such as 'All rights reserved. No part of this publication may be reproduced or transmitted, in any form or by any means, without prior permission', or 'All rights reserved. No part of this publication may be reproduced, stored in a retrieval system, or transmitted in any form or by any means, electronic, mechanical photocopying, recording or otherwise without prior permission of (name of the publisher) or of the original copyright-holder.' If the copyright-holder is willing to allow part or all of the publication to be reproduced the document may say so – often with the rider that the source of the information must be acknowledged. It is unlawful to break a copyright and while there is no doubt that much copyright material is reproduced illegally (and escapes penalty either because the copyright-holder is unaware of what is going on or perhaps does not want the publicity that a court action might involve), the penalties for breaking copyrights can be severe. In an office the most likely areas to be affected by copyrights are the reprographics section, computer programming and microfilming. If you look at any newspaper or magazine you will find that at some point either the world copyright symbol will appear – with or without a printed warning – or there will be just a written warning. Most material published by government departments is Crown copyright and it is illegal to reproduce it without written permission. Very often a fee is payable.

QUESTIONS

1. Describe how you would prepare the following.

   a spirit master using five colours;
   an ink duplicator stencil – handwritten or typewritten;
   an offset-litho plate – handwritten or typewritten.

2. What is the essential difference between copying and duplicating?
3. What materials are suitable for:

copying?
duplicating?

4. List the most important steps to be followed when using:

a spirit duplicator;
an ink duplicator,
an offset-litho machine;
a direct electrostatic copier;
an indirect electrostatic copier.

PROJECT

Produce a file on the current models of spirit duplicators, ink duplicators, offset-litho machines, diazo copiers, heat-transfer machines, dual-spectrum copiers and electrostatic copiers – direct and indirect. From your file produce a report recommending the 'best buys' in each range.

THE TRAINING AND QUALIFICATIONS REQUIRED FOR OFFICE WORK

Before entering the world of office work it is important that young people are made aware of the personal qualities and qualifications required in the various jobs. It is essential that the would-be office worker finds out the qualifications required as early as possible so that the correct courses can be taken before leaving school or qualifications can be obtained at school which will lead to the appropriate training after school. For most young people at school the first crossroads comes at the end of the third year when choices have to be made about courses in the fourth and fifth years which lead to the taking of the various public examinations. While it is not essential that 'commercial' courses are taken at this stage the would-be office worker would be well advised to seek the guidance of the careers service at school or the appropriate careers service outside school.

19.1 PUBLIC EXAMINATIONS

There is a wide range of bodies offering qualifications for both the person at school and the one who has left school or college and who requires further training and qualifications. All the examining bodies issue full details of the syllabus of each area of study and before undertaking training it is advisable to make a study of them.

The *General Certificate of Education* provides proof of ability at two levels, Ordinary ('O') level and Advanced ('A') level.

The *Certificate of Secondary Education* is awarded to candidates who reach the required standards in each of the subjects offered by the various examining boards. The examination is usually offered at one level only and it is usually taken at the end of the fifth year at school.

At the time of writing it seems highly probable that the CSE and GCE examinations will be combined in one common examination. There are several pilot 16+ examinations in existence – the purpose being to evaluate the effects of offering such examinations. These examinations are offered to any person over the age of 16 and certificates are issued to candidates who are successful in meeting the various requirements. One future title of the new examination may be the GCSE - *General Certificate of Secondary Education*.

The *Royal Society of Arts* offers a wide range of courses which can be taken at school or college as the result of full-time or part-time study by candidates of all ages. Unlike the GCE and CSE examinations which are offered only once or twice a year, the RSA examinations are offered up to four times a year at the various stages – I, II or III.

The *London Chamber of Commerce and Industry* offers a wide range of courses which can be taken while candidates are at school or college as the result of full or part-time training.

The *Business Education Council* offers a unified national system of non-degree courses for people whose occupations fall within the broad area of business and public administration. Colleges of Further Education, working on their own or together with other colleges, offer, subject to the approval of the BEC, courses leading to three levels of awards, General, National, and Higher.

19.2 PART–TIME STUDY

People at work may obtain part-time study in one of three ways. *Day-release* study is obtained when an employer gives an employee time off work to go to college for regular study – a day per week, two half-days or a combination of both and some evening study. *Block-release* is obtained when an employer allows an employee to study for a month or six weeks at a time, for example, during a year. If an employer is not prepared to allow an employee day-release or block-release the solution may be evening classes. *Evening classes* are offered by colleges and evening institutes to any person who is prepared to give up one or two evenings a week to attend classes (and do homework if requested) to obtain qualifications.

19.3 GENERAL QUALIFICATIONS

All office/secretarial jobs require employees to reach recognised levels of ability in English Language in particular and a range of other subjects in general. Many require an ability in Arithmetic or Mathematics (or Calculations). As a general rule, employees who hope to obtain a well-paid job should be prepared to offer four or five subjects including English and Mathematics. People wishing to take up clerical/secretarial posts should offer proof of ability in the appropriate skills – shorthand, type-writing, office practice and so on. As microcomputers become common-place it is reasonable to expect that in the near future employers will expect proof of some knowledge and understanding of their functions and mode of operation. The following list outlines some of the duties of people engaged in a range of office jobs.

19.4 COMPUTER OPERATOR

Although computers can save time and money they have to work to instructions – and those instructions must be given by people such as *systems analysts* – who look into possible answers to problems – *programmers* – people who present information to computers in a form that they can understand – and *operators* – people who actually operate the machines.

19.5 COUNTER CLERK

The range of work offered is very wide and depends on the body employing, hence the training required varies considerably. The qualifications required vary as much as the range of work offered. Counter clerks must be able to get on with other people, be able to write and record neatly, usually be able to operate a calculator (of some kind) and be proficient in using a telephone. A clean and tidy appearance is an important personal qualification.

19.6 FIGURE CLERK

Figure clerks need to be able to write figures neatly on record sheets and other documents, to be able to spot errors both in their own work and that of others, to be able to talk about figures to others – for example, when talking over the telephone to customers complaining about invoices and so on – and to operate calculators. In many firms clerks are trained on the job, with higher qualifications usually obtained at the local colleges as the result of part-time study.

19.7 GENERAL CLERK

All clerks have to handle large quantities of paper – filling in forms, sorting and filing information and so on. An *office junior* may be responsible for collecting the post before sorting it and opening it and distributing it, visiting the bank and Post Office as required, answering the telephone, meeting visitors, making the tea and a whole range of jobs including operating the various machines found in the office. Other clerks may be responsible for dealing with a certain number of customers of a firm, filing, job vacancies, ordering stock, answering letters, using the telephone and so on. Most clerical work training is provided on the job – some firms offer day-release or encourage employees to go to evening classes. Some general clerks are employed by particular firms; others work for agencies who send them to where there is a short-term shortage. Most firms look for qualifications – often qualifications in English.

19.8 OFFICE MACHINE OPERATOR

Most offices use a wide range of machines and so have to employ people to operate them. An *accounts clerk* will have to use an accounting machine to work out the totals of invoices and orders which will certainly involve working out taxes such as VAT. Stock records need to be kept up to date and this again will involve the use of calculators and similar machines. A

Visual Display Unit Operator (VDU) or terminal operator operates a machine which is linked to a computer and presents information on a screen in a form which can be read. The operator can feed information into the computer (which may be miles away) or ask the computer for information which is presented on the screen so that it can be copied or used as required. VDU operators require training to be able to understand the various computer programs because computers only accept information presented in a certain way – that is, on punched cards, punched tape, tape or discs. A *keyboard operator* is responsible for preparing the information for the computer. It is essential that keypunch operators work quickly and with accuracy; their work is checked by other workers called *verifiers*. Most machine operators are trained on the job and pay and promotion is based on efficiency and experience. The range of machines varies from firm to firm.

19.9 RECEPTIONIST

A receptionist is responsible for looking after callers at the firm, both those with appointments and those callers without appointments. A receptionist has to be able to look after callers, announce them, take them to the right person, or show them the way. If the receptionist is very busy, she should provide tea/coffee/reading material, etc., for those who have to wait for appointments, be tactful with unwanted callers, make appointments for those callers who do not have appointments and need to see individuals at the firm, book theatre tickets, train tickets, air tickets and so on as required, book accommodation, find out where addresses are, use street maps, travel timetables, look up all kinds of information – or seek it from other sources – and many more jobs. Many receptionists have to type information, make bookings and keep records. Some receptionists have to be able to understand medical terms – especially those employed by doctors and dentists. Many are responsible for the switchboard and looking after the petty cash. All receptionists must be able to get on with other people – even difficult ones. Training is often very informal, many receptionists are often simply shown what to do by older people. Some firms run their own training schools; others run courses linked with colleges or offer part-time training in such subjects as typewriting, shorthand and accounts. It is very difficult to become a receptionist straight from school because firms want people with experience. While qualifications are important and some firms ask for them, most firms require people with personality, maturity, good looks and the ability to speak well.

19.10 SECRETARY

A *junior secretary* may be expected to work for several people while a *personal secretary* will work for one particular person. Secretaries may be responsible for dealing with both incoming and outgoing mail, sending replies to letters, filing information, using the telephone, meeting people, making appointments, operating the various machines found in the office, taking shorthand or audio-typewriting, making/typing reports of various kinds, being responsible for ordering stock for the office, looking after the petty cash and any one of hundreds of jobs required by her employer. A senior secretary may even act for her employer in his absence - keeping him fully informed of what has happened while he is away. A good secretary will know all about the firm for which she works and be able to turn her hand to a wide range of jobs as the situation demands. Any secretarial course - no matter how good it is - will provide only the basic training and the final 'polish' will come with experience. Good typing speeds are essential, 40 words a minute being the minimum, while high shorthand speeds, over 100 words a minute, or good audio skills are invaluable. Most employers look for a good general education in addition to training in office skills while the ability to offer proof of ability in English language is often essential. Many secretaries are required to speak a second language - especially if the employer is involved in the export trade. In addition to being a 'Jack of all trades' a secretary will be expected to be able to use a telephone well, file, type, take dictation/audio type, write neatly and make records as well as get on with others.

19.11 TELEPHONIST

A telephonist working for a private firm may be responsible for the switchboard at the firm and the associated jobs which go with dealing with the telephone. Such an employee must know the various extension numbers at the firm and be able to deal with all kinds of calls - those from both welcome and unwelcome callers. There is an increasing demand for people who can speak other languages. Most employers look for good qualifications in English, accurate spelling is vital, and many require all-round general qualifications. A clear and pleasant voice is a 'must'. Many telephonists are men.

19.12 TELEX OPERATOR

Many firms are connected to the telex service so that information can be received and transmitted quickly at any time of the day or night. Many messages are sent out on typed punched tape - so a telex operator must be able to produce the tapes used as well as dial the required codes before sending messages. Some messages are typed straight into the telex machine - so the ability to type with accuracy is vital. It is extremely useful if operators can memorise telex codes - to save having to look them up each time. Messages may be received on a VDU or on punched tape or as a tear-off message typed straight on to a roll of continuous stationery. Training is basically learning how to operate a telex machine - it takes between one and six months. Qualifications usually include a good general education, the ability to be able to type with accuracy, an ability to memorise codes and a sound knowledge of geography.

19.13 TYPIST

Most firms use typewriters of various kinds although not all employ people simply to type. A *copy typist* reproduces work prepared by others – the demand for copy typists is rapidly falling as an increasing number of sophisticated machines are being used. A *shorthand typist* takes dictation from a superior and types back the information. An *audio-typist* types information dictated on to an audio mahcine ready for the dictator (author) to sign. Some typists work on their own; others are employed in the typing pool. The range of work may include the typing of orders, invoices, statements and other business documents, letters, envelopes, reports, memos, minutes, masters for stencil and spirit duplicators, legal documents, accounts and so on. Most employers require proof of the ability to type, a minimum speed of 30 words a minute, and the ability to take dictation either in the form of shorthand or the ability to operate an audio machine. Qualifications may be obtained at school or college, in the training schools operated by the firm, as the result of part-time training or even by self-teaching – although there is a need for some public qualification. An English qualification is often essential and many firms often insist on a range of certificates.

19.14 CLERK TYPIST

Clerk typists are expected to perform a range of jobs depending on the employing firm. In some firms the work is mainly filling in forms and keeping records, more clerical work than typing work; in others the work may involve a lot of typing and little filing work. Some clerk typists have to meet large numbers of people on a face-to-face basis; others may have to use the telephone a great deal. Some clerk typists may find that their work is little more than copy-typing; others may find that it is like that of a junior secretary; it all depends on the employer. Many employers look for certificates in a range of subjects and some demand typing and audio/shorthand qualifications. Clerk typists must be able to use a telephone, file, to type, take notes and keep records. An English qualification is very useful, as is a qualification in Arithmetic (Calculations) in many offices.

19.15 FILING CLERK

In some organisations filing is left to specialists while in others it is performed by general staff. The amount of filing to be done will depend on the size of the business and the method used will depend on the nature of the material to be filed. Training is usually given on the job by senior staff and the qualifications required may vary from four or five subjects, including English Language on a nationally recognised certificate, to the ability to work to rules in a methodical manner. Chapter 14 on filing gives some indication of the nature of the work involved.

QUESTIONS

1. What is day-release? What is block-release?
2. List the qualities and qualifications you would expect from each of the following:

A private secretary	An office junior
A telephonist	A computer operator
A receptionist	A telex operator

FINDING

AND APPLYING FOR A JOB

20.1 FINDING THE RIGHT JOB

The school or college employment agencies will provide a great deal of information about jobs in your locality and they will be able to put you in touch with the government agencies responsible for employment. Local newspapers contain advertisements seeking employees for a wide range of jobs and these should be read daily. Private employment agencies keep details of jobs available and you would be well advised to consult them – while there is nothing like having a friend or relative to advise you of situations which are vacant even before they are generally advertised. While seeking a job you should be realistic about your own capabilities and the kind of job you hope to obtain – do not oversell yourself or underestimate your talents.

20.2 APPLYING FOR A JOB

Once you have seen or heard of, a job that you think you might like you should waste no time applying for it. If the advertisement invites you to send for application forms do not be afraid to make a telephone call and ask for them to be sent to you because in this way you will save at least a day. If you are invited to write for application forms do so in your best handwriting, but if your handwriting is poor and you can type then type your letter. It is vital that your letter does not contain errors of any kind, either spelling or grammatical.

If you are invited to apply for a job by letter you should handwrite your letter by choice but a well-typed letter is to be preferred to a badly written one. In your letter you should state the following:

What job you are applying for – and where you have seen it advertised.
Your full name and address. Add your telephone number if you have one.
Your date of birth and your age.
Your education to date.

Your qualifications. If you are awaiting the result of examinations you should state which examinations you have taken and when you expect the results.

Your previous experience – if you have any. If you have a part-time job say so.

If you are already in full-time employment you should state your full working experience to date and give details of any training you have undertaken.

The names and addresses of persons to whom reference may be made concerning your suitability for employment – if you are still at school it is usual to give the name of the head teacher.

The earliest date on which you could start work. If you are still at school or college say when you will be leaving.

If testimonials are requested you should enclose copies only.

A referee is a person to whom a potential employer can go to for information about you. Before you give the name of a person you must ask that person if you may do so and give the correct name and address of that person together with any qualifications. A referee is not bound to give a favourable report on you if he or she feels that some aspect of your character or training is lacking. As you will not see what a referee says about you (unless he or she chooses to show you) choose people who will give you a favourable report.

A testimonial is a written statement about you given by any suitable person who knows you. Testimonials are headed 'To whom it may concern' and are addressed to any potential employer and copies only should be sent. Copies of testimonials should be headed 'Copy'. Naturally you will only use testimonials which are favourable to you.

If you have to fill in a form of application do so in your best handwriting after you have read the form carefully to look for any specific instructions such as 'Use block capitals'. Sometimes you are invited to submit a letter of application with the form. If you feel that an application form does not contain sufficient space to give all your particulars use a separate sheet of paper to add further relevant details.

No matter what method is used when applying for a post, check for spelling and grammatical errors. Many employers will automatically reject any application which is badly presented or contains errors.

20.3 IF YOU ARE INVITED TO ATTEND FOR AN INTERVIEW

If you are invited to attend for an interview you should write and accept the offer without delay. If you are invited to telephone your acceptance you should do so. Make a careful note of the date, time and place of the interview together with documents or material you are asked to take with you. If you do not know where the interview address is use the local *A to Z* to find it and if necessary go to the address before the due date to find out how to get there and how long it takes.

20.4 **INTERVIEWS**

Take care to attend for an interview looking your best, bearing in mind that a potential employer will not expect to see you dressed in unsuitable clothing. Remember to dress for the occasion; if your 'best' outfit is 'way out' do not wear it, but find something more suitable. Make sure that you 'look the part' and are neat and tidy.

Arrive at the place of the interview in good time so that you can get your bearings and do not arrive in a state of panic. When you arrive, announce yourself. Many firms show you round before the interview, and if you are invited to go on a tour take care to note what is going on so that you can ask suitable questions if invited to do so or can reply to questions asked about your tour. If possible find out who is to interview you – it may be one person or it may be several. You may be asked to take a test of some kind – a spelling test, an English or Arithmetic test and, in the case of a typist or shorthand post, tests of your skill. Be prepared for a test and take the necessary material with you.

When you are finally called for interview do not take a seat until invited and then look at the person(s) interviewing you – do not look down. You may be introduced to the person(s) interviewing you – try to remember their names, but do not be afraid to write them down as they are introduced. Ask about their positions if you are not told. Speak naturally and do not be afraid to look at the person asking the question. Keep to the point and answer the question asked – not the one you would like to be asked. While you should be brief in your answers do not reply with one word – sell yourself. Be honest about your abilities and speak the truth at all times. If you want the job say so and make it clear that you are prepared to work hard at it – show that you have ambition and are keen to learn. If, when you are called for interview, you have decided that the job is not for you – say so. This will save you and the interviewer time and trouble and it is better to be honest from the start rather than to be seen to have changed your mind later. If you are offered a post and you want it, accept it. If you feel that you would like to go home and think about the offer say so, and guarantee to let the firm know next morning. You may be told that others have to be interviewed and you will be informed at a later date; do not be afraid to ask when that date will be.

20.5 **STARTING A NEW JOB**

Once you have been offered a job you may be required to have a medical examination – and this you must take if you want the job. If you are still at school a medical examination will be given before you leave. In any case the examination will not take longer than a few minutes and is simply to ensure that you are fit enough for the job in hand.

When you start work you may be asked to produce the following documents:

Your birth certificate – to prove your age.

A medical certificate.

Your examination certificates.

A P45 tax form – see Section 22.10.

Your National Insurance particulars. If you are still at school you will be given these by your Youth Employment Officer before you leave. See also Section 22.9.

20.6 CONTRACT OF EMPLOYMENT

When you accept a post you will be given a Contract of Employment. This contract will state the conditions under which you are employed and what your rights are. You must be told such information as:

The date on which your employment started.

Your rate of pay or the method to be used to calculate your wages/salary.

When you are to be paid – weekly or monthly.

The terms under which you are employed, including the hours you have to work.

Details concerning your holidays – how much holiday you are allowed and when you will be allowed to take it.

What happens if you are sick or injured and cannot work.

Details of any pension schemes.

How much notice you must give should you want to leave – and how much notice you must be given should the firm wish to discontinue employing you. If your employment is for a limited period only the dates should be stated.

In addition to this information you will be told your rights under the **Trade Union and Labour Relations Act** and the **Employment Protection Act**. This information will include your rights in connection with trade unions and in connection with any dispute with your employer. (At the time of writing it seems certain that the Employment Protection Act will be amended or repealed – you will be told the current position at the time of your employment.)

20.7 PERSONAL FILE

Once you have been appointed a file on you will almost certainly be opened and in it will go the job description, specification and personnel specification (if they have been drawn up – see Section 1.4), your application form and any documents relating to your application, details of your medical record if available and your personal record card. This card will probably have to be filled in by you when you start to work and on it will go your personal details: age, date of birth, address and so on. In addition a card, or space on the original card, will be used to record details of your performance while at the firm. This information will include details of any absence, training, experience, general information, wages/salary – and any information which will be of value when the time comes for you to be promoted – or leave the firm.

20.8 LEAVING A JOB

Sooner or later people leave jobs for a variety of reasons – retiring, promotion, etc. Before you leave you must find the amount of notice that you must give – this will be found in your Contract of Employment. It is usual to resign in writing, by means of *a letter of resignation*. In this letter you must state when you intend leaving – the date from which your notice is to take effect. It is polite to say why you are leaving and there is little to be gained from leaving 'under a cloud' – you may find that later you need to make reference back to your employer. If you have contributed to a pension fund you may be able to transfer this to your new job – or draw out your contributions. You will need your *insurance card* and *tax form* (P45) when you leave.

ACTIVITY

Make a study of one or more of the following and make a report of not more than 3000 words giving the main points of your chosen area(s) of study. The Contracts of Employment Act 1972 (and other related Acts), the Employment Protection Consolidation Act 1978 (and its related Acts) and the latest Trade Union and Labour Relations Act (at the time of writing the 1974 Act and its related legislation is under review).

QUESTIONS

1. What is the difference between a reference and a testimonial?
2. What information is contained in a Contract of Employment?
3. What information would you expect to be kept in a personal file?

THE LAW RELATING
TO EMPLOYMENT

As well as the hiring and firing of staff and the legislation connected with these activities the Personnel Department – see Section 1.4 – is also responsible for seeing that other governmental regulations are observed. In addition to health, safety and working conditions, see later in this chapter, there are several other Acts which affect terms of employment. Among these the following are worthy of attention but because legislation is constantly changing you are advised to keep a record of new Acts.

21.1 HEALTH, SAFETY AND WORKING CONDITIONS

The Health and Safety Act of 1974 is the most important Act covering working conditions in offices and business premises and incorporates most of the earlier 1963 Act dealing with offices, shops and railway premises.

The Offices, Shops and Railway Premises Act 1963

The 1963 Offices, Shops and Railway Premises Act brought the working conditions of people engaged in offices, shops and railway premises under the law and extended the protection to these people to bring it in line with workers in other areas of industry. The Act is concerned with the physical working conditions, safety, first aid and fire precautions and should be read together with:

The Fire Precautions (Factories, Offices, Shops and Railway Premises) Order 1976.
The Fire Certificates (Special Premises) Regulations 1976.
The Fire Precautions (Non-Certificated Factory, Office, Shop and Railway Premises) Regulations 1976.

The 1963 Act defines the premises to which the Act applies and then sets out various headings such as general requirements, fire precautions, responsibility for complying with the provisions of the Act, exemptions, overlapping with the provisions of other Acts, notification of accidents and enforcement. The main provisions are as follows:

1. Anyone intending to employ people in office, shop or railway premises is required to send notification (in the prescribed form) to the local authority responsible for enforcing the general provisions of the Act.
2. All premises, furniture, furnishings and fittings must be kept in a clean state.
3. Rooms where people work must not be overcrowded – regard must be taken of the number of people in each room and the amount of space occupied by such things as furniture, fittings and machinery.
4. Space standards must be observed.
5. A reasonable working temperature standard must be observed – not less than 16°C (60.8°F) after the first hour. There are regulations concerning the method to be used for heating premises.
6. Ventilation must be adequate.
7. Lighting must be suitable and sufficient.
8. Suitable and sufficient sanitary conveniences must be provided and these must comply with the prescribed regulations.
9. Suitable and sufficient washing facilities – including the supply of clean, running hot and cold water or clean, running warm water, and soap and clean towels or other suitable means of cleaning or drying – must be provided.
10. Drinking-water must be provided.
11. Arrangements must be made for clothing not worn during normal working hours and clothing not taken home.
12. There are requirements concerning seating arrangements.
13. Eating facilities must be provided in certain situations.
14. Floor, passages and stairs must be safe and specified regulations must be observed.
15. Dangerous parts of machinery must be fenced and guarded. There are regulations concerning the cleaning of machinery.
16. Regulations cover the loads people are expected to carry.
17. There are first-aid provisions – first-aid boxes or cupboards containing first-aid requisites must be provided and be readily accessible.
18. There must be fire escapes which conform to regulations. Certain premises must be inspected and certified by the appropriate fire authorities. Fire drill regulations must be followed.
19. Certain accidents must be notified to the appropriate authorities.

The Health and Safety Act 1974

Under the Health and Safety Act employers are responsible for the health and safety of employees, with particular regard to the use of machinery, the training of staff in safety procedures and the general working environment. It is also the duty of all employees to take reasonable care of their own health and safety and that of others. While it is the responsibility of the Personnel Department to see that the 1974 Act is carried out at particular firms it is the *Factory Inspectorate* which is responsible for seeing that this Act and the 1963 Act are administered and enforced.

The Health and Safety Executive issues a wide range of leaflets and booklets on all aspects of the 1974 Act and these should be obtained and studied.

ACTIVITY

Obtain copies of the various Acts previously discussed together with any new Acts affecting terms of employment from your school, college or local library and spend some time looking through them. If you were responsible for keeping your employer up to date on the legislation affecting terms of employment at your firm, what steps could you take?

21.2 SAFETY IN THE OFFICE

As offices become increasingly concerned with machinery and materials of many kinds there is a growing awareness of the need to prevent accidents. Many of the machines used are potentially dangerous – guillotines cut fingers just as easily as they cut paper, automatic staplers can staple fingers as easily as documents if not used with care, duplicators can catch the unwary, electric connections can be dangerous – and so on. Many of the materials used are highly inflammable, particularly some fluids used in spirit duplicating and cleaning, while others must not be used in a confined space because of the fumes given off. *All* people employed in offices must be made aware of the need to take care and the Health and Safety Executive and the Home Office publish information concerning these matters. The Civil Service publishes a handbook for supervisors, *Is My Office Safe?* (HMSO, 1978; ISBN 0 11 6302232). This handbook should be obtained and studied: the following points are taken from pages 17–19 of it.

APPENDIX 1

Health and safety in the office

Specimen handout

The Health and Safety at Work Act 1974
You are required by law to take reasonable care for your own health and safety at work and that of others who might be affected by your acts or omissions. Moreover, you must co-operate with your employer in enabling him to meet his legal obligations – e.g. you must not intentionally or recklessly interfere with or misuse anything provided in the interests of health and safety.

A safe working place

Many accidents at work are caused by falling. Be on your guard against:

worn or missing stair-treads
missing or damaged handrails
worn floor-coverings
slippery floor surfaces
broken glass, etc.
trailing telephone or electric leads.

Bumping into things is another cause of injury. Don't leave in corridors or passageways obstructions such as:

furniture
cartons
trolleys.

Furniture can cause accidents. Don't:

leave your desk drawer open
put too much weight in the upper drawer of filing cabinets or open more
    than one drawer at a time – the cabinet might tip towards you
position furniture where sharp corners could cause injury.

Don't stand on swivel chairs or anything else which is insecure.

Fire precaution

Fires don't just happen: there is always a cause.

Use ashtrays – not the waste paper bin.
Dispose of waste paper and other flammable material regularly.
Switch off machines at night and remove the plugs.
Don't stand portable heaters where they can be knocked over or where
    they might set light to things.
Don't place paper, towels or clothing near portable fires or on storage
    heaters.

Take extreme care in the use and storage of flammable liquids:

Don't use naked flames, e.g. matches, cigarette lighters.
Replace caps or stoppers of containers at once after use.

Mop up any spillage and store mopping up material in a closed metal con-
    tainer prior to final disposal.
Never prop open a fire door.

Fire precautions

Read the fire instructions NOW. Find out, if not stated:

whether you should use the fire extinguisher
the arrangements for evacuating visitors and disabled colleages
alternative exit routes – should your normal one be blocked.

Should it be necessary to pass through smoke to reach an escape route:

Inhale as little as possible.
Keep near to the floor if the smoke is dense.

If your route is impassable due to very dense smoke, close the door of your room and use the telephone to state your position. Make your presence known by standing at the window. Prevent smoke penetration around the door by sealing with whatever materials are available.

Don't use the lift – you might be trapped.

Electrical equipment
Look out for and report:

loose connections
unearthed equipment
damaged cables
defective insulation
overloaded circuits
broken switches
worn or dangerous appliances
trailing leads
liquids which if spilt could cause a short circuit.

Don't tinker with electrical equipment.

Machinery
Read any operating instructions.
Don't meddle with any safety guard.
Don't clean machinery when it is in motion.
Learn how to stop any energy supply in an emergency.
Guard your fingers when using guillotines.
Don't tinker with lift mechanism.

Lifting and carrying
There is less strain when lifting heavy loads if you bend your legs and keep
    your back straight.
A burden shared is a burden halved.
Two journeys may be better than one.
Be able to see over the top of the load.

First aid
Who is your nearest first-aider?
Where is your nearest sick room/first-aid box?

(*Is My Office Safe?* (pp. 17–19)

APPENDIX 2

Am I safety conscious?
Specimen self-questionnaire

Ask yourself the following questions and make sure you know the answers both in your own interest and that of your colleagues and visitors to the office. If the questions raise any doubts at all resolve those doubts either by taking appropriate action yourself or by consulting your supervisor.

1. I should take reasonable care at work because:

   (a) It is in my own interest.
   (b) I might otherwise cause injury to other people.
   (c) I am legally bound to do so.

   Tick those reasons which seem correct.

2. Is there anything I do in my work activity which might cause me to:

   (a) Fall?
   (b) Injure myself against a sharp edge?
   (c) Trip over?

3. Is there anything I do in my work activity which might conceivably cause injury to others?
4. Are there any steps which I can take in doing my job which might help prevent fires from starting in the building where I work?
5. What action should I take if I see a fire door open?
6. If I detect a fire how do I raise the alarm?
7. In the event of a fire am I expected to use a fire extinguisher?
8. Where is the nearest fire extinguisher? Should I need to use it would I know how?
9. What is the signal to evacuate the building?
10. In an evacuation who would take care of disabled colleages and visitors to the office?
11. Am I familiar with the escape routes from the buildings? Have I tried them out?
12. If I had to travel through a smoke-filled area what could I do to lessen the worst effects of smoke?
13. Where is my exact assembly-point in an evacuation of the building?
14. What would I do if all exit routes were blocked?
15. What, if any, highly flammable substances are used by my colleagues in the area where I work?
16. What action should I take on finding a fault in electrical equipment which seems to make it unsafe for use?
17. Do I need any further instruction in the safety aspects of equipment I use to do my job?

18. How can I avoid strain when lifting?
19. How do I summon first-aid?

(Ibid. pp. 20–2)

21.3 SECURITY IN THE OFFICE

Offices contain both equipment and information which are valuable; hence both need protecting from loss or theft.

21.4 EQUIPMENT

Most machinery has some form of identification stamped on it – type-writers, for example, can be identified by their serial numbers. Records should be kept of these numbers and machinery which is not identifiable in this way should have some form of identification attached; an engraving tool can be used to mark items. All items should be locked in a secure but convenient place when not in use. Drawers, windows and doors should be locked when premises are not in use and keys should be accounted for – it may be advisable to limit the number of people with access to all keys. The crime-prevention branch of the local police will give individuals and firms free advice on matters of security and will advise on the use of special locks to doors and windows as well as alarms. Insurance companies will often insist on specified precautions being taken before they will insure homes and business premises. Combinations of safes should be known only to those with the authority to open them. Apart from equipment in general use, that in stock should also be kept under close check and the ordering, delivery and withdrawal of supplies from stores should be the responsibility of a person in authority. Stocktaking should be thorough and regular.

21.5 INFORMATION

Many firms possess information which might be of value to a competitor – details of new products which are being developed, methods of production, plans for expansion and so on. Employees have a responsibility to take care of this information and in many firms sensitive information is available to very few people, usually executives and senior staff. All classified information should be accounted for and files should be locked when not in use. Desk diaries and correspondence containing sensitive information should be kept secure. Telephone conversations concerning such information should be discouraged. Documents, and even carbon paper which might give away some vital information, which are no longer required should be passed through a shredder. Dictation tapes with important information should be wiped clean after use. Confidential staff records should be seen only by those who are entitled to see them and their circulation must be limited. In some firms procedures are enforced limiting access to important information either by a system of colour coding or by numbering/naming documents and issuing them only on a signature. The Civil Service has its own procedures and secret information is available only to those who have signed the Official Secrets Act. Some firms, banks in particular, require employees to sign a document at the time of appointment agreeing to keep confidential matters secret. No employee should discuss business matters of a confidential nature outside the business; conversations between employees at the same firm can be overheard wherever they are held. Secretaries in particular must ensure that they do not disclose details of information which might come to their notice, either as the result of being asked to work on it or through the actions of others who should have taken more care. Any confidential documents should be kept under cover in files or cabinets when not in use so that a casual visitor is unable to see them.

Students taking public examinations, in particular, must take care not to confuse questions on office safety with those on office security – the matters are not the same!

QUESTIONS

1. What are the main provisions of the Health and Safety at Work Act 1974?
2. Outline the steps which should be taken to ensure maximum security in an office.
3. Outline the steps which must be taken to ensure maximum safety in any office.

PROJECT

Produce an indexed file containing the current regulations relating to terms and conditions of employment. If you are at work comment on how far the working conditions and terms of employment as laid down in the regulations apply to your situation.

WAGES, SALARIES
AND OTHER FORMS
OF REMUNERATION

People employed in all forms of work expect to be paid and there are several ways in which payment for work is calculated.

22.1 A WAGE

A wage is a negotiable amount paid either for a certain number of hours worked (in which case the wage may be a fixed regular sum) or for how much is undertaken in a given time – usually a week. *Hourly rates* are usually calculated on the basis of a *flat rate* for a certain number of hours (usually called the *basic rate*) with extra payment for hours worked over the basic rate. For example, if a worker was paid £3.00 an hour for a 35-hour week with time and a half for the next five hours and double time for the rest – and he worked 50 hours in a week – he would be paid as follows:

	£
35 hours at £3.00 an hour (the flat rate)	105.00
5 hours at £4.50 an hour ($1\frac{1}{2}$ × £3.00 – time and a half)	22.50
10 hours at £6.00 an hour (2 × £3.00 – double time)	60.00
50 hours worked Total	£187.50

Piece-work rates are rates paid for completing a given amount of work. For example, a typist might be paid 50p for every twenty-five envelopes addressed. If she addressed 750 envelopes she would be paid £15.00 (750 ÷ 25 = 30. 30 × 50p = £15.00). A man paid £2.00 for fitting doors and who fitted twenty doors would be paid £40.00. Just as an hourly-paid worker may be paid more for working longer hours so a piece-work worker is paid more for completing more.

22.2 CLOCK OR TIME CARDS

Most hourly-paid workers are required to clock in and out of work using a time clock and a card. A **Time Recorder Clock** is placed near the entrance/exit of a firm and each hourly-paid employee has a time or clock card. The card is usually headed with the name of the worker, his/her number, the week being worked – department and so on. When the employee goes to work he/she takes his/her card from the 'Out' rack and inserts it into the Time Recorder and presses it so that the machine records the time in the 'In' column. The card is then placed in the 'In' rack. When the worker leaves work he/she takes the card from the 'In' rack, inserts it into the machine to record the time he/she leaves work and places the card in the 'Out' rack – after checking that the time has been correctly entered in the 'Out' column. Any overtime worked may be recorded in a separate column. A typical example of a clock card is given in Figure 22.1.

On the card is a column showing the total number of hours worked each day while at the foot of the card is space for the wage for the week to be calculated.

22.3 THE WAGES CLERK

The wages clerk is usually responsible for a number of tasks and one of these is to work out the total number of hours worked each day of the week by each hourly-paid employee, using the time or clock card. Once the total number of hours for each day has been worked out the total for the week is found. Using the normal, or basic, hourly rate for normal hours worked and the overtime rate for any hours worked above the normal time (overtime) the wages clerk works out the total pay for the week.

Some firms deduct time, often a quarter of an hour, from workers who clock in/out more than two minutes after/before the quarter/half/three-quarters of an hour. For example, if a worker clocks in at 8.33 and out at 12.30 he/she would be credited with $3\frac{3}{4}$ hours and not 4 hours – because 8.33 is three minutes after the half-hour. The same worker clocking in at 1.35 and out at 4.27 would be credited with $2\frac{1}{2}$ hours and not 3 hours because 1.35 is more than two minutes after 1.30 and 4.27 is more than two minutes before 4.30 – he/she would have been credited with that quarter of an hour if he/she had waited until 4.28 to clock out.

22.4 GROSS PAY

Gross pay is the total amount due each week or month before any deductions for tax, National Insurance and so on. These calculations are also the responsibility of the wages clerk and are discussed in Section 22.6.

22.5 A SALARY

A salary is an annual sum paid for particular duties and it is usually paid each month, each month's salary being one-twelfth of the annual sum. If a

Fig 22.1 *time card – not filled in*

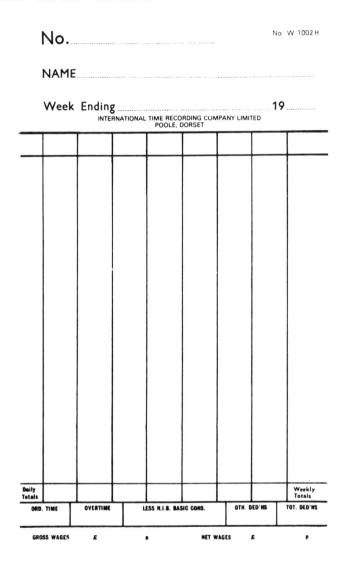

worker is paid an annual salary of £3 120 the monthly gross payment will be £260 (£3 120 ÷ 12 = £260). Most salaried staff are not paid for overtime, but have the knowledge that each month's gross salary will be the same.

Other forms of remuneration include commission and fees. *A commission* is usually paid to people employed in selling goods and is often based on a percentage of total sales. For example, a person might be paid a commission of 10 per cent on all sales and if he/she sold goods worth £1 000 his/her commission would be £100 – 10 per cent of £1 000. Very often people engaged in selling goods are paid a flat-rate basic salary with commission on all sales so that the more they sell the more they earn. *Fees* are sums of money usually paid to professional people for undertaking given tasks – for example, a dentist may charge a fee of £25.00 for every tooth filled while a doctor may charge £20.00 for every visit to a private patient, and a solicitor may charge £35.00 for giving advice about making a will.

Expenses are not normally regarded as part of taxable income since they are sums of money paid out to compensate workers for money spent in the course of undertaking a certain task in connection with their full-time occupation. For example, a person who uses his/her car to take some mail to the Post Office, a distance of six miles, might be paid expenses at the rate of 30p per mile, giving a total of £1.80. Expenses are best thought of as compensation for expenses incurred on behalf of the worker's employer. Earnings over a certain figure and expenses may be taxable (the amount varies according to the budget).

Many workers are paid wage or salary increases for a number of reasons. A *merit* increase may be paid to an employee who reaches a higher standard of work – for example, a typist might be given a rise for reaching fifty words a minute. Some salaried workers are paid *increments* which are annual increases for working at a particular place or staying in a particular profession. For example, an employee might be paid a starting salary of £6 000 with annual increments of £120 for ten years – after which time he/she will be on top salary of £7 200, always assuming that there are no annual salary increases in the meantime (in reality this is not the case and the top salary would be greatly in excess of this figure). *An incentive scheme* is designed to encourage employees to work harder and stay with a firm: sometimes the payment is paid on the performance of a whole group of workers. Profit-sharing is a form of incentive payment whereby the workers are given a percentage of the firm's profits – or given shares in the firm. Some firms offer workers a *bonus* if targets are exceeded – a sum of money above normal payment and the offer is an incentive to the workers to work hard.

22.6 DEDUCTIONS FROM WAGES AND SALARIES

All people have to make a return giving particulars of their income to the Board of Inland Revenue. **Income** is the total amount received by a person in a year and this may include a wage or a salary, interest on savings, rent from property, dividends from shares, commission, fees, a pension – or any combination of these. Expenses are not normally regarded as part of income although tips are. People who work for others usually pay any tax due as they earn their income – **PAYE** or Pay As You Earn – while self-employed people pay their tax in lump sums in two equal instalments. The first instalment is due on 1 January in the fiscal year and the second is due six months later. So far as office work, and the wages department in particular, is concerned it is PAYE which is paid and for the purposes of this section tax paid by the self-employed is not discussed. The PAYE system aims at a precise cumulative balance every week in the year between salaries/wages earned and tax collected.

Deductions from wages and salaries are of two kinds – statutory and voluntary. *Statutory deductions* are those which must be deducted from wages and salaries and of these income tax and National Insurance are of immediate concern. *Voluntary deductions* which an employee might agree to be deducted from her wage or salary include payments to a savings scheme, payments to a holiday fund, a union or professional association fee paid weekly or monthly or a contribution to a charity.

Income tax is liable to be paid on all income and the rate is charged on the basis of the *fiscal year*, which runs from 6 April one year to 5 April the following year and should not be confused with a calendar year, which runs from January to December. The method used to collect income tax from employees is PAYE. Under this system employees pay tax as they earn their money and it has the advantage that they do not have to find large sums of money at the end of the year. Income tax is deduced from income by the employer each week or month and is paid by him to the Inland Revenue on behalf of the employee.

Each worker is allocated a *code number* (signifying the tax allowances attracted by the individual) by the Board of Inland Revenue after they have filled in a *tax claims* form. Tax allowances are given for the following:

expenses incurred and which are not reimbursed by the employer (the regulations are governed by very strict rules);
interest paid on building society loans – for own house purchase and up to levels decided in the budget;
personal – single people are allowed less than married people;
dependent relatives.

The list of allowances is liable to change at any time, as are the amounts, and students are advised to check by asking at the local tax office. It is important that every individual should check his/her code number to see that the allowances are correct. When all the allowances have been added together the Inland Revenue issues a code number which shows the total allowances given – that is to say, how much money can be earned before income tax must be paid. This code number should be given to the employer to show him how much tax-free pay to allow. The code number does not tell your employer how the code number is arrived at so that your personal details remain hidden from him. All income over and above your tax-free allowance is liable to tax, but the rate will depend on your gross income.

22.7 CALCULATING TAX DEDUCTIONS

Each employee is given a tax deduction card (P11) by the employer and on each pay day the wages department must enter the following details:

Fig 22.2 *form P11*

Deductions working sheet P11 (New)				Employee's surname *(in BLOCK letters)*		
Employer's name						
Tax District and reference				National Insurance no.		Date of birth *in figures* Day , Month

	National Insurance Contributions			MONTH number	WEEK number	Pay in the week or month	To
	Total of Employee's and Employer's Contributions payable 1a	Employee's Contributions payable 1b	Employee's contributions at Contracted-out rate (included in column 1b) 1c			2	3
	Bt. fwd. £	Bt. fwd. £	Bt. fwd. £	B.F. from Mth. 7	B.F. from Wk. 30	£	Bt fw
				6 Nov. to 5 Dec.	31		
					32		
					33		
					34		
				8	35		
				6 Dec. to 5 Jan.	36		
					37		
					38		
				9	39		
				6 Jan. to 5 Feb.	40		
					41		
					42		
				10	43		
				6 Feb. to 5 Mar.	44		
					45		
					46		
				11	47		
				6 Mar. to 5 April	48		
					49		
					50		
N.I. Cont'n Table Letter ▼					51		
				12	52		
					§		
‡				‡ N.I. LETTER: Enter letter identifying contribution table used when making first entry on sheet and on any subsequent change of table. N.I. TOTALS: Enter in columns 1a, 1b and 1c separate contribution TOTALS for each table used.			

P11 (New)   *Keep this form for not less than 3 years after the end of the ye*

275

First two forenames		Tax Code†	Amended code†				Year to 5 April
no. etc.	Date of leaving *in figures* Day | Month | Year		Week/Month no. in which applied				19......

PAYE Income Tax

	Total free pay to date as shown by Table A	Total taxable pay to date	Total tax due to date as shown by Taxable Pay Tables	Tax deducted or refunded in the week or month *Mark refunds "R"*	For employer's use
	4	5	6	7	
£	£ ▬▬▬	£ ▬▬▬	Bt. fwd. £	£ ▬▬▬	

PAY AND TAX TOTALS:

◀ Previous employments ▶

◀ This employment *(Mark net refund "R")* ▶

† If amended cross out previous code.

§ Complete this line if pay day falls on 5 April (in leap years 4 & 5 April). See Week 53 instructions in the Employer's Guide to PAYE.

Employee's Widows & Orphans/Life insurance contributions in this employment   £

Holiday pay paid but not included in column 2   £

...ich it relates, or longer if directed.

D8252224 20,000,000 11/80 J. Higgins & Sons (Printers) Ltd. A2214

the amount of gross pay due each week or month - column 2;
the total amount earned so far in the fiscal year - column 3;
the amount of tax-free pay to which the employee is entitled - column 4;
the total taxable pay - column 5;
the total tax due to date - by reference to the tax tables - column 6;
the tax deducted or refunded in the week or month - column 7.

National Insurance details - discussed later - are entered in columns 1a and 1b. The tax deduction card must have entered upon it the code number of the employee, his/her name and the name of the employer. The code number usually consists of two parts; a figure and a letter. The figure indicates the amount of tax-free income; the letter indicates, for example, L for a single person or H for a married person. Any changes to the code must be notified by the employee to the tax office which will, in turn, inform the employer.

In order to deduct tax an employer has to use *tax tables* issued by the Board of Inland Revenue to all employers. Copies of the tables can be seen at the local central library, the tax office, or by asking the employer. The tax tables consist of two books:

Table A book shows the Free Pay Tables for each week or month of the financial year. Each code number is shown and with it the amount of tax-free pay to date.
Tables B to D book show the Taxable Pay Tables.
Table B shows the tax due on taxable pay to date (the pay to date less the free pay to date) up to weekly or monthly limits.
Table C shows the tax due where the limits exceed those given in Table B.
Table D are a set of shortened ready reckoners for each of the higher rates of tax. These are used as directed in Table C and for codes in the D series.

Full details of the PAYE system are given in the *Employer's Guide to PAYE* issued periodically by the Board of Inland Revenue.

22.8 TAX DEDUCTIONS OR REFUNDS

Tax deductions or refunds are based on the amount of gross pay less any contributions to a superannuation scheme. Deductions for National Insurance or any voluntary deductions must be made later.

22.9 NATIONAL INSURANCE

Pensions for retirement, widowhood and invalidity consist of two parts: a *basic flat-rate pension* and an *additional pension* related to the earnings on which an employee pays contributions above the qualifying earnings level necessary for the basic pension. Employees who are members of an ocupational pension scheme which meets the requirements laid down can be *contracted-out* of the additional pension for retirement and part of the additional pension for widowhood by their employers. As a rule, employees who are contracted-out are still eligible for a basic pension from the State scheme but obtain their additional pension from their occupational scheme. Students who are interested in learning more about the contracting-out requirements should obtain leaflet NP 23 from their local Social Security Office. National Insurance contributions for employed earners, employees and office-holders (an employed earner is any person who is gainfully employed either under a contract of service or as an office-holder in an office with emoluments (profits arising from employment) chargeable to income tax) are related to their earnings and are collected together with income tax under the PAYE procedure. They consist of:

(i) *primary Class 1 contributions* from employed earners;
(ii) *secondary Class 1 contributions* from employers and other paying earnings.

Liability for contributions from both employees and employers are subject to lower and upper earnings limits which are empressed in weekly terms (even though earnings may be paid at monthly or other intervals). The lower and upper limits are reviewed each year and students should obtain leaflet NI 208 if they wish to learn the current amounts. The leaflet is obtainable from the Post Office. If earnings do not reach the lower limit there is no liability for contributions from either the employee or the employer, but if earnings reach, or exceed, the lower limit contributions have to be paid on the whole of the earnings (those below and above the lower earnings limit).

An employer may contract his employees out of part of the State scheme - details are given in leaflets NP 23 and NP 29.

Employee's contributions (when not contracted-out) are payable at either:

the standard rate (table A of the National Insurance contribution tables - leaflet CF 391, obtainable from the Department of Health and Social Security);
the reduced rate (Table B), payable by certain married women and widows; or
is not liable for contributions (Table C), because he/she is over pension age or has made other arrangements to pay contributions.

Employer's contributions (when employees are not contracted-out) are at the same rate, whichever of the above categories of contributions applies to the employee.

ACTIVITY

Students who wish to learn more about National Insurance should obtain leaflet NP 15, *Employer's Guide to National Insurance Contributions* from the local office of the Department of Health and Social Security together with any other leaflets currently available.

National Insurance deductions are entered on the P11 in columns 1a and

1b. A column is provided for employee's contributions at the contracted-out rate when this applies. The amounts payable are given in the National Insurance contributions tables (CF 391) issued by the Department of Health and Social Security.

National Insurance contributions help to pay for a number of cash benefits and these include: unemployment payments, sickness benefits, payments for injuries received at work, maternity payments should a woman have a child, a widow's pension should a woman's husband die before she reaches the retiring age, a retirement pension; a death grant is payable on death.

National Insurance numbers are allocated to all contributors by the Department of Health and Social Security and the numbers enable contributions to be correctly entered on the accounts of individuals; the system for the employed is given above and differs from that used for the self-employed. Most people are given their National Insurance number, which remains the same for life, as they start their first job. The numbers consist of 2 prefix letters, 6 figures and a suffix letter e.g. AB654321C. The suffix letter (which may be A, B, C or D) has no connection with the letter of the contribution table applicable to an employee. *Young people* are usually allocated their NI numbers in the year in which they reach 16 years of age. Shortly before leaving school they are given their *NI number cards* advising them of their numbers. An employee must give his NI number to his/her employer on request.

National Insurance contribution tables, as indicated earlier, are issued to employers annually by the Department of Health and Social Security and these show the amounts of the various contributions.

Table A is for use for employees over the age of 16 and under pension age (65 men, 60 women), but exclude those married women and widows liable to pay contributions at the reduced rate and those employees for whom form RD 950 is held.

Table B is for use for those married women and widows authorised to pay their contributions at the reduced rate. These employees must produce a valid certificate to this effect on form CF 383 – the 'certificate of election'. Form CF 380A – the 'certificate of reduced liability (printed in green) – may be held for some women who began their current employment before 6 April 1980.

Table C is for use for employees not liable for primary employee contributions. These are either:

(i) employees over pension age (above) including those previously contracted-out;

(ii) employees in not-contracted-out employment for whom the employer has been notified (on form RD 950) that primary employee contributions are not due for that employment.

Income tax weeks are successive periods of seven days – the first of which starts on 6 April – in each income tax year. The first income tax week is 6–12 April inclusive, the second is 13–19 April, the third is 20–26

April – and so on. The complete weekly income tax calendar is given in the *Employer's Guide to PAYE*. Any odd day or days at the end of the last complete tax week in the year is/are treated as a whole tax week.

Income tax months are successive periods in each income tax month running from the 6th day of one month to the 5th day of the following month. The first income tax month is from 6 April to 5 May, the second is 6 May to 5 June, the third is 6 June to 5 July – and so on. The complete monthly income tax calendar is given in the *Employer's Guide to PAYE*.

Using the tables
Follow the instructions given in the tables. Briefly these are:

1. At the beginning of the tax year or, if later, when the employment starts or the employee reaches the age of 16, select the contribution table relevant to the employee and his/her pay interval. (The tables do not show all amounts of income but progress in steps, for example, £80.00, £80.50, £81.50 – and so on.) Enter the table letter (A, B or C) in the first NI Contribution Table Letter space provided at the bottom of P11.
2. If, during the year, it is necessary to change to another table, draw a line under the last entry on P11. Enter the totals of contributions paid up to the time of the change against the first table letter and then insert the letter of the new contribution table on the next NI Contribution Table Letter line.
3. At the end of the year complete the 'Totals' box for the contribution table letter then in use.

Where substitute annual documents are used the identifying letters must be entered in the employer's pay records so that at the end of the year deduction documents may be completed to show the table letters used and the relevant totals of contributions.

The calculation of contributions should be noted from a current copy of CF 391 as they are liable to change and any information given here may be irrelevant.

Contributions to income tax and National Insurance deducted from an employee during a tax month must be paid, by the employer, to the Collector of Taxes within fourteen days of the end of that month.

22.10 CHANGING A JOB

When changing a job the employee is issued with a **P45** (see Figure 22.3) by the employer holding the tax deduction card (P11).

The P45 is in three parts and the original must be filled in by the employer holding the P11 – the back of the original is coated with carbon paper so that copies are made on Parts 2 and 3.

Part 1 is sent by the employer to the Tax Office dealing with his affairs as soon as employment ceases.

Fig 22.3 *form P45*

P45 — Details of EMPLOYEE LEAVING — PART 1

	District number	Reference number
1. PAYE reference		

2. National Insurance number

						Mr. Mrs. Miss

3. Surname *(Use BLOCK letters)*

First two forenames *(Use BLOCK letters)*

4. Date of leaving *(in figures)*	Day	Month	Year **19**

5. Code at date of leaving
If Week 1 or Month 1 basis applies, please also write "X" in the box marked "Week 1 or Month 1"

Code | Week 1 or Month 1

6. Last entries on Deduction Card	Week or Month number	Week	Month
If Week 1 or Month 1 basis applies, complete item 7 instead	Total pay to date	£	p
	Total tax to date	£	p
7. Week 1 or Month 1 basis applies	Total pay in this employment	£	p
	Total tax in this employment	£	p

8. Works number		9. Branch, Contract Department, etc.	

10. Employee's private address ....
....
.... Postcode......................

11. I certify that the details entered at items 1 to 9 above are correct.

Employer

Address

Date   Postcode

INSTRUCTIONS TO EMPLOYER

● Complete this form according to the "Employee leaving" instructions on the P8 (BLUE CARD).

● Detach Part 1 and send it to your Tax Office **IMMEDIATELY.**

● Hand Parts 2 and 3 (unseparated) to your employee **WHEN HE LEAVES.**

● IF THE EMPLOYEE HAS DIED, please write "D" in this box and send ALL THREE PARTS of this form (unseparated) to your Tax Office **IMMEDIATELY.**

For Tax Office use

For Centre use		
Amended	M/E	P

P45   HPB 1166 5/80

Parts 2 and 3 are joined together – and must not be separated by the employee, who must hand them intact to his/her new employer. The new employer keeps Part 2 and sends Part 3 to his/her Tax Office. The two Tax Offices confer and the employee's file is transferred to the new employer's Tax Office.

As can be seen from the example of a P45, the form shows:

1. The employer's PAYE reference number.
2. The employee's National Insurance number.
3. The employee's surname, status (Mr, Mrs, Miss, etc.) and first two forenames.
4. The date of leaving the last job.
5. The Code at the time of leaving.
6. The last entries on the deduction card (P11) – also item 7. Items 6 and 7 show the total pay in the current employment and the total tax paid in the current employment (the amount paid in the fiscal year to date).
8. The works number.
9. The branch or department in which the employee is working at the current place of employment.
10. The employee's private address.
11. The employer's name and address.

Should a new employee fail to produce a P45, he may have lost it or does not want (for whatever reason) to hand it over, the new employer should send a **P46** to the Tax Office and prepare a new P11. Tax will be deducted at the *emergency rate* until the Tax Office issues further instructions.

22.11 CERTIFICATE OF PAY AND TAX DEDUCTIONS

After 5 April each year the employer is required to give a certificate of pay and tax deductions to each employee in his employment on that date and from whose pay tax has been deducted. The certificate, **P60** (see Figure 22.4), should show the total amount paid to the employee during the year ending on that date and the total tax, less refunds, deducted.

22.12 RETURN OF P11

All employers must send to the Collector of Taxes, not later than 19 April each year, all P11s together with a covering certificate. These cards will show all earnings, PAYE deductions and National Insurance contributions for the previous year.

22.13 ABSENCE FROM WORK THROUGH ILLNESS

Any employee absent from work because of illness should:

1. Ask his/her doctor for a medical certificate. Both sides of this certificate must be filled in and the certificate sent to the local office of the

Fig 22.4 *form P60*

†*DO NOT DESTROY*

P60

Certificate of pay and tax
deducted   YEAR 1980-81

Employee's National Insurance number				Code at 5 April 1981 ▶	

Employee's surname	Employer's reference

First two forenames (or initials)	Works No. (if any)

PAY AND TAX	PAY	TAX
1. In previous employment(s) in 1980-81 taken into account in arriving at the tax deductions made by me/us	£	£
2. In this employment		

I/We certify that the particulars given above include the total amount of pay for income tax purposes (including overtime, bonus, commission etc.) paid to you by me/us in the year ended 5 April 1981, and the total tax deducted by me/us (less any refunds) in that year.
Employer's
name
*(in full)*_____

Address
(in full)

TO THE EMPLOYEE

†*Keep this certificate. It will help you to check any Notice of Assessment which the Tax Office may send you in due course.*
A duplicate form P60 cannot be supplied.

P60 (1980)

Social Security (Some employers ask that the certificate be sent to them first and they send it on to the Social Security.)

2. If the doctor issues a form or a note other than the statement the employee should send it to the local office of the Social Security with a letter – containing his/her name, address, National Insurance number if known (it is a good idea to keep it in your diary), and date of birth.

3. Inform his/her employer – unless done at point one above.

4. Return to work on the date given on the statement. If no date is stated the employee must ask for another statement when the first expires and send it to the local office of the Social Security. A statement which does not state when an employee may return to work is an *'open'* statement – a *'closed' statement* is one giving a date. Before an employee can return to work after being issued with an 'open' statement his/her doctor must issue a 'closed' statement.

The local office of the Social Security makes sickness payments, which are based on earnings, to those sending in a medical statement or certificate. During the time off work National Insurance contributions are not payable –

a contribution is credited once the Department of Health and Social Security is satisfied that an employee is unable to work.

22.14 VOLUNTARY DEDUCTIONS

Some employees undertake voluntary deductions from their wages or salaries. One such voluntary deduction may be a SAYE deduction – **Save As You Earn**. A SAYE scheme is a savings contract in which an employee agrees to make regular monthly payments to an approved savings scheme. The contract is normally for five years – 60 monthly savings. Interest is paid (tax-free) on the savings – the employee can opt to withdraw the savings and the interest or to leave the savings for a further two years – during which time no further payments are made – and in return will receive a bonus amount of interest (also tax-free). Details of SAYE schemes are liable to change so check at the local Post Office, bank or building society.

ACTIVITY

1. Find out – from the local tax office or library – the current rates of income tax.
2. Find out the current National Insurance rates.
3. Find details of the current SAYE schemes.

22.15 THE PAYMENT OF WAGES AND SALARIES

Most workers are paid their wages in cash which is placed inside a wage packet. On the outside of the wage packet will be details showing who is being paid and how the payment is made up. Typical information will include:

the name of the employee;
department and/or works number;
gross pay – how it is made up;
details of all deductions;
net pay – pay after deductions.

Some wage packets are designed with a window so that the employee can check the contents before opening the envelope – in this way errors can be avoided before the envelope is opened. Details of the payment may be printed on the outside of the envelope or included on a pay slip inserted into the envelope.

22.16 PAYMENT INTO A BANK OR BUILDING SOCIETY ACCOUNT

Many employees prefer to have their wages or salary paid directly into a bank, Girobank or building society account and firms are happy to do this – it lessens the risk of a wages robbery resulting from the firm having to collect cash from a bank in order to make up wage packets. The usual method of payment directly into a bank, building society or Post Office account is by means of credit transfer. (For details of this method see the section on banks and the Post Office Girobank.) Instead of receiving payment in cash the employee receives a *wages or salary slip* on which is listed his/her name, works number, gross pay, deductions (listed) and net pay. The *net pay* figure is the amount which has been credited to the account of the employee who draws money out of the account as required (see Figure 22.5).

Fig 22.5 *a salary advice slip*

GROSS TO DATE	TAX TO DATE	TAX CODE	DATE	PERSONAL NO	NAME
4205.00	1060.50	110 L	31 01 xx	23 14 9845	ROBERTSON J S

ANNUAL REMUNERATION	BASIC PAY		GROSS PAY		NATIONAL INS NO
5046.00	420.50		420.50		ST 956713

SUPERANN	N I	OTHER DEDUCTNS	TAX	TOTAL DEDUCTNS	NET PAY
25.03	23.67		106.05	154.75	265.75

In Figure 22.5 J S Robertson has been informed that on 31 January from his/her gross pay of £420.50 for the month £106.05 has been deducted for income tax, £23.67 for National Insurance (NI) and £25.03 for Superannuation (Superann) – a total of £154.75 for the month. His/her annual remuneration is £5046.00 and so far this year £1060.50 has been paid in tax. His/her net pay for the month is £265.75 (basic pay less deductions).

Fig 22.6 *a wages slip*

WORKS NUMBER	TAX CODE	GROSS WAGE	TAX	DEDUCTION REFUND (C)	NATIONAL INSURANCE	OTHER DEDUCTIONS	NET WAGE	PAY WEEK
P3491	135L	85.00		9.15	4.90	2.00	68.95	36

In Figure 22.6 the employee received a gross wage of £85.00 in Tax/Pay Week 36. From this wage has been deducted £9.15 for income tax, £4.90 for National Insurance and £2.00 for some other deductions – details have not been given. The worker picks up £68.95 after the total £16.05 deductions.

ACTIVITY

What other information is given on the above wages slip?

22.17 PAY IN HAND

Many firms pay a week or a month in arrears, depending on how often payments are made, and this is called 'keeping pay in hand'. This practice gives the firm time to make the calculations required to make deductions from wages or salaries. When an employee leaves the firm he/she receives a double payment the last time a payment is made. Firms will often give workers an advance (to tide them over the first period when they begin work) if this system is operated.

22.18 FLEXITIME

Some firms try to improve output and the general working conditions of employees by use of flexitime. All workers are expected to be present during certain hours called *core time* but within limits they are allowed to choose when they will work to make up the rest of their time. Workers may opt to work earlier or later than normal - to miss the traffic rush, for example - or to work long hours on some days so that they can have time off, for a variety of reasons, on others. The use of flexitime allows workers to work when it suits them - and so work to better advantage when they do. A further advantage from the point of view of the employer is that when flexitime is introduced workers tend to work more regularly and do not take time off for such things as medical appointments.

QUESTIONS

1. Define a wage, a salary and income.
2. Outline the system used for assessing and collecting taxes on income.
3. What are the following used for?

    P11   P45
    P46   P60

4. What is flexitime and how does it operate?

SOURCES OF INFORMATION

Nobody knows everything and even those people blessed with photographic memories (people who see material and are able to recall it in every detail) do not recall all they see. A good office worker records everything required to writing and files it where it can be found when needed and learns where to look for facts which are required from time to time and about which she is, until the time of the inquiry, unaware.

23.1 MEMORY AIDS

Memory aids connected with filing are to be found in Section 14.10 on filing; other aids include *address books* for the storage of important names, addresses and telephone numbers; *diaries* for the recording of matters of importance both in the past and future; *minutes* of meetings and *copies* of letters, reports and other documents; *card indexes* of a range of material such as personal details of employees and addresses, for example; *tickler systems* to provide information in advance of events; *visual control boards* for indicating such details as stock control, the progress of projects, the movement of staff, details of holidays and so on; *strip indexes* - for such material as telephone numbers and addresses - are just a few examples.

ACTIVITY

You have just been given a list of memory aids - can you add to it?

23.2 GENERAL INFORMATION

Although it is highly unlikely that any one individual would be expected to find information using all the sources listed below, they do provide a wealth of information when trying to solve the problem of 'where to start looking', when faced with the problem of finding information on unfamiliar topics.

23.3 OUTSIDE REFERENCE SOURCES

An office or a firm cannot be expected to carry unlimited stocks of reference books – although some large firms do have extensive libraries.

The local library will certainly have a range of reference books covering a wide range of topics. If an individual library does not have a particular book the librarian will probably know where to obtain a copy – and may be able to offer it on loan. Many central libraries offer a telephone information service and will try to provide information as requested. This may take some time and it is advisable to give the reference section as much time as possible to answer requests for assistance.

Trade Associations and Chambers of Commerce keep large numbers of records and can supply a wide range of information.

Newspapers often have library facilities and keep back copies of newspapers for reference. They usually like advanced notice if the inquiry involves editions which are not current – less than a month old.

Government offices hold large quantities of information and much of this is available on request either free of charge or for a nominal fee.

Foreign embassies will gladly supply information about their particular country in response to either a written or telephoned request.

Professional associations and institutes, such as the Institute of Bankers, provide information and assistance in their own particular areas.

Banks provide a wide range of free information on a variety of topics including reports on the economic conditions in foreign countries, trading conditions and market trends, reports on companies, advice on tax and other matters – as well as the usual banking services.

The Citizens' Advice Bureau offers a great deal of help including that on legal aid and buying and selling (consumer protection).

The Government publishes much free information in the form of regular publications such as its *Economic Progress Report* which is prepared by the Information Division of the Treasury. **The European Economic Community** has several regular free publications and a range of services and other publications. In London the Press and Information Office is at 20 Kensington Palace Gardens, W8 4QQ. **The European Free Trade Association** publishes a monthly *EFTA Bulletin* and offers a range of services. Free copies of the bulletin are available from Press and Information Service, European Free Trade Association, 9-11 Rue de Varembe, CH 1211, Geneve 20. If copies are ordered through the distributors of the bulletin a small charge may be made.

The above list is not exhaustive and you would be well advised to keep a list, not only of those given but any others you discover, and so provide yourself with a personal general information service.

23.4 REFERENCE BOOKS

The range and number of reference books kept in any one particular office will be decided by the type of work undertaken in that office and a good secretary will select a range of books to meet the needs there. Too many reference books – and reference books which are out of date – are as bad as too few books on a narrow range of subjects. It is impossible in this section to list all the books which might be used and students must make their own selection to meet the situations as they find them.

A good dictionary will provide the correct spelling, meaning, pronunciation, derivation and part of speech of each word and may also contain a great deal of extra information in the form of lists of abbreviations, words and phrases in common use from foreign languages, mathematical symbols, the derivations of Christian and surnames and details of metric symbols. The individual must strike a balance between a small limited dictionary and the huge volumes found in large libraries.

An **encyclopaedia** will provide a wide range of accurate information – usually in alphabetical order, and copies of such publications as **Encyclopaedia Britannica, Chambers'** or **Everyman** should be kept where appropriate. **Pears Cyclopaedia** is published every year and can be relied upon to give a wide range of information including Events, Prominent People, the Law of England, General Information, Gazetteer of the World, Ideas and Beliefs and a world atlas. In many small offices it is to be preferred to the larger encyclopaedia because of its range of topics and ease of reference.

An **atlas** provides much information in addition to maps – population statistics, temperature information and location of industries and raw materials, for example.

The Post Office Guide is a 'must' for the mailing room because of the up-to-date information it contains on a wide range of Post Office services. The supplements should be inserted as they arrive. **The British Telecom Guide** gives full details of telecommunications.

The telephone directory provides details of telephone services and the names, addresses and telephone numbers of people in the area. Directories for other areas can be obtained – although a 'set' for the whole country is not a normal proposition.

The **Yellow Pages Directories** give details of services offered in particular areas as do the **Industrial and Commercial Yellow pages**. The **Green Pages** give a brief description of the apparatus and services available from British Telecom.

Various **A to Z** publications detail information as to locations and the appropriate books for the required area should be obtained – there is no need to obtain copies for areas not covered by your firm/office.

The AA and RAC handbooks provide information about hotels, garaging facilities, half-day closing, population and maps as well as the services offered by each organisation. The information is particularly useful when planning accommodation, trips and itineraries. The advice services offered by both bodies should be consulted – details in the handbooks, providing you, or the firm, are a member.

A ready reckoner is useful for making calculations – although the cheap modern **calculators** are making this task increasingly easier.

Shorthand writers and typists may find a **shorthand dictionary** or a **typewriting dictionary** very useful.

ABC Guides are published with information on *Railways, Coaches and Buses, Shipping,* and *Airways.* Current editions must be obtained because the information becomes dated.

Whitaker's Almanack is published annually and contains a wide range of information on world events, the Government, statistical information and such miscellaneous information as trade unions, banking, the arts, weights and measures, and so on.

The Stock Exchange Year Book provides information on companies and investments, etc.

Roget's Thesaurus of English Words and Phrases arranges words in groups according to their meanings – as opposed to a dictionary, where they are arranged in alphabetical order.

Modern English Usage by H. W. Fowler is a standard reference book on English usage.

Forms of address are to be found in such publications as *Whitaker's Almanack* and a good dictionary but for specialist information the following should be consulted.

The Army List, The Navy List and *The Airforce List* – for details of serving officers;

Black's Titles and Forms of Address;

British Qualifications – for details of degrees and qualifications granted by British universities;

Burke's Genealogical and Heraldic History of the Landed Gentry;

Crockford's Clerical Directory – for details about the Church of England. Other religious bodies publish similar directories.

Debrett's Peerage and Titles of Courtesy;

The Dentists List – for details of registered dentists;

Diplomatic Service List – for details of British representatives overseas;

Directory of Directors – for details of joint-stock (limited liability) companies and directors;

Kelly's Handbook to the Titled Landed and Official Classes;

The Law List – for details of legal people (solicitors and barristers, etc.);

The Medical Register – for details of medical practitioners;

Who's Who – for details of eminent living people.

The Municipal Year Book and Public Utilities Directory provides a great deal of information about local authorities in England and Wales – the names of chief officers, population matters and so on.

The Guide to British Enterprise (Dun & Bradstreet Ltd) lists the names and addresses, subsidiary or parent companies, field (s) of activity/activities, names of directors and nominal capital for a selection of prominent firms in the United Kingdom.

The Annual Abstract of Statistics gives a wide range of statistical information on such matters as population, manufacturing trade, transport, overseas finance, local government, etc.

Croner's Reference Book for Employers provides information on legislation passed by Parliament and a monthly amendment is provided to keep information up to date.

Kelly's Directory of Manufacturers and Merchants lists, alphabetically, manufacturers and suppliers of goods and services.

Street Guides are invaluable when finding the location of roads and streets, etc., in all parts of the country. Guides should be purchased for any relevant areas.

Ordnance Survey maps cover the country and contain much detailed information about the location of lines of communication, towns, villages and other settlements, as well as the physical geography of the country. The relevant maps should be obtained, as and when required, from H.M.S.O. or any good book shop. The exact location of roads and streets, etc., on new developments may not be found in the Street Guides or on the Ordnance Survey maps – it takes time for these reference sources to be brought up to date and development is taking place all the time. **The Planning Department** of the local government authority concerned will be able to provide the latest information about new developments.

ACTIVITY

Visit your local central library (your local lending library might not have a large reference section) and make a list of other reference books which contain the kind of information you might be required to find. As you find a new source of reference add it to your list and keep the list for later use.

Answer the following:

1. Where would you expect to find details of the currency used in foreign countries and the exchange rates?
2. What book would give you details of books in print?
3. What publication gives details of Parliamentary speeches?
4. Where would you expect to find details of all members of the Board of Directors of a company with which you were about to start trading?

23.5 TELECOMMUNICATIONS SOURCES

The above questions, and the research they involve, should extend your list of sources of information but two further sources should be considered: that transmitted in addition to the normal television programmes and that transmitted via the telephone system – Teletext and Prestel.

Teletext comes in the form of magazine pages which can be read from a television screen – provided the television set is equipped to receive the information. The BBC service is known under the general heading of **Ceefax** – 'seeing facts'. At the time of writing Ceefax is broadcast on BBC 1 and **Orbit** on BBC 2. The ITV service is called **Oracle** – 'Optional

Reception of Announcements by Coded Line Electronics'. The magazines are transmitted in words and diagrams and are constantly up-dated to give the latest information available. Each magazine has an index to enable pages to be selected as required and selection is made by using a special remote control keypad – the information required can be superimposed over a normal TV programme. The range of information available is very wide and is constantly being expanded – it includes news, weather, sports, quiz games, finance headlines, food guide, entertainments, consumer news, *Financial Times* Share Index, travel information and technical information, to name but some of the items available.

Prestel is the name given to the information system provided by British Telecom and to receive it a television set has to be connected to a telephone – by pressing buttons on a small key pad (which looks rather like a calculator) the information selected is displayed on a television screen. There will be over 1 000 000 pages of information available when the system is fully operational. The information is stored in a computer and is constantly being up-dated – the information being supplied by any organisation booking space in the computer. When the system is used in the home or office the local telephone rate is charged plus a charge for the Prestel service itself. In addition some firms in the system make a charge for the information they provide – although some firms make no charge. Prestel will tell you what the charge is for each page before you call it. Individuals at home can call up a vast range of information ranging from the local weather forecast to what is on offer at their local supermarket while business organisations can call up such information as airline schedules, manufacturing and service industry guides, foreign-exchange rates, business news, development reports, legal facts and a vast range of technical information. In the near future it will be possible for any business to have its own Prestel-linked programmable terminal so that information can be fed into the system as well as being taken from it. This will enable any small business to use the facilities of a huge computer for a range of tasks – including stock control, accounting or any planning tasks.

The basic difference between Prestel and Ceefax and Oracle is that Prestel is a two-way system using telephone lines while the broadcast services are a one-way system giving, by comparison, a limited range of information. When Prestel is fully operational any firm with a terminal will be able to offer information to the computer as well as take from it. The service is being extended into a worldwide viewdata service and is currently being sold in Europe, the United States of America and the Far East. See the *Telecom Guide* for current details of Prestel services.

QUESTIONS

1. List ten reference books that you would expect to find in any general office and state the kind of information found in each.

2. How do the Ceefax and Oracle services operate and what kind of information is offered?

PROJECT

Make a study of the Prestel service. Your study should not exceed 5 000 words excluding diagrams.

VISUAL AIDS

The collection of information is vital to the understanding of a wide range of business and everyday events and can show past and present trends as well as indicating possible future trends. A businessman, for example, might like to compare trading figures over weeks, months or years to see if there are general trends which will assist future planning. An insurance company is interested in such details as the comparison of age, weight and height of individuals and life-expectancy – or the comparison of jobs and road accidents – and so on. Just as it is important to collect and store information it is essential to present the information in a way which is easy to understand and in a way which will enable comparisons or decisions to be made. An office worker might be expected to present material in an attractive as well as an informative manner and there are a number of ways of doing this. No matter what method is employed it is useful to remember that *colour* can add to the attraction and usefulness of displays and so enhance their value. When presenting information some thought about the tools to be used may help presentation.

24.1 BASIC DISPLAY KIT

A basic display kit should consist of a range of materials and it is a good idea to build one to suit your particular needs.

Papers should be obtained in suitable sizes and colours. Normal A4 (bond) paper will be used for typed displays but larger displays may require the use of *poster-sized paper* – the B series. *Sugar paper* is both relatively cheap and readily available in a range of colours. *Graph paper* will save time when used to display statistics which are presented in the form of line graphs.

Graphite pencils are available in a range of hardnesses and have the advantage that they can be sharpened as required and they are easy to erase should an error be made. The hardness of graphite pencils is stamped on the pencil itself and a shading chart indicates what degree of hardness is suggested for each particular use. The chart gives some indication of the effect of each hardness. Berol offer a range of *fine line leadholders* which enable lines of a consistent thickness to be drawn without sharpening – an ordinary pencil gives a line which varies in thickness depending on the degree of sharpness. As well as offering leads of a consistent thickness for each particular task, Berol offer them in a range of hardnesses. *Filmograph pencils* are particularly useful on plastic draughting films while *coloured pencils* are available as coloured 'leads' or the more traditional crayon type. (It is worth remembering that if material is being prepared for photographing a sky blue pencil should be used for positioning material because it does not show on a photograph.) As well as selecting the appropriate pencils care should be taken to use the correct eraser for each kind. *Pure rubber* erasers should be used for erasing pencil marks, ink and typing erasers should be used with ballpoint pens and typed material; filmograph erasers should be used with filmograph pencils.

Line markers are available in a range of thicknesses and use water-based ink, which is washable and can be used to lay one colour over another, or waterproof permanent ink. *Water-based* inks should only be used for display material which is to be kept dry – for outside displays the *waterproof permanent* type should be used. Line markers enable 'liquid' colour to be handled cleanly and easily without the need to use *brushes and paints* – which might be used in certain kinds of large displays. *Fine-line pens* are available in a range of colours and with a range of tips. *Ballpoint pens* are chiefly used in general writing, *plastic-tipped* pens for data processing where fine detailed work is carried out, *micropoint pens* are used in accounts sections where there is a space limitation while *nylon fibre* pens have the same use as ballpoint pens.

Pens using nibs of various sizes are available for a number of lettering purposes and should be used with *inks* of the appropriate base and colour. Special pens are available for use with waterproof inks.

To ensure consistency when *lettering* it is often advisable to use a *stencil* which has the letters of the alphabet cut out together with figures and some symbols. Use should be also made of *adhesives* of appropriate kinds – some *impact adhesives* are difficult to work with should material have to be moved about but are invaluable where drying is important. *Spot adhesives* are available, in the form of a pencil, which enable adhesive to be placed exactly. *Gummed paper* is useful as is *cellulose tape* – Scotch 'Magic' transparent tape is non-reflective and is useful for repairing damaged displays and drawings. A pencil sharpener, a sharp knife, ruler (clear plastic by choice), scissors, coloured drawing-pins, a long-armed stapler and a draughtsman's board, or a desk with a hard surface, should make up the rest of the basic kit.

24.2 BAR GRAPHS

Bar graphs, or *pillar graphs* as they are sometimes called, are a useful aid for showing the comparison between two or three sets of figures, usually over a limited period of time, for example a year. The table below shows the average monthly temperature (in degrees Fahrenheit) at three holiday resorts.

Months	Hvar	Pula	Split
February	54	49	51
March	58	53	53
April	64	63	64
May	72	70	73
June	79	79	80
July	84	84	86
August	82	84	86
September	79	77	77

This information has more visual appeal if it is presented as a bar graph. This graph would look better in colour – each resort being given a distinctive colour. A key has to be provided to show each resort; the left-hand vertical line shows the temperature and the line at the bottom shows the months. It is easier to use graph paper when preparing bar graphs than to use plain paper. As well as showing comparisons a bar graph also indicates trends. The temperature graph shows that the months warm up until they tend to reach a plateau in July and August before starting to cool in September.

Fig 24.1 *bar graph*

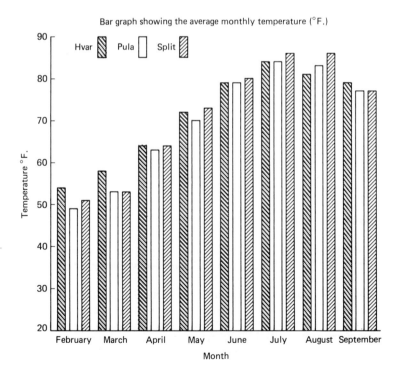

If, instead of leaving the columns separate, they are joined, the graph is called a *histogram*. The table of the monthly takings of a department in a large store can be presented in the form of a histogram. The left-hand vertical line shows the amount of takings in £000s and the bottom line shows the months. When preparing a bar graph you must only use figures which are similar in size (see Figure 24.2).

Fig 24.2 *histogram*

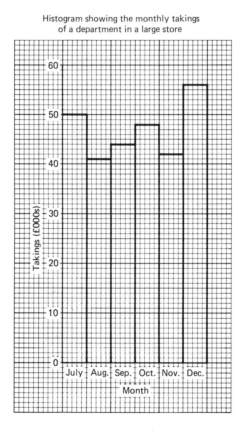

Histogram showing the monthly takings
of a department in a large store

24.3 CHARTS

Charts are particularly useful for showing the position of items. Most of you will be familiar with the keyboard chart below showing the position of keys on a typewriter (see Figure 24.3).

A simple chart or diagram is useful, in particular, for showing placement. Imagine the problem of explaining to a friend the exact seating arrangements in your classroom or lecture theatre.

A bar chart or **horizontal line chart** is rather like a bar graph turned on

Fig 24.3 *typing keyboard chart*

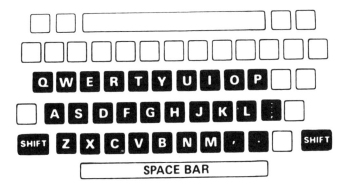

its side. This table, showing the number of pairs of shoes sold by a firm in selected European countries, has more visual impact if it is shown as a bar chart. A bar chart is useful for showing comparisons. (see Figure 24.4).

SHOE SALES IN SELECTED EUROPEAN COUNTRIES

Country	Pairs of shoes sold
Belgium	2 500
Denmark	2 000
France	3 500
Germany	4 600
Italy	1 200

Fig 24.4 *bar chart showing shoe sales to selected European countries*

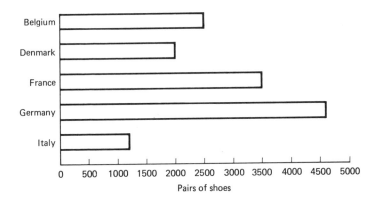

A pie chart is also useful for showing comparisons – when the total amount is known. A circle is drawn and portions making up the full amount are ruled off. If an insurance company received its premium income as follows: United Kingdom 25 per cent, United States 37½ per cent, Netherlands 12½ per cent, Australia 6¼ per cent, Canada 6¼ per cent and the Rest of the World 12½ per cent this could be shown as a pie chart (see Figure 24.5). While the figures presented as a statement might not have a great deal of meaning they do have more significance as a pie chart. (A protractor is a useful aid in the production of pie charts - each 3.6° represents 1 per cent.)

Fig 24.5 *pie chart showing percentage of premium income received from the world*

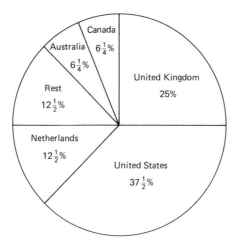

24.4 LINE GRAPHS

Line graphs can be used to show a wide range of information - particularly when there are upwards and downwards movements. Line graphs are best produced on graph paper and the largest sheet which is conveniently available should be used. Providing the statistics are of comparable figures, two or three items can be plotted on the same graph to show trends and comparisons. Colour is an added advantage if more than one item is being plotted. Care should be taken when joining the points on a line graph. Like *all visual displays*, line graphs *should* be *clearly labelled* - without a title any information is useless.

A graph plotting more than one item is sometimes called a *multiline graph* (Figure 24.6).

24.5 MAPS

Maps are useful for showing a wide range of information - population density, roads, rivers, mountains, rainfall, vegetation, location of raw materials, etc. - all the usual information contained in an atlas. By using such devices as coloured drawing-pins it is possible to highlight the location

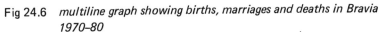

Fig 24.6 *multiline graph showing births, marriages and deaths in Bravia 1970–80*

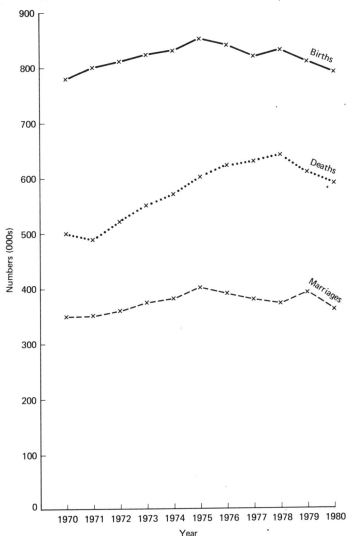

of certain projects, the whereabouts of staff on tour, and so on. If you had to draw the attention of potential buyers to a range of goods you were offering in various parts of the country, one way of doing this would be to pin lengths of coloured ribbon or tape to the locations on a map and link them to piles of leaflets containing information on your products.

24.6 **TYPED TABLES**

Typed tables (tabulations) are a quick and easy way of displaying statistical information. The tables in this chapter could be typed – or written – out for effective display.

24.7 **MODELS**

Simple models are often a quick and easy way of illustrating a particular point and they have the advantage of offering a three-dimensional picture of the information being presented. Cubes of coloured wood, for example, could be used to show the amount of sales by a company over a period of time – each block representing a given value of sales (each 20-mm. cube could represent 100 units and a total unit of 600 sales would be made up of six blocks). An estate agent offering houses for sale on an estate might locate simple models of houses on a plan of the estate – different colours could be used to indicate those sold and those for sale.

Visual control boards (discussed in Chapter 11 on stock control) should be used for a wide range of information. Can you remember some examples?

24.8 **COLOUR TRANSPARENCIES**

Colour transparencies produced on acetate film for overhead projection are a useful way of presenting a wide range of information to a large audience. The transparencies can be produced in colour and when projected sections can easily be masked off (to show selected data only). Using overlays it is possible to build up pictures – selected information is produced on each of a number of single transparencies which are laid one on top of the other as the picture is built up. The use of 35-mm. transparencies (as taken by any 35-mm. camera) can be projected to illustrate points to a large audience.

When producing visual aids it is worth remembering that each particular problem has several probable solutions and very often there is no 'right' way of presenting statistics.

ACTIVITY

Present the information contained in each of the illustrations in this section in a different way – remember that there is always more than one way of displaying information.

QUESTIONS

1. What is a bar graph and what kind of information is it best used for?
2. What is a histogram and what kind of information is it best used for?
3. What kind of information is best illustrated using a model?
4. What are line graphs and what information is best illustrated using them?

APPENDIXES

A.1 CORRECTION SIGNS

People working in an office may use a form of shorthand signs to indicate the corrections required in any piece of work – typed material or material produced on a word-processor, for example. The signs originated in the printing trade and are still sometimes called **Printers' Correction Signs**. The following list contains those used by most examining bodies. Usually a sign is made in the text at the point of error while a further sign or signs in either margin provide more details.

SIGNS IN THE TEXT

Sign   *Meaning*

/   Something is incorrect. See either margin for correction.
ʌ   Something has been left out. This sign is called the caret.
⌒   Close up a space.
∾   Change round the order of the word or letters indicated.
⌐   Start a new paragraph.
⌐⌐   Do not start a new paragraph – continue with the old one.
......   Leave the word(s) in – ignore the crossing out.

SIGNS IN THE MARGINS

Sign   *Meaning*

Caps or uc   Change the letter(s) indicated to capital (upper-case) letters.
lc   Change the letter(s) indicated to small (lower-case) letters.
Put in a space where indicated in the text.
Close up   Close up a space where indicated in the text.
NP or Para   Start a new paragraph where indicated.
|~| Put in a hyphen.
|—| Put in a dash.
trs   Change round the order of the words or letters indicated.
stet   Let it stand – leave in the word(s) indicated by the dots.

℗ ℗ Put in a comma or full stop as indicated.
ᵞ ᵞ Put in single or double quotes as indicated.
ℒ Leave out the word(s) indicated. The sign is made by joining the letters *d e l* (the first letters of the word 'delete') in one outline.

In addition to using correction signs, balloons and arrows may be used to indicate the exact position of material.

A.2 MISCELLANEOUS ITEMS

Aerosol sprays are available for a variety of office functions – air-freshening, deodorising, cleaning surfaces and machinery, telephone disinfectant and so on.

Anglepoise lamps enable light to be directed as required for particular tasks – the lamps can be angled at any position and they have a heavy base to prevent tipping.

Archive boxes are used for storing records which are used infrequently and they are available to take a range of paper sizes.

Attaché cases are used to carry a range of materials – particularly documents. Sales representatives often carry **sample cases.** Both attaché cases and sample cases are available in a range of sizes – often with combination locks for security.

Bins are used for a variety of purposes and their design reflects the use to which they are put. **Storage bins** are usually larger and more robust than **waste-paper bins** which should be designed with an eye to fire precautions.

Blackboards or chalkboards may be used to illustrate points or convey information.

Whiteboards are used with water-based pens and are wiped clean with a damp cloth.

Blotting pads are used for ink to be dried quickly.

Blotting paper is very absorbent and is often used in drawing offices and art departments where work has to be dried quickly.

Brushes are used for a range of purposes and are designed, with natural or synthetic bristles, to meet particular needs such as pasting glue or cleaning typewriters.

Clipboards provide a firm surface on which to write – the documents are fastened to the board by means of a bulldog clip or some other form of clip.

Clips are used for a range of purposes and there are many designs. **Bulldog clips** are available in a range of sizes and are used for fastening several documents together. **Paper clips** are made of wire and are available in a range of sizes and designs. They are used to fasten documents together temporarily and because they tend to fasten together or on to other documents they should not be used for filing purposes – staples should be used instead. **Foldback clips** perform the same function as bulldog clips but are often more convenient to use since the 'handles' can be folded over to prevent protrusions.

Dampers are used to moisten sticky labels and are available in a range of sizes and designs for various applications.

Dispensers are used for a range of functions – with cellulose tapes, stamps, string and so on. Many have a cutting edge built in to save time.

Eyelets are metal or plastic inserts used to reinforce holes punched in various materials using a **punch**.

Finger cones are usually made of rubber and are used to facilitate the counting or handling of sheets of paper – they grip the paper better than bare fingers.

Legal departments use **tapes** of various colours to fasten legal documents as well as **treasury tags** to fasten sheets of paper together.

Office furniture is designed to meet the demands of the various office situations. Chairs and desks should conform to the **British Standards Institution (BSI)** recommendations – although many well-designed items fall outside these recommendations. Any good office-equipment catalogue will show the range of furniture available. *A study of office furniture and the BSI recommendations could form the basis of an excellent project.*

Perforators and **punches** are available in a range of sizes for a host of applications, but in particular for making holes in sheets of paper which are to be housed in files. **Reinforcers** made of gummed paper (often itself reinforced with fabric) are used to protect the holes made in sheets of paper which is to be housed in a file. **Drills** are used to make holes in material which cannot be perforated or punched – either because it is too hard or is too thick.

Rubber bands are often purchased by weight and are available in a range of sizes and thicknesses. They are often used to fasten documents together temporarily.

Stapling machines are used to fasten sheets of paper together. They are available in a range of sizes and take **wire staples** in a range of sizes and strengths. A **long-armed stapler** is used to fasten documents of a large size and an **electric stapling machine** would be used in an office where large quantities of documents have to be fastened together. If documents are to be attached temporarily the stapler should be adjusted to bend the wire staples outwards – in which case they act as a pin. If the documents are to be fastened permanently the stapler should be adjusted to turn the staples inwards and over. A **staple extractor** may be used to remove staples.

String and **twine** may be made of natural or synthetic material and used for binding or packing purposes. The use to which the string or twine is to be put will determine the strength and colour of the material used.

Tally counters may be hand- or desk-mounted and are used when counting documents, individuals and so on.

Trolleys provide mobile working surfaces or storage areas and are used to house a range of equipment (telephones, typewriters, duplicators, etc.) and items (office trays, etc.).

INDEX